ROUTLEDGE LIBRARY EDITIONS:
URBAN STUDIES

Volume 24

URBAN AND RURAL CHANGE IN WEST GERMANY

URBAN AND RURAL CHANGE IN WEST GERMANY

Edited by
TREVOR WILD

LONDON AND NEW YORK

First published in 1983 by Croom Helm Ltd

This edition first published in 2018
by Routledge
2 Park Square, Milton Park, Abingdon, Oxon OX14 4RN

and by Routledge
711 Third Avenue, New York, NY 10017

Routledge is an imprint of the Taylor & Francis Group, an informa business

British Library Cataloguing in Publication Data
A catalogue record for this book is available from the British Library

ISBN: 978-1-138-89482-2 (Set)
ISBN: 978-1-315-09987-3 (Set) (ebk)
ISBN: 978-1-138-05207-9 (Volume 24) (hbk)
ISBN: 978-1-138-05208-6 (Volume 24) (pbk)
ISBN: 978-1-315-10528-4 (Volume 24) (ebk)

Publisher's Note
The publisher has gone to great lengths to ensure the quality of this reprint but points out that some imperfections in the original copies may be apparent.

Disclaimer
The publisher has made every effort to trace copyright holders and would welcome correspondence from those they have been unable to trace.

Urban and Rural Change in West Germany

Edited by TREVOR WILD

CROOM HELM
London & Canberra
BARNES & NOBLE BOOKS
Totowa, New Jersey

Croom Helm Ltd, Provident House, Burrell Row,
Beckenham, Kent BR3 1AT

British Library Cataloguing in Publication Data

Urban and rural change in West Germany.
1. Regional planning – Germany – Social aspects
2. Regional planning – Germany, West – Economic aspects
I. Wild, Trevor
307'. 0943087 HT395.G/

ISBN 0-7099-2715-0

First published in the USA 1983 by
BARNES & NOBLE BOOKS
81 ADAMS DRIVE
TOTOWA, New Jersey, 07512

Library of Congress Cataloging in Publication Data
Main entry under title:

Urban and rural change in West Germany.

1. Germany (West) – Social conditions – Addresses, essays, lectures. 2. Germany (West) – Economic conditions – Addresses, essays, lectures. I. Wild, M.T. (Martin Trevor), 1940-
HN445.5.U72 1983 306'.0943 83-6350
ISBN 0-389-20392-0

Typeset by Elephant Productions, London SE19
Printed and bound in Great Britain

CONTENTS

FIGURES

TABLES

Tables

ACKNOWLEDGEMENTS

The completion of this book would have been impossible had it not been for the kind assistance of the following: Keith Scurr, Derek Waite and Andrew Bolton of the Department of Geography, University of Hull, for drawing all the figures; Brian Fisher of the same department for his photographic work and advice on photographic reproduction; Derek Attwood of the Department of German, University of Hull, for his careful translation of Chapter 9; the University of Hull for its financial assistance in covering the costs of translation; the British Academy and the Social Science Research Council for their generous sponsorship of the research for my personal contributions; lastly, but not least, my wife and children for their undying patience and encouragement during the long hours of writing and editing. To all these people and institutions I express my deep gratitude and sincere thanks.

Trevor Wild

GLOSSARY OF GERMAN WORDS AND PHRASES

Note: Plural endings are given for nouns which are appropriately referred to in the plural form in the text.

Altstadt, ¨–e: the historic core of a city
Anerbenrecht: a type of single-inheritance custom
Angestellte, –r: white-collared worker
Angst: anxiety
Anwerbestopp: ban on foreign-labour recruitment (1973)
Arbeiter: blue-collared worker
Arbeiterbauer, –n: worker-peasant
Arbeitsamtsbezirk (Abz), –e: labour-market area
Aussiedlung, –en: outsettlement involving locational shifts of farms from villages into new consolidated holdings
Autobahn, –en: motorway
autogerechte Stadt: car-orientated city
Baureifesland: investment land
Bausubstanz: composition of building
Bebauungsplan: buildings plan
beschränkte Flexibilität: 'restricted flexibility'
Betriebskolonie, –n: company-housing community
Betriebswohnheim, –e: company-owned hostels, usually for single guestworkers
Blockern, –e: street-block interior
Brachland: fallowed land, excluding that associated with normal agrarian practice
Bundesamt: federal office
Bürgerinitiative: citizens' initiative, equivalent to Residents' Action Groups
citynahes Gebiet, –e: zone of mixed land uses immediately outside the commercial core of a city
Deutsche Bundesbahn (DB): federal railway
Dörferneuerung, –en: village renovation
Drei-oder Mehrfamilienhaus, ¨–er: apartments
Durchbau: complete renovation involving the interior gutting of a building
Einfamiliehaus, ¨–er: individual dwelling (non-apartment)

Einkaufszentrum, -zentren: shopping centre
Ergänzungsgebiet, –e: inner zone of urban-rural fringe
Ertragsmesszahl: yield measurement of soils
Fernpendelnwanderung, –en: long-distance travel to work on a periodic basis
Flächennutzungsplan: land use plan
Flurbereinigung: field consolidation and reorganisation
Funktionsgesellschaft: functional society
Fussgängerbereich, –e: pedestrianised area
Gartenvorstadt, ⸚e: garden suburb
Gastarbeiter: guestworker
Geest: sandy heathland
Gemeinde, –n: local authority; in rural areas equivalent in size to parish or commune
Gemeindeverband, ⸚e: unions of rural Gemeinden, usually to provide prestige services such as schools or health clinics
Geschäftswohnung, –en: apartment building with ground floors occupied by shops or other small businesses
Haufendorf, ⸚er: compact, irregular villages; the commonest type of traditional village in West Germany
Heimatstil: homely style; a trend in housing provision which was important in many German cities during the interwar period
Hinterhaus, ⸚er: apartment building within a streetblock interior
Huckepack: 'piggy back' railway operation
Innenstadt, ⸚e: 'interior city'; i.e. the commercial core and its near surrounds
Isoliertestadt, ⸚e: isolated city
Kleinbauer, –n: small peasant farmer
Kleinsiedlungen Wohnheim, –e: 'colonies' of small detached houses, usually built for refugees in the late 1940s and early 1950s
Kneipe, –n: corner pub
Kreisstrasse, –n: county road, equivalent to secondary road
Land, ⸚er: federal state
Landesstrasse, –n: state roadway
Landkreis (Lkr).), –e: county district; a West German administrative unit which has little power, but is very useful for mapping purposes
Ländlichesuburbanisierung: rural suburbanisation
Loess: wind-blown glacial silt, usually providing very fertile soils
Mietwohnung, –en: rented dwelling, usually an apartment
Naturschutzgebiet, –e: nature conservation area
Neugliederung: post-1968 redrawing of administrative areas

Ödland: all fallowed land
Randzone, –n: outer zone of urban-rural fringe
Realerbteilung: partible inheritance
Reich: German Empire
Regionale Stadt, ⸗e: regional city
Reihenhaus, ⸗er: terrace-row house
Regierungsbezirk, –e: administrative region
Rohbauland: development land
Sanierungsgebiet, –e: improvement area, usually in inner cities
Sanierungskern, –e: core of improvement area
'S' Bahn, –en: high-speed commuter railway
Schaffe eine menschliche Stadt: the shaping of a city fit for people
Schwerpunkt, –e: concentration point
Siedlungschwerpunkt: settlement concentration point
Sozialbrache: social fallow
soziale Marktwirtschaft: Social Market Economy
Sozialschwache: socially deprived persons
Sozialwohnung, –en: social housing
Stadtbahn, –en: city tramway
Stadtdistrikt, –e: urban district
Stadtkern, –e: the urbanised core of a city region
Trabantenstadt, ⸗e: satellite town
'U' Bahn, –en: underground tramway
Umlandzone, –n: urban-rural fringe
Unland: land which has no potential use
Verbindungsbahn, –en: connecting tunnel on 'S' Bahn system
Verbrauchermarkt, ⸗e: hypermarket or superstore
Verdichtungsraum, ⸗e: urban agglomeration
Vergleichseinkommen: parity income
Verkehrsbund, –e: joint passenger-transport companies, usually run by local authorities
Verstädterte Zone, –n: middle zone of urban-rural fringe
Wirtschaftswunder: economic miracle
Wohnen im Grünen: living in the green
Wohnungshalde: 'housing mountain' of the mid-1970s
Zeitgeist: spirit of the age
Zwischenstädtegebiet, –e: the area lying between two or more closely positioned cities

PREFACE

There are many important facets to the special identity of West Germany, but particularly notable are its unique political configuration, its eventful historical background, its pace of economic development and economic restructuring, its huge rise in average personal affluence and, not the least, its far-reaching changes in the interactional relationships between its cities and countryside. Taken together these features and trends have set the stage during the last three decades for a steadily increasing interest among British and American writers, teachers, students and readers. At first, literature in the English language on West Germany tended to be insular and to fall into the category of encyclopedia-type texts. These produced many facts and figures, but left the reader to select the most relevant issues. More recently, writers have adopted thematic approaches which have provided a greater degree of insight. Yet, because of the fast rate of change in West Germany, there is always a need to add to and to update the issues and perspectives which are contained in these themes.

The thematic approach underlies this book, which, under the general heading of 'Urban and Rural Change in West Gemany', calls on the expertise of six university teachers who have each had considerable research experience in West Germany. When read in combination, their contributions not only explore the various changes which are evident in West Germany's mosaic of cities, towns, villages and countryside, but also focus in a critical way upon the problems which have arisen, and the planning strategies which have been implemented for their solution.

The chapter headings do not complete the list of issues and themes which are covered in this book. There are several, including the course of postwar economic development, the affluence movement, demographic change, imbalances between the regions and, of course, the salient effects of West Germany's rich historical legacy, which are so strongly interwoven that it is wiser to discuss them at appropriate stages in the text rather than treat them as separate entities.

Three editorial improvisations have been made to assist the reader. First, the naming of places, regions and topographic features, many of which have both German and English appellations, follows a consistent procedure of using English names only for the largest cities and most widely known regions, rivers, hill ranges and lakes. For example,

Köln is written as Cologne, *Rheinland* as Rhineland and *Mittelgebirge* as the Central Uplands; but less familiar cities and geographical features are written as they appear in German literature, for example Koblenz instead of Coblence and Frankenschweizland instead of Franconian 'Switzerland'. The second improvisation concerns the use of German words and expressions. These have to be employed where they add to the understanding of the text. Some can be easily translated into English, but wherever there are potential difficulties a note (usually in parentheses) is made of the English connotation. To simplify further the reader's appreciation, a short glossary of the more frequently used German words and phrases, with their English translations, precedes this Preface. Lastly, the text has to refer to a large number of regional and topographic names. Most of these can be identified on the first map of this book, Figure 0.1.

Figure 0.1: Guide to Regional Terms Commonly Referred to in Text

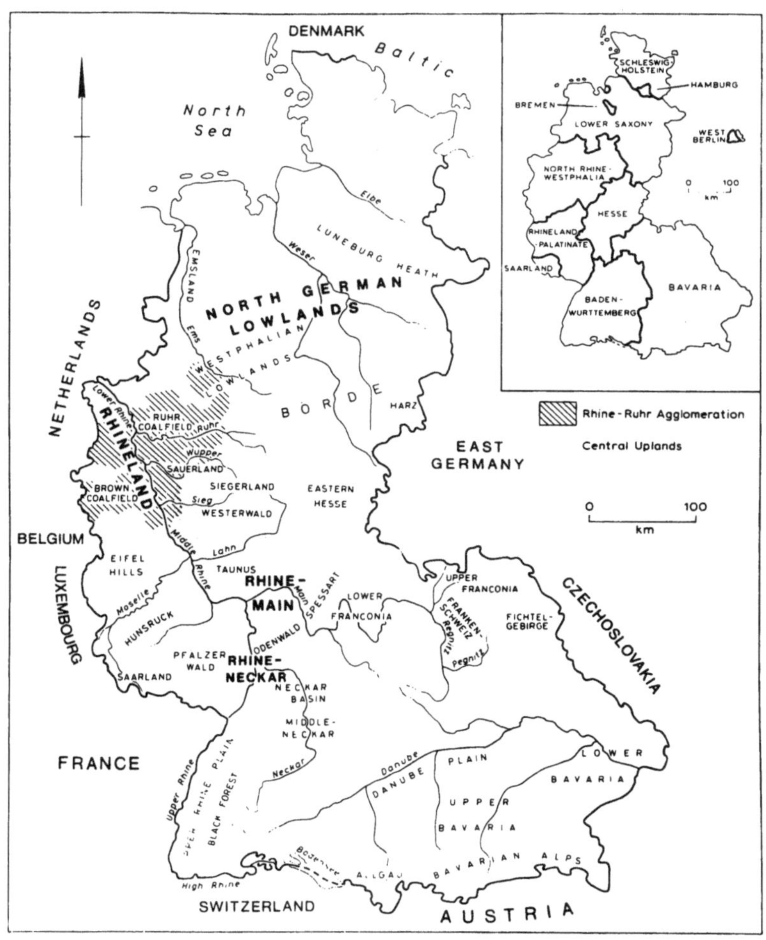

1 INTRODUCTION: THE PATTERNING OF CITIES AND RURAL AREAS IN WEST GERMANY

Trevor Wild

Perusal of any standard atlas map of western Europe which shows the distribution of cities and intervening spaces, brings to light a remarkable range of international differences. Very noticeably, West Germany, with its diffuse pattern of major cities and intricate arrangement of rural areas, represents one end of the diversity spectrum. Indeed, these two interrelated characteristics are so crucially important in the spatial organisation of West Germany, that a perspective on the realities of their spatial expression is needed by any student of urban and rural change within this highly individualised country. This, therefore, will form the theme of the introduction to this book: moreover, it will be a focus of interest which will serve to acquaint the reader with an appropriate geographical setting for the text which follows.

The Distribution of Cities

The distinctiveness of West Germany, in terms of its lack of a dominating 'metropolitan' capital and its frequency of major 'regional' cities, has been described recently in the following factual statements:

> When it is compared with those of other west European countries, the urban structure of West Germany is distinguished first and foremost by the absence of a national focus as dominating as a capital city such as Paris, London, Madrid or Brussels. If West Berlin is left aside as a special case, Hamburg with 1,688,000 inhabitants is the largest single centre . . . Yet this city accommodates only 2.7 per cent of the national population, a remarkably low proportion when one considers figures for other 'primate' cities. Comparisons with France and the United Kingdom, to take perhaps the two most obvious examples, show corresponding percentages of 16.2 per cent for Greater Paris and 13.9 for Greater London . . .
>
> Another outstanding characteristic is the significant number of large regional centres . . . Again comparisons with France and the United Kingdom are revealing, for while West Germany now has thirty-two cities with populations above 200,000, these two countries

have only twenty-one and twenty respectively. Above the 500,000 mark the difference is even more striking, with West Germany having as many centres of this size as France and the United Kingdom together.[1]

There is no single explanation for the diffuse distribution of major cities and metropolitan functions in West Germany. A common fallacy is to attach too much weight to the political events of the early postwar years, namely the division of Germany, the bisecting of Berlin (4.3 million inhabitants in 1939, representing 7.0 per cent of the *Reich* population), the creation of a federative system of regional government and, lastly, the choice of Bonn, hitherto just a small provincial city, as the 'provisional' federal capital. These decisions served to amplify, rather than initiate, an urban system and framework of city-size relationships which, apart from some interesting individual changes in rank positioning during the postwar period, had already been well established. Accordingly one has to turn to historical factors of causation.

The origins of the West German urban system can be traced as far back in time as the Middle Ages, when the German territories lying to the west of the river Elbe were fragmented into a chaotic assemblage of numerous duchies, principalities, ecclesiastic 'states' and independent imperial cities, each competing against its neighbours for political and economic power. In many instances this rivalry tended to heighten the functional importance of historic urban centres often out of all proportion to their local resources and geographic location. This 'upgrading' of provincial cities increased in scale during the sixteenth, seventeenth and eighteenth centuries. This, the so-called 'Age of Princes', was an era not only of widening economic interaction between trading centres, but also one of intensifying political competition in which a select number of expanding territories sought to strengthen their prestige and influence by constructing all the ostensible trappings of a *de facto* nation state. One of the most notable features of the latter trend was the proliferation of state capitals, and through this the granting of a clearly defined regional status to an extensive list of West German cities.

With few exceptions, the size and functional standing of these regional cities was greatly enhanced during the industrial revolution. In reviewing this critical period, writers consider that the 'take-off' phase belonged to the 1870s, and the fastest pace of industrialisation took place during the following three decades.[2] It is important to stress that, unlike the British experience, these major events of economic history *postdated* the main wave of construction of Germany's provincial railway network. Indeed, the point can be further emphasised by noting that during the 'railway era' of the 1850s, 1860s and early 1870s most sponsors of state railway systems decided to focus their main routes on established regional capitals instead of towns and cities with optimum combinations of industrial resources. Consequently, over the nation as a whole, the German tradition of diffuse 'city regionalism' was reinforced, rather than altered, during the industrial revolution.

In the economic development of postwar West Germany two major sets of advantages have been derived from this historical legacy. In the first place, the existence in this country of as many as 15 major regional centres and 52 other large cities, all with present-day populations above the 100,000 level, means that there is a wide replication of the organisational requirements for nurturing modern industrial and commercial growth. Indeed, one is very much tempted to think along the lines that the regional availability of such essential needs as financial facilities, research and advisory institutions, concentrations of skilled labour and adequate communications infrastructures represents one of the most important, if least publicised, growth factors behind West Germany's outstanding postwar economic success.

The second set of advantages accrues from the repeated ranges of services which these numerous large cities provide both for their own communities and their wider catchment areas. In the large majority of cases they cover an impressive variety of central-place functions which include all the social, cultural and consumer prerequisites for attaining high 'quality-of-life'. In total, about 75 per cent of West Germany's population lives within easy travelling distance to at least one *Regionale Stadt*,[3] a proportion which serves to underline the extensiveness of an increasingly city-oriented consumer society.

Although it is far more effective than in most other west European countries, even in West Germany the geographic distribution of regional cities falls some way short of the theoretician's notion of equal spacing and functional balance. In the Rhinelands a particularly strong degree of political fragmentation during the Middle Ages and the Renaissance, followed by rapid economic development during and after the industrial revolution, produced a concentration of centres (38 out of the total 67) distributed along a broad tract of territory stretching from Recklinghausen in the northern Ruhr to Stuttgart in Baden-Württemberg (Figure 1.1). Indeed, within this so-called 'Rhine axis' or 'urbanised core' of West Germany, one can recognise three constellations of cities:

Figure 1.1: West Germany: Distribution, Size and Functional Importance of Major Cities

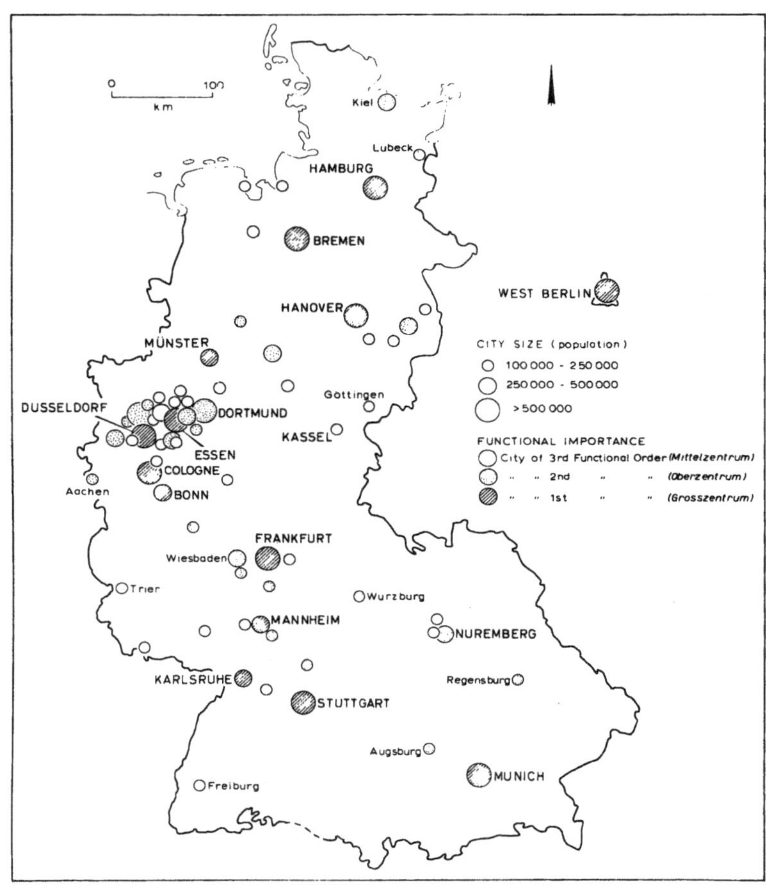

Source: The functional classification of 100,000-plus cities is based on the system which G. Kluczka defines and describes in 'Zentrale Orte und zentralörtliche Bereiche mittlerer höherer Stufe in der BRD', *Forschungen zur deutschen Landeskunde*, vol. 194 (1970).

first and foremost, the Rhine-Ruhr region, with as many as 23 municipalities with 100,000-plus populations; secondly, the Rhine-Main region, which has five such centres including Frankfurt, Wiesbaden and Mainz; thirdly, the Rhine-Neckar region, where the cities of Mannheim, Ludwigshafen, Heidelberg, Karlsruhe and Pforzheim are likewise positioned only short distances apart from each other. These three regions are clearly over-provided with metropolitan facilities: they are also overburdened with the types of environmental problems which are universally associated with a vigorous and polycentric type of urban-growth process.

Moving away from the Rhine axis, the distribution of major cities becomes progressively sparcer. Indeed, east of a line drawn from Münster to Frankfurt and Stuttgart, and west of a line drawn from Aachen to Karlsruhe, the principal feature in Figure 1.1 is the occurrence of what German geographers refer to as *Isoliertestädte* ('isolated' cities). The largest examples are Hamburg, Munich, the Nuremberg conurbation, Bremen and Kassel, but the list can be extended to include centres such as Trier and Freiburg in the west and Kiel, Lübeck, Göttingen, Würzburg, Augsburg and Regensburg in the east. The wide separation of these cities means that their hinterland areas, or *Umlandzonen*, do not overlap (Figure 1.2). Beyond the confines of the Rhine axis and its offshoots, therefore, there are extensive parts of West Germany which, even under today's conditions of much-improved regional road and public-transport networks, still do not have easy access to metropolitan functions and amenities. Fittingly described as 'the peripheral regions', in all cases their remoteness poses a severe handicap to their general economic development and enhancement of material quality of life. With ample justification, those federal and Land authorities which institute and direct policies of regional development have, since the early 1950s, consistently focused their attention and resources on tackling this problem. For more than a decade its solution (and also that of the rapid decline in the farming occupation) was seen to lie in the promotion of industrialisation. It is significant, however, that since 1969 and the introduction of the 'Joint Task for the Improvement of Regional Economic Structures',[4] a growing emphasis has been placed on improving the central-place functions of all areas deemed to have been deficient in urban facilities. The cornerstone of this strategy is the selection of certain small to average-size towns for investment in the three crucial fields of infrastructure provision, expansion of public services and fostering of local businesses. Its full effect has yet to be seen, but given time this deliberate manipulation of the urban spatial system and extension of urbanism will most likely prove to be a major factor in reducing the inequalities between West Germany's city-orientated areas and its rural residuals.

Figure 1.2: West Germany: Major Cities and their *Umlandzonen*

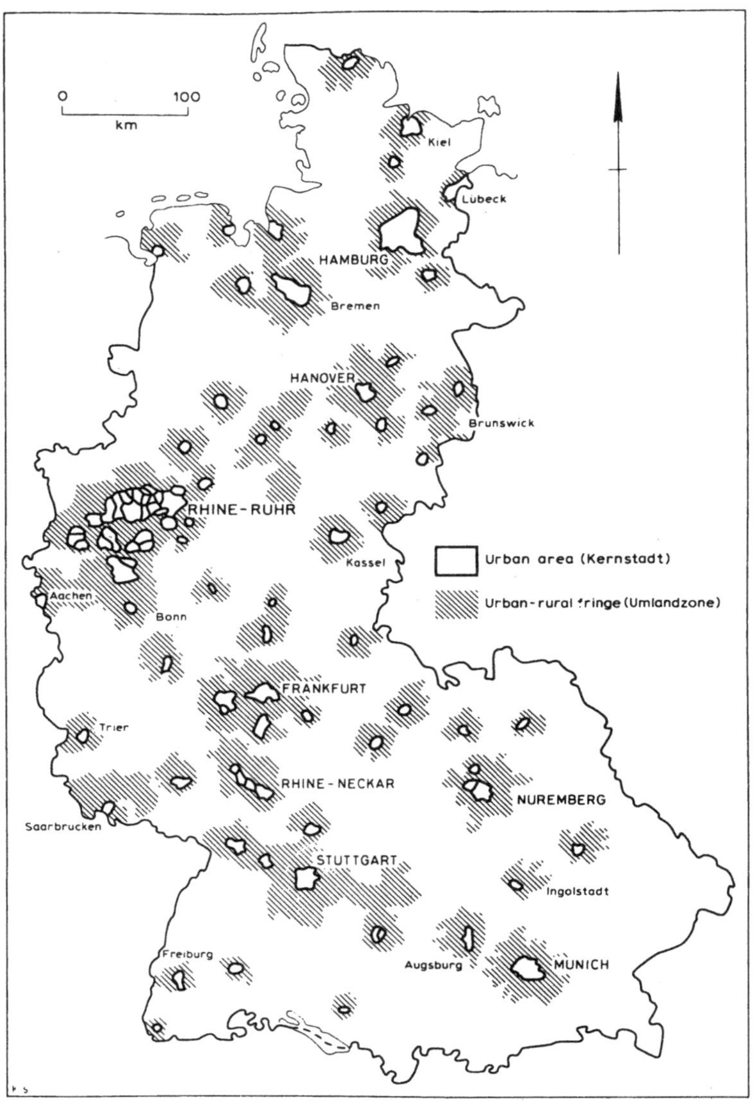

Source: Die Akademie für Raumforschung und Landesplanung, ***Stadt und Stadtraum*** (Veröffentlichungen der Akademie für Raumforschung und Landesplanung, Hanover, 1974), pp. 169 ff.

The Distribution of Rural Areas

The diffuse, if by no means perfect, distribution of major cities, with their hinterland areas and protruding development axes, has produced a highly fragmented pattern of non-urbanised interstices. Accordingly, there is no regionality in West Germany comparable in scale and contiguity with say *le désert français*, the 'Highland Zone' of Britain or the interior of the Italian *Mezzogiorno*.

Until the publication of the 1970 federal census, German academics commonly defined rural areas in terms of the predominance of the farming occupation. In 1950 farmers had represented more than 33 per cent of workers in as many as 241 of West Germany's 425 *Landkreise* (county districts). These are shown in the first of the three maps presented in Figure 1.3. Even at this early date, several years before the full outbreak of the rural suburbanisation process, one is confronted with a broken pattern. Separated from each other by the emergent Rhine axis and the alignment of 'old' industrial regions running north-eastwards across the country from Aachen to Brunswick, four major – but irregularly shaped – tracts of shaded territory can be recognised: first, a collection of rural areas stretching from eastern Hesse, through central and eastern Bavaria, to the Austrian frontier; secondly, the belt of countryside which, with major interruptions around the cities of Bremen and Hamburg, extends eastwards from the Emsland to Schleswig-Holstein and Lüneburg Heath: thirdly, a linear cluster of rural Landkreise occupying much of southern Baden-Württemberg and western Bavaria; fourthly, a more compact grouping in the Eifel-Moselle-Hunsrück regions to the west of the Rhine.

The second map in Figure 1.3, representing the distribution in 1961, depicts a much smaller number of rural Landkreise; the reduction coming as a response to a major wave of occupational change away from farming and mainly into manufacturing industry. This shift was nationwide, but it was particularly effective in locations not far away from the Rhine axis and the vicinity of large cities. The result was a marked geographical shrinkage and greater fragmentation of rural areas. These two trends gained in momentum after 1961, and by 1970, the date of the third map, only 20 remote Landkreise qualified for shading.

Measured in occupational terms, West Germany has experienced a massive retreat of rurality. This has been demonstrated in Figure 1.3 within the standard mapping framework of Landkreis districts. But it has also occurred even at the parish level, for today less than one in ten *Gemeinden* can still count farming to be the principal source of

Figure 1.3: West Germany: Rural Areas Defined by Importance of Farming Occupation, 1950, 1961 and 1970.

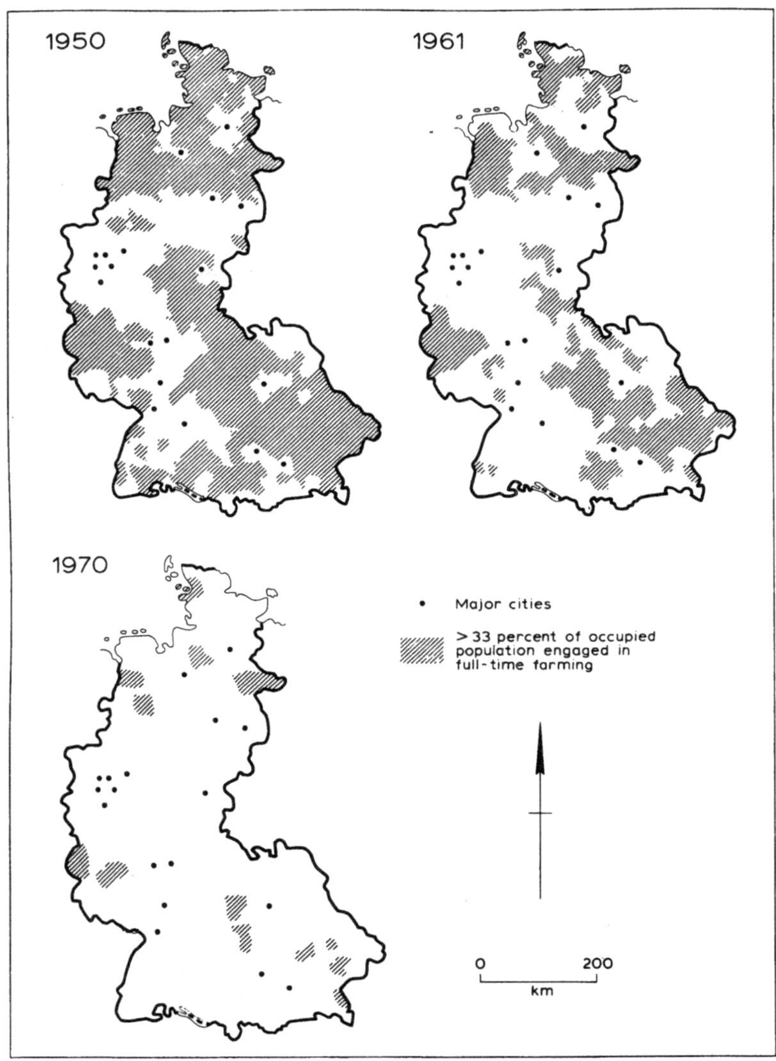

Source: Based upon data contained in Institut für Raumforschung, *Informationen Sonderhefte: Kreiszahlen zur Raumordnung* (Institut für Raumforschung, Bad Godesberg, annual reports).

Figure 1.4: West Germany: Rural Areas by Modern Definition

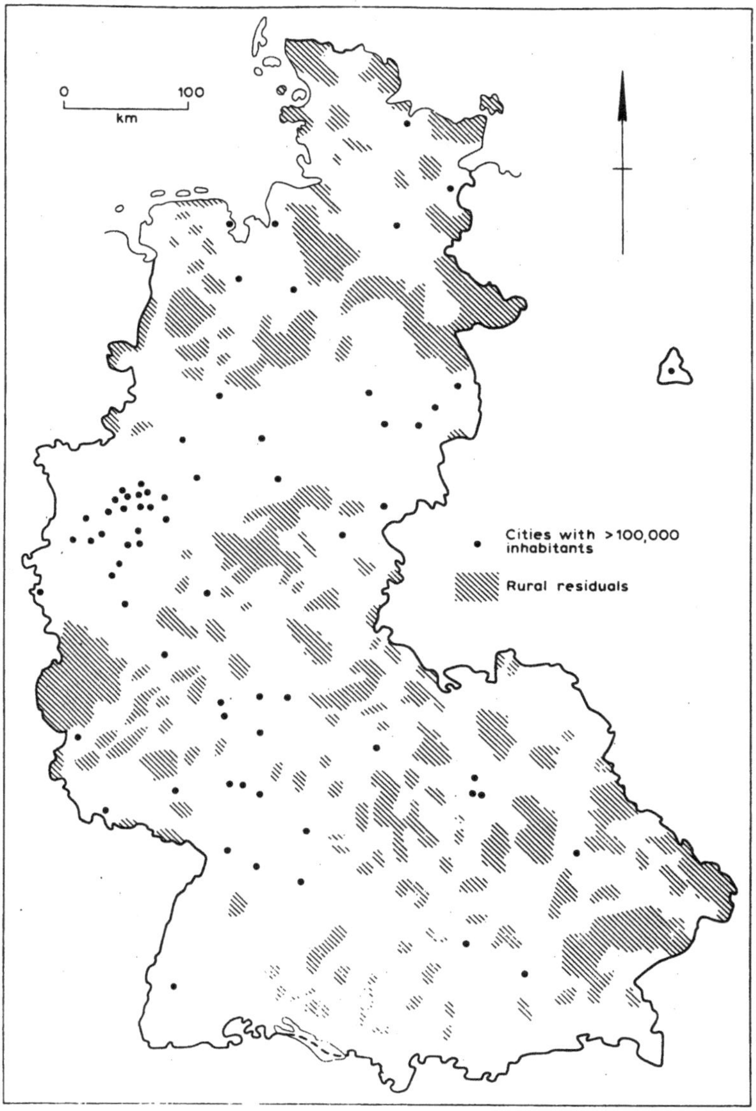

Source: Simplified from G. Isbary, 'Areas of sound structures and living conditions', *Veröffentlichen der Akademie für Raumforschung und Landesplanung*, vol. 57 (1970), Abblatt Beilage 9.

livelihood. Since the 1970 census, therefore, most authorities in West Germany have modified their conceptual definition of rural areas. In so doing they continue to recognise the importance of the agricultural base, but also turn to a more complex identification which embodies such relevant ingredients of the rural scenario as population densities, communications facilities, distance from employment centres, average household incomes, arrangement of settlement sizes and central-place structures. By aggregating these indicators it is possible to draw much more meaningful maps of rural areas, and Figure 1.4, based on the work of Isbary in 1970,[5] performs this task. The distribution that emerges from the exercise realistically highlights the spatial intricacy and complexity of West German rurality. Altogether, more than 100 separate rural areas are identified, ranging in size from just a handful of Gemeinden to territories of more than 2,000 km^2 extent. The majority are to be found within those peripheral parts of the country where farming retains a well-above-average occupational significance. But also represented are a number of isolated and 'non-urban' industrial retreats where the predominant settlement unit is the manufacturing or mining village. These share with the other shaded areas in having the four critical attributes of remoteness from large urban centres, inadequate central-place structures, having more than one-half of their population living within communities of less than 5,000 inhabitants and (as a result of the recent downturn in industrial employment) suffering insufficient local job provision.

The rural areas of Figure 1.4, therefore, are disadvantaged in almost all important respects other than their living environments and natural scenery. But, unlike the situation in other west European countries, the haphazard configuration and geographic identity of West Germany's rural problem, more often than not, renders it very difficult to apply regionally based solutions. Moreover, under present-day conditions of demographic decline, economic recession, reductions in job opportunities and intensifying cuts in transport budgets, it is likely that the spatial expression of modern connotations of rurality will endure rather than decline.

Notes

1. M.T. Wild, *West Germany, a Geography of its People* (W.Dawson & Son, Folkestone, 1979, and Longman Group, Harlow, 1981), p. 190.

2. There is some confusion, however, over the German term *Die Gründerzeit*. Translated as 'the foundation period', this has connotations in both the economic

and political evolution of Germany. The 'period' itself belongs to the 1870s, and more specifically the first few years of Bismarck's Second German Empire.

3. E. Böventer, 'Regional Economic Problems in West Germany' in E.A.G. Robinson (ed.), *Backward Areas in Advanced Countries* (Varenna, 1969), pp. 171-95

4. With some minor modifications to its spatial application, the Joint Task still forms the basis for present-day, federal regional development strategy. For a full account see Wild, *West Germany*, pp. 137-42.

5. G. Isbary, 'Areas of sound structures and living conditions', *Veröffentlichen der Akademie für Raumforschung und Landesplanung*, vol. 57 (1970), Abblatt Beilage, 9.

2 POSTWAR DEVELOPMENT AND PLANNING OF WEST GERMAN CITIES

Joe Hajdu

Germany's rich urban heritage, and in particular its outstanding contribution to urban form and architectural styles, was an underlying feature of the pioneering treatise on the west European city written by Dickinson in 1951.[1] Although for several years after its publication this book was generally regarded as a definitive work on the subject, it was based primarily on prewar research observations, and more than a generation has passed since its compilation. There is a need, therefore, to review the current state of the city in West Germany, its postwar development, the planning problems which have been presented and, last but not least, the changing perception of solutions which are deemed to be appropriate to these problems. Many similarities can be seen between the West German urban experience of the recent past and that of cities in other highly developed societies of the western world. But the form which urban change has taken, and the type of urban planning problems, has had characteristics which are peculiar to West Germany. The reasons for this are to be found largely in the special morphology of the West German city, the devastating impact of the Second World War on its fabric and, lastly, the spectacular nature of socio-economic change since 1945.

Postwar urban development in West Germany can be viewed within the context of a series of overlapping phases in which one priority is superseded by another and certain policies evolve which are then modified or overturned. This chapter is based on the recognition of four such phases: first, the phase of immediate-postwar reconstruction: secondly, a phase of rapid urban population growth, economic expansion and quickly rising affluence; thirdly, a phase characterised by mounting environmental concern and pressures for the retention of the traditional urban fabric; finally, the current phase of newly emerging urban problems at a time when West German cities are entering a period of relative economic austerity.

The First and Second Phases

The first phase, that of postwar urban reconstruction, began soon after the ending of hostilities in 1945; but it did not achieve full expression until after the currency reform and economic 'take-off' of 1948. It continued until the mid 1950s, and throughout this period the most urgent priority was the provision of residential accommodation for vast numbers of people in the severely bomb-damaged towns and cities. The arrival of about 11.5 million refugees and expellees into West Germany during the first postwar decade aggravated a housing shortage which had already assumed crisis dimensions as a consequence of wartime destruction. Homes had to be provided at the fastest possible rate, and obviously the finer points of urban planning had to be overlooked in this massive building programme. The urgency of this task, the problems of complex property-titles and the general conservatism of the German city-dweller meant that a large proportion of the rebuilding was little more than a crude restoration of the prewar urban fabric.

By the affluent standards of present-day West Germany the sizes of these early postwar homes were small, and their bathrooms, kitchens and heating systems were simple. Yet the sheer physical scope of construction is impressive, rising from under 300,000 dwelling completions in 1948 to 460,000 in 1952 and 568,000 in 1955. Since 1945 more than 17 million homes have been built, and today over two-thirds of all dwellings in West Germany were constructed during the postwar period. An international comparison is revealing; during the period 1949-72, for every thousand inhabitants, the number of dwellings completed in West Germany was 198, but in the United Kingdom, France and the USA the corresponding figures were only 129, 135 and 157 respectively.[2]

In the mid 1950s it was realised that a simple quantitative approach to city reconstruction was not enough. Most urban areas were starting to surpass their 1939 population levels, and significant intra-urban population movements were taking place. Underlying these changes was the drift of rural people to the cities as employment opportunities expanded in the booming West German economy. Moreover, until the building of the Berlin Wall in 1961, the inflow of refugees from the East continued at a high rate, with most of these people also being drawn towards the larger and more prosperous urban centres. At the same time, rising affluence meant that increasing numbers of established city-dwellers were able to set their sights on larger, better-appointed homes spaced at lower densities. This encouraged a shift from the generally small and crowded apartment blocks of the inner-urban precincts, outwards to new detached, semi-detached and duplex homes being built in the urban–rural fringe. This critical period of the late 1950s and early 1960s, therefore, became a phase of marked urban change motivated not only by urban population growth, but also by an increasing demand for more spacious homes in a 'green' environment.

The latter trend was largely accommodated through the conversion of rural land to urban housing on the edges of most large cities, and through the residential expansion of formerly agricultural villages within commuting distances to centres of employment. These parallel processes produced those zones of low-density residential sprawl, which by the mid-1960s were becoming all too apparent features in the expanding structure of the West German city and its immediate hinterland. Because the 1949 Basic Law of the German Federal Republic gave the main powers of town planning to local government (at the *Gemeinde* level), the balance between land speculation and land-use planning in this 'residential fringe' varies greatly from one municipality to the next. In some cases, adoption of local architectural styles and attention to environmental sensitivity has created attractive, harmonious housing estates; in others, however, speculative builders have been allowed to produce developments which are uninspiring in design and entirely out of character with the existing settlement fabric of the urban–rural fringe.

Not all of the population pressure in and around cities could be accommodated by these two processes of 'free' urban development. There was also a need for local governments, planners and building companies to turn to a more co-ordinated and controllable type of solution. Owing to rapidly increasing land values inside the built-up urban areas, and also due to the huge difficulties faced in any public-sponsored quest for property acquisition, redevelopment schemes comparable to British models were unpractical. Accordingly, several city authorities, mostly those administrating urban centres with particularly heavy influxes of rural migrants and refugees, concentrated their resources on the building of *Trabantenstädte* (new satellite towns) on easily obtainable 'green-land' sites.[3]

The Trabantenstädte

The planning, construction and management of the Trabantenstädte is usually undertaken by a consortium of bodies, including city housing departments, building firms, housing co-operatives and banks and finance companies. In most cases either the *Land* or federal government has made cheap finance available on condition that a certain proportion of the dwellings are to be let at pegged rentals to people meeting the criteria for social-housing help. From the late 1950s to the early 1970s, a number of large West German cities developed satellite new towns on an extensive scale; for example, Bremen-Neue Vahr (built for an envisaged population target of 30,000), Hamburg-Osdorfer Born (18,000), Dusseldorf-Garath (30,000), Frankfurt-Nordweststadt (45,000), Mannheim-Vogelsang (20,000), Nuremberg-Langwasser (60,000) and Munich-Perlach (60,000). West Berlin has two Trabantenstädte: Gropiusstadt in the southeast portion of the metropolitan area extends over a site of 248 ha, and has more than 15,000 homes for nearly 40,000 people; the Märkische Viertel in the north has 17,000 dwellings on 392 ha, and accommodates a population of around 50,000. The degree to which these communities function just as giant dormitory suburbs varies considerably. However, as far as the provision of services is concerned, attempts have usually been made to create an independent viability, with reliance on the parent city being limited to highly specialised retail, cultural and professional facilities.[4]

It is worth turning now to the example of Nurember-Langwasser where construction work started in 1957 on a 541-ha site, 6 km away to the southeast of the city centre. Like most settlements of its type, Langwasser lies within the administrative area and jurisdiction of the city, but an extensive tract of residual public forest (the Nürnberger Reichswald) separates it from the edge of the contiguous built-up area. It also provides for valuable environmental and recreational needs, and includes a well-designed system of walker's paths, cycling tracks and children's play areas, all within easy reach of the residents of Langwasser. The new community has been planned on the basis of a series of neighbourhood units set within a carefully arranged layout of 'green' wedges (Figure 2.1). The only building structures permitted within these wedges have been kindergartens, schools and sporting venues. Land-use planning has ensured the separation of incompatible activities, with particular attention being given to the positioning of the 26-ha industrial zone and the framework of streets and roads. Another important feature, and one which is very typical of the West German satellite town, is the highly developed pattern of retail facilities. No home in Langwasser is more than 300 m walking distance from at least one neighbourhood shopping cluster. The whole community focuses on the centrally-situated *Franken-Einkaufszentrum*. Opened in 1969 and subsequently provided with a 'U' Bahn link to the city centre, this is easily the largest suburban retail complex in Nuremberg. In addition to its 35,000 m² of shop-floor space, its list of services has recently been extended to include a community hall, library, an adult education group (*Kulturwerk Langwasser*) and several clubrooms.[5]

Figure 2.1: Plan of Nuremberg-Langwasser

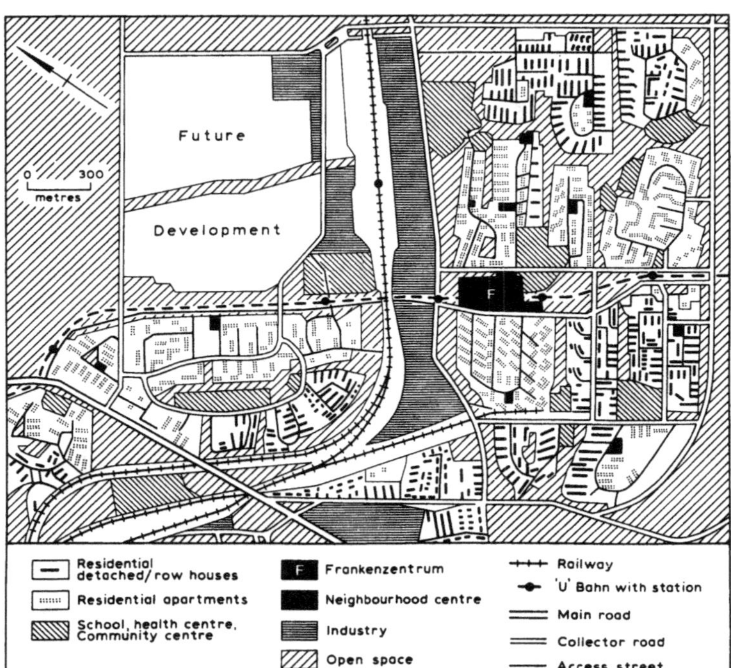

Source: Gemeinnützige Wohnungsbaugesellschaft der Stadt Nürnberg, *Nürnberg-Langwasser, Stadtteil im Grünen* (H. Gröschner, Nuremberg, 1975), Appendix Location Map.

As much as 43 per cent of the Langwasser site is occupied by residential development, while a further 35 per cent is given over to roads, parking spaces and green space. The remaining 22 per cent of the land has been zoned for such uses as retailing, manufacturing, railways, schools and sports centres. By British standards the population density (approximately 185 persons per residential ha) is high. This is due to the heavy emphasis on apartment construction, which today accounts for as much as 80 per cent of the settlement's total housing stock. The concentration on multi-dwelling residential buildings, however, has had two important practical advantages: on the one hand it has allowed the widespread use of cost-saving, prefabricated methods of construction; on the other, it has enabled the domestic heating system to be centralised at the neighbourhood level.

One of the original aims in the planning of Langwasser was the creation of between 5,000 and 6,000 industrial jobs. To date, 34 manufacturing firms have been attracted to the community, but these provide work for only 2,100 persons – less than 20 per cent of Langwasser's 'active' population.[6] This shortfall means that in the sphere of workplace-residence relationships there is a high degree of interdependence with many other parts of Nuremberg. The problem was most acutely felt during the late 1960s and early 1970s, but since then it has been eased in three successive stages: first, by the provision of direct road access to the city's encircling Autobahn 'box'; secondly, through the completion of the 'U' Bahn link to the city centre; thirdly, as a result of the expansion of new work opportunities on the extensive Europa Canal industrial estate, which is within an easy bus or car-journey distance of less than 5 km from central Langwasser.

The City Centres

During the 1950s and early 1960s urban planners in West Germany were not only forced to seek solutions to mounting population growth and demand for residential accommodation, but also had to cope with escalating pressures of economic and social change on the central areas of cities. One particularly visible symptom of such change was the rapid proliferation of commercial office buildings and the larger-scale types of retail outlets. These developments, linked as they were to periodic bursts of property speculation, were very much to the fore in the growing dislocation of the traditional balance between the residential and work functions of the 'interior' city.[7]

Today this balance is fast disappearing, but writers still regard it as a distinctive and fundamental characteristic of the West German city. The decline of what may be described as 'central-city living' is a long-established and well-documented trend in the USA and in Britain, but in West Germany it was seen as a symbol of the destruction of a treasured aspect of the urban heritage and an unwelcome disruption of sensitive, social and (local) political values.

Frankfurt is an extreme, but not atypical, example of what has been happening. Here, the number of people living in the *Innenstadt* area (city centre and immediate surrounds) declined from 42,000 in 1939 to just 13,000 in 1974. Much of this population loss belonged to the district known as Frankfurt-Westend. Until the 1960s the Westend, which lies between the main railway station and the historic core of the city, was an area of mixed land uses consisting mainly of pre-1914 apartment buildings, workshops, retail premises and other small businesses.[8] As part of a general policy of advancing Frankfurt's role as West Germany's leading banking and financial centre, the municipal authorities published a plan to facilitate the expansion of office development to the west of the Altstadt and central business district. This plan, and the subsequent property boom of the late 1960s and early 1970s, transformed the Westend from what had once been a typical pre-First World War urban landscape to a district dominated by a 'Manhattan-type' skyline. The numbers of Westend properties changing hands, in which the buyer intended to demolish and rebuild, rose from 13 in 1967 to 43 in 1968 and as many as 66 in 1969, before falling to 20 in 1971 and 12 in 1973. However, the price of these transactions rose continuously, averaging DM 946 per m^2 of land in 1967, DM 1,491 in 1969 and DM 2,406 in 1973.[9] Moreover, the Westend property boom of 1968-73 was in effect the peak of a longer-term trend which had been apparent since the early 1960s, and during the period from the 1961 to the 1970 census had produced a 24 per cent increase in Westend jobs, but a 23 per cent drop in the local population.[10]

In addition to the pressures of commercial growth, city centres and their near surrounds came under the quickly growing threat of the motor car. In West Germany a pronounced 'take-off' in car ownership occurred in the late 1950s (see Figure 7.2). It was followed by a phase of spectacular expansion during the next decade, when the average density of cars in cities of over 100,000 inhabitants increased from 143 vehicles per km^2 to 605.[11] What was initially welcomed as a trend increasing the accessibility of city centres, soon led to anxiety over the problems of congestion and impeded traffic flow. Many city centres, especially those which had inherited a medieval street pattern, had to be replanned, and municipal authorities were all too easily tempted to implement proposals for the '*autogerechte Stadt*' – the city which will do justice to the needs of the motor car. Designs for meeting these needs varied considerably from city to city. In Hamburg and Frankfurt, for example, the Altstadt was bisected by the construction of a new arterial road. Other cities, such as Cologne and Munich, used the sites of demolished fortification lines to build multi-lane ring roads around the central area. The earliest, and arguably the most successful, autogerechte Stadt was Hanover, where the large amount of wartime devastation was seen as an opportunity to remodel the entire traffic pattern of the central business district.[12] Previously Hanover's through-traffic had been carried along one or other of the city's nine arterial roads, and had been forced to converge on the Altstadt where only two streets, Kröpke Strasse and Steintorstrasse, permitted easy movement. However, only three years after the end of the Second World War the municipality produced a plan which sought to eliminate all through-traffic from the city centre. This was to be achieved through the building of an internal ring road, with some sections following the line of the old city wall and others being laid out within a severely bombed residential and industrial zone. The construction work commenced in November 1949, and because of this early start the project was not only concurrent with the beginning of the general postwar construction of central Hanover, but was also able to take a unique position amongst West German cities in predating (by several years) the upsurge in urban traffic congestion.

The Third Phase: Environmental Concern and Reappraisal of Priorities

The accumulating effects of urban change ranked highly amongst the targets of the wave of social criticism which spread through the Federal Republic during the second half of the 1960s. That this should occur on such a widespread scale was a shock to the many politicians and civic administrators who felt that the rebuilding of West Germany's war-ravaged cities, the management of urban traffic and the overcoming of the postwar housing crisis, were all highly creditable achievements. But the critics argued that these were essentially monuments to a type of technological and engineering progress which on numerous occasions had proved itself to be detrimental to the urban environment and the social milieu. More moderate versions of this view eventually found acceptance among members of the planning profession, with writers such as Albers and Bahrdt[13] taking an analytical approach to a debate which hinged on three principal foci of controversy.

First and foremost was the pre-eminence which the previous generation of planners had given to the motor car. By the late 1960s, however, the unending increase in traffic and its demand for parking and driving space was seen both as a threat to the fabric of the 'interior' city and as the prime instigator of urban sprawl and the destruction of the countryside. In some cases 'anti-car' pressure groups were able to force the postponement or cancellation of sections of newly proposed metropolitan ringroads; in other cases they led the protest against inner-city road projects, especially those which were designed to run through residential areas.

The second cause of discontent was the loss of residential accommodation in many inner urban areas. This was frequently related to the space needs of large commercial companies and property speculators, and became an outstanding target for student protest and anti-establishment political activism. Not surprisingly, one of the first of several flashpoints occurred in Frankfurt-Westend. Here, in 1973, groups of local residents and political 'extremists' occupied apartment buildings which were about to be demolished by property developers. The police intervened and violent clashes followed,[14] setting a pattern of disturbances which soon spread to one after the other of West Germany's major cities.

The third issue, the criticism levied at the Trabantenstädte, turned attention away from the interior city and towards the city outskirts. In the sense that they were designed as clearly separated settlements in which (in theory at least) every attempt was made to enable the inhabitants to harmonise between residential accommodation, relaxation and shopping, the building of these satellite towns had been influenced by the British 'Garden City' movement and the guidelines set down by the 1933 Charter of Athens. But, notwithstanding the merits of their physical planning, their general environment was seen by many to be structured to provide a setting for buildings rather than to facilitate social contact. People felt isolated in their bleak, concrete-faced apartments, while quite commonly amenities were slow to arrive and there was a serious lack of local employment provision. Organised criticism sometimes brought results.[15] In Bremen-Neue Vahr, for example, a residents' action group was able to force the building companies to extend their development plans in 1971 to include a community centre, some hobby rooms and a medical-welfare complex. Similar residents' pressure in Cologne-Chorweiler, a Trabantenstadt which at one time had been notoriously deficient in social amenities, succeeded in making the developers turn their attention to the creation of much improved systems of neighbourhood centres and walkways.

While sporadic improvements were being made to the quality of life in the satellite towns, the very concept of the planned 'greenfield' community was under challenge. In 1971 two Munich architects, Lembrock and Fischer, staged an exhibition in which they referred to man's need for the variety, colour and vibrancy which only an established city can provide. They wanted the emphasis in urban endeavour and appreciation to swing back to the older, prewar residential areas which were able to satisfy these conditions but, at the same time, were suffering from increasing levels of congestion, noise and pollution. The exhibition, which carried the title of 'Profitopolis, or Mankind Needs Another Type of City', drew a very positive response, and is now seen with hindsight as a major turning point in postwar thinking on the West German city.

The Rediscovery of Urbanity

Whereas the first two postwar decades saw an emphasis on city reconstruction, urban expansion and planning for the motor car, the period since the mid-1960s has been one of growing homage to the principle of '*Schaffe eine menschliche Stadt*' (the shaping of cities fit for people). This change of attitudes has become particularly apparent in two special contexts.

The first is the reappraisal of planning policies for the historic city cores, where it was felt that there was a pressing need for arresting, if not reversing, the postwar trend of overwhelming commercialisation. Thus, local authorities were encouraged to soften what many people saw as a dominantly materialistic image of their city centres, and by way of response by-laws were amended to facilitate the Altstädte becoming places for relaxation, social meetings and street entertainments. During the 1970s, therefore, open spaces in almost every sizeable West German city suddenly saw the appearance of informal vendors' stalls, musicians' corners, pavement artists and open-air cafés. Proliferation of these 'happenings' could not have occurred without an abrupt departure from traffic-orientated planning and its neglect of the pedestrian.

The second context is the rediscovery of the positional and social advantages of inner-city living. Out of this new perception has arisen a keen desire to create a better harmony in urban investment policies between the hitherto stigmatic, prewar apartment areas and the extensive modern housing development on the outskirts of cities and in the widely spreading urban-rural fringes. The residential quarters of inner-city districts, with their rich architectural heritage, their large numbers of local shops, pubs and small businesses, and their proximity to the Altstadt, are deemed by many writers to be on a more 'human' scale than any type of postwar suburb.

Having outlined these two fundamental changes in urban thinking, it is now worth directing our attention to the 'key' planning issues of central-area pedestrianisation and residential conservation.

Central-Area Pedestrianisation. In West Germany the earliest pedestrian malls, invariably situated within the historic city cores, were created as a 'surrender' to the inability of narrow, ancient streets to cope with the twin pressures of growing traffic congestion and increasing numbers of shoppers. However, necessity became a virtue as the social and environmental benefits of pedestrianisation became apparent. Since the late 1960s the proliferation of pedestrianised areas, or *Fussgängerbereiche*, has been spectacular: 96 had been established in West Germany by 1970; three years later their numbers had increased to 214, and by 1980 the total had passed 500.[16] Counts of shoppers and other visitors walking along streets, immediately before and immediately after pedestrianisation, have been made in several cities. Without exception, the results indicate a substantial expansion in numbers of potential customers.[17] Moreover, there are reports of resultant rises in retail turnover, and there is frequent mention of shopowners dropping their initial stance of opposition to the process and offering unqualified support.[18]

However, the drawing of people into the pedestrian malls has often been done at the expense of a decline in business in adjacent streets.[19] To overcome this problem, some cities have extended their original Fussgängerbereiche to include as many central shopping streets as possible. But as the size of the pedestrianised area increased, so did the nearby problems of traffic flow and vehicle access. In most city centres municipal traffic engineers have channelled motor cars around the pedestrianised area and through a system of one-way streets. The complexity of traffic planning is typified by the example of Munich (Figure 2.2) where the pedestrian malls, focusing on the axial Neuhäuser Strasse, make through-traffic impossible. It has been diverted onto an inner ring road from which a series of looping entrants and exits provide access to the rear of the Fussgängerbereich. Car drivers are able to leave their vehicles in well-positioned, off-street or underground parking lots. Only delivery vans and service vehicles are allowed to enter the pedestrianised area, their intrusion being restricted to the time between 10.30 p.m. and 9.45 a.m.

In recent years the provision of car-parking space around the edges of pedestrianised areas has come under increasing criticism. Indeed, in some cities it has been argued that, apart from improving the retail environment, all that the pedestrian malls are achieving is the pushing of congestion and noise from one central location to another. The answer to this problem lies in innovations and investments in public transport, especially those which are geared towards improving the accessibility of the retail and business quarters. At present as many as 16 cities in West Germany have built, or are in the process of completing, their own underground tramway systems. The commonest method of constructing these 'U' Bahnen is to select the most viable of the pre-existing, surface tram routes, and where these enter the central area, to put new lines in shallow tunnels just below the street level.

Figure 2.2: Traffic Planning and Pedestrianisation in Central Munich

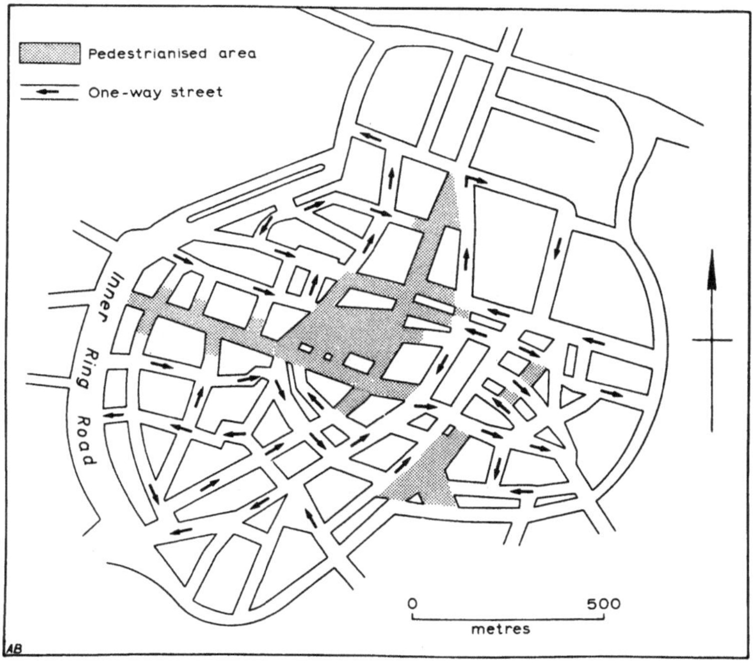

Source: Kompass Verlag, *Kompass-Stadtplan München* (H. Fleischmann Geographischer Verlag, 1980).

However, in addition to the 'U' Bahnen some cities are building underground railways which are designed to provide even faster movement from suburbs to the central business district. Frankfurt has already completed such a line (part of the extensive Rhein-Main 'S' Bahn –

high-speed commuter railway – system) providing an essential rapid-transit link from the satellite community of Frankfurt-Nordweststadt to the heart of the city's pedestrianised area. Underground railways, with stations conveniently placed at intervals of between 800 to 1,000 m from each other, have also been laid underneath the central areas of Stuttgart, Hanover and Munich. A significant portion of the funds for these expensive projects has come from tied grants financed out of federal government resources. The 1975 Public Transport Act made this possible. However, since then the initial confidence in prospects of early repayment is receding rapidly during the present phase of economic recession and heavy increases in operating costs.

Concurrent with this change in general economic conditions there has been some further criticism of pedestrial malls, both from the traffic-management and from the environmental point of view. In 1978 a report sponsored by the *Bundesministerium für Raumordnung, Bauwesen und Städtebau* (Federal Ministry for Regional Planning, Building Affairs and Urban Development), argued that if all that pedestrianisation had achieved was to move congestion and pollution from the central business district to the immediately adjoining *City-nahesgebiet*, or mixed-use zone, then it had not contributed very significantly to the overall improvement of the urban environment.[20] Moreover, the report argued further that higher retail turnover was an inadequate compensation for increased pressures and blight in adjacent areas. There are some signs of a positive response to this criticism. This has taken two forms: first, over the last few years, the development of pedestrian precincts in which commercial aims are blended in with environmental and conservation policies (rather than the other way round); secondly, the introduction of new models of traffic management aimed at moderating the all-too-abrupt transition from pedestrian street to congested access way. Central Bonn is an example of the former; central Göttingen illustrates the latter.

Pedestrianisation in Central Bonn. The Altstadt area of Bonn is one of West Germany's finest examples of how careful and sympathetic planning can blend together the commercial, environmental and cultural needs of a modern city centre. This achievement, which has been completed with remarkably little destruction of Bonn's rich and varied architectural legacy, has been brought about through an enlightened policy of civic design in which pedestrianism, conservation and transport planning have all played important parts.[21]

Central Bonn consists of a tight concentration of buildings whose layout, despite some considerable wartime destruction, is still largely determined by a medieval street pattern (Figure 2.3). The traditional ecclesiastic and commercial functions of the city remain strongly entrenched in the spacious *Münsterplatz* (cathedral square) and *Marktplatz* (market place). These two focal features of Altstadt-Bonn are linked by Remigiusstrasse, a narrow, 250-m-long, street which, with its three department stores and its various speciality shops, has the highest pedestrian flows in the city. By the mid 1960s Remigiusstrasse had become virtually impassable for road traffic, and in 1967 the decision was taken to close it to all vehicles except delivery vans. That same year another shopping street leading off from the Marktplatz, Stern Strasse, was subjected to pedestrianisation. These two pioneer attempts at reducing traffic congestion in the main retail streets and giving shoppers easier access to their venues represented the first phase in the creation of Bonn's Fussgängerbereich. A few years later, however, thought was given to the design of a much more extensive network of traffic-free malls, along which people could conduct their business as well as relax and enjoy the passing scene from outdoor benches, cafés and restaurants. The city authorities maintained that the centre of Bonn should be not only a pleasant and safe environment in which to shop, but should also be a place where it is safe to stroll, meet people and be entertained. In accordance with this concept the second phase of pedestrianisation was implemented during the early 1970s. By 1975 the traffic-free zone of central Bonn had been extended to include almost all the principal shopping streets and most cinemas, restaurants and historic buildings. This required a comprehensive traffic-management plan in which the two most important features were, first, the widening of the inner ring road running around the edges of the Altstadt, and secondly, the construction of large underground car parks underneath the Marktplatz and Münsterplatz. Subsequently, the completion of the Bad Godesberg-Bonn *Stadtbahn* and 'U' Bahn line, with an underground station below the Hauptbahnhof and another close to the university, further facilitated access to the 2,200 m of pedestrianised streets.

The third phase in the pedestrianisation of central Bonn recognised the value of conserving salient historic and cultural features of the Altstadt townscape. Of particular significance was the work undertaken within the market-place precinct. This included the restoration of the splendid early eighteenth-century town hall and the 'facelifting' of a row of highly prized, late medieval buildings. Once these two tasks had been completed, the municipality turned its attention on the

Münsterplatz, where the dominant townscape 'element' was the late Romanesque cathedral. To date three important projects in the Münsterplatz scheme have been completed: first, the resurfacing of the square itself, using dark-grey paving stones to match the trachyte texture of the traditional buildings; secondly, the refacing (in vernacular style) of a group of late nineteenth-century commercial buildings; thirdly, the reconstruction of a large, postwar department store whose original, discordant glass-frontage has happily been replaced by a more appealing exterior of stucco and stonework.

Figure 2.3: Pedestrianisation in Central Bonn

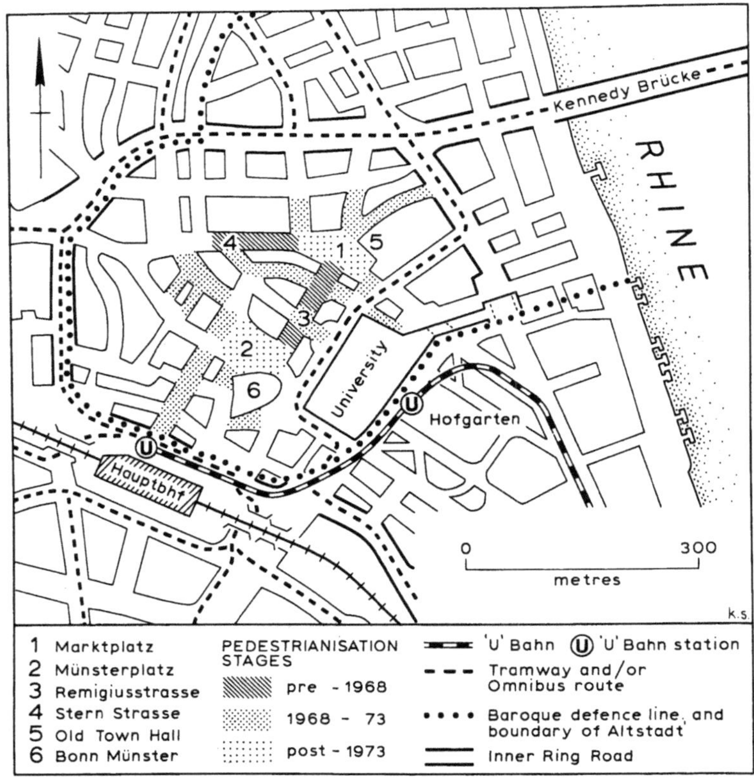

Source: Wilhelm Stollfuss Verlag, *Stollfuss Stadtplan, Bonn* (W. Stollfuss Verlag, Bonn, 1979).

Pedestrianisation in Central Göttingen. Similar elements of 'humanisation' and townscape conservation are also to be seen in the pedestrianised area of the Lower Saxony city of Göttingen. However, it is in the sphere of traffic management that central Göttingen is deserving of special mention.[22] In this city planners were made strongly aware of the types of problems which could arise through limiting pedestrianisation to just one or two major retail streets. Hence, they adopted a policy of developing a large Fussgängerbereich, which by 1977 had a total street length of 2,250 m. Göttingen, however, is a small city with a population figure of around 120,000. Accordingly, a pedestrianised area of this extent meant that it encompassed almost the entire central business district, including all of its retail core, most of its office district and sizeable parts of the surrounding mixed-use zone. A complete prohibition of motor traffic in such a large area would have been very difficult; the answer, therefore, was to institute gradations of restriction. In this system the focal shopping street and adjoining streetblocks form a totally traffic-free zone. This, however, is surrounded by a second zone in which traffic restrictions do not apply to buses, delivery vans and residents' cars. Their flow through this zone, however, is regulated by a one-way network, severe parking restrictions and a speed limit of just 30 km h. The obstacles presented to the motorist in trying to negotiate a way through this part of central Göttingen mean, to all intents and purposes, that through-traffic is forced to follow a newly provided system of orbital roads running round the built-up area of the city.

It should not be concluded from the examples of central Bonn and central Göttingen that policies of reorganising patterns of traffic movement and giving preference to pedestrians over the motor car have everywhere met with unqualified support. In some West German cities a difficult central-area layout, ill-prepared planning or a strong motor-car lobby have led to the constriction, and occasional abandonment, of pedestrianisation schemes.[23] In other instances, the spatial definition of the Fussgängerbereich has remained tightly drawn around a mere handful of shopping streets. Almost invariably these cases are to be found in cities where the balance of local pressure groups is weighted in favour of financial and trading interests which, as a general rule, tend to place greater importance on the convenience of motorised clients than they do on environmental improvement.

Urban Renewal and Conservation in Prewar Residential Areas

Since the late 1960s there has been a growing feeling in West Germany that the first generation of postwar city planners had all too readily been prone to 'writing off' the nineteenth and early twentieth-century urban fabric. A conference held in West Berlin in 1976 gave publicity to the new mode of thinking, in particular the reappraisal of the architectural contribution and social cohesion of pre-1914 residential areas. This meeting, mainly attended by planners and architects, was sponsored by the Council of Europe and was titled 'The Big European Cities and Change – a Future for their Past'. Two quotations from German delegates articulate the chief foci of discussion: first, Breitling's statement that,

> The tremendous problem of urban renewal which confronts us today has arisen from the fact that our concepts of what people need, and concepts as to what city structures best meet today's requirements, have led us to believe that historic districts of the late nineteenth century are merely the residue of a decadent period which has no claims to longevity.;[24]

secondly, Günther's view that

> not only must we take into consideration the urban infrastructure and the material value of the buildings to be rehabilitated, as well as their historical importance and architectural value, but we must also determine what meaning the area undergoing rehabilitation has for its residents and what bonds exist between these residents and their environment.[25]

The change in attitudes was backed by a spate of planning legislation – the 1971 Act for the Promotion of Urban Development, the 1976 Act for the Promotion of Urban Development and the 1977 Housing Modernisation Act – which by the end of the 1970s had allowed most major West German cities to introduce programmes directed at the renovation of their prewar residential areas. As far as the improvement of inner-city housing districts is concerned, the reader can turn ahead to the next chapter of this book, where a description and critical appraisal is made of the Elberfeld-Nordstadt scheme within the prewar apartment zone of the Wuppertal conurbation. However, as an illustration of the quickness and extent of the changing perception of nineteenth and early twentieth-century residential environments, the revival of interest in the old housing 'colonies' of the Ruhr coalfield is of special interest.

Rehabilitation of Ruhr Housing Colonies. The industrial revolution in Germany, which began in earnest during the 1870s and was completed by the time of the outbreak of the First World War, was primarily based on the tremendous expansion of mining and steel production in the Ruhr coalfield. The industrialisation of this region necessitated a massive influx of people, not just from the neighbouring rural areas, but also from parts of the German Reich as far away as Pomerania, Mecklenburg and German Silesia. Then, as the period progressed, the more enlightened colliery owners and steel cartels sought to reduce the shock of their employees' occupational transition from farming to mining or factory work. The companies did this by creating new housing estates with village-style environments. Normally positioned within easy walking distance to pithead or factory, these settlements, with their usual emphasis on cottage-type dwellings, quickly came to form distinctive features of the Ruhr landscape. The large majority were built during the period 1880-1914, the most famous being Krupp's Kolonie Margaretenhöhe which was completed in 1905 on a site within the northern outskirts of Essen. By 1939 as many as 311,363 'colony' dwellings had been built in the Ruhr, and in some municipalities, such as the Emscher cities of Bottrop, Recklinghausen and Gelsenkirchen, they accounted for nearly half the housing stock.[26] However, about two-thirds of them were destroyed during the course of the Second World War, and many of those which survived carried serious structural damage.

Residential reconstruction within the Ruhr was mainly in the form of rebuilding the devastated apartment quarters of the larger towns and cities. Accordingly, little attention was paid to the deteriorating state of the workers' colonies, most of which were situated in outer-suburban locations. Indeed, further decay and depletion of these settlements followed in the wake of the wave of pit closures during the 'coal crisis' of the late 1950s and early 1960s. Quite often entire colonies were sold to investors or developers who were far more interested in the value of the actual site than they were concerned with the community which had grown up on it. However, the expulsions of many redundant miners and steelworkers, and their resettlement in newly built high-rise flats (in many cases situated some considerable distance away from the demolished colony), did have the effect of making people realise the special virtues of the old cottages, especially those with individual gardens and traditional architectural styles. In some instances during the 1970s the activities of developers led to the formation of local residents' action groups, a well-known example being the protest group in the Rheinpreussen-Siedlung on the outskirts of Duisburg, where there continues to be a protracted conflict between the property owner and a tenant population which has repeatedly refused to move.

Also during the 1970s there was an awakening interest in the conservation of surviving miners' colonies. In 1973 the oldest of these settlements, *Kolonie-Eisenheim* (1844) in Oberhausen, was designated as a housing development worthy of preservation and public investment.[27] Since then there has been an increasing number of instances where municipal authorities are not only intervening to prevent evictions, but are also taking active steps to facilitate tenants purchasing their cottages. In addition, city housing departments in the Ruhr have been given the freedom and powers to sponsor the 'conserved' modernisation of colony dwellings. Already several settlements have benefited from this type of civic intervention, none more so than the Lippe-valley community of *Kolonie-Beisenkamp*. Lying within the jurisdiction of *Gemeinde* Datteln (one of the larger local authorities in the northern fringe of the Ruhr coalfield) Beisenkamp first became a focus of interest in 1975 when a firm of architects and planners was commissioned to draw up a general conservation and rehabilitation plan.

Beisenkamp had been built in a style which sought to replicate some of the features of villages in the residents' homeland of East Prussia. A winding 'rustic' street pattern and variety in the alignment of houses had been deliberately designed to counter the sameness of roof lines and the standardised dimensions of doorways and window frames. In recent years the closure of the parent colliery has raised the unwelcome prospect of the sale of the whole settlement, and with this the loss of cheap rental accommodation which several families had enjoyed for three generations. Compensation payments made by Datteln council and the Land (North Rhine-Westphalia) government on behalf of the owners of the colony, however, ensured the continuation of tenancies. Money was also made available for the modernisation of a large proportion of the dwellings. Meanwhile, the 1975 plan provided not only for the retention of the general building line and street pattern, but also for the preservation of such valued architectural features as the high-gabled roofs, the attractive wooden shuttering and the balanced arrangement of windows and doors (Figure 2.4). Each of these had to be reconciled with any future enlargements of the cottages, and accordingly external alterations and additions are only permitted at the rear of the houses. As far as the frontages are concerned, the strict restrictions on 'improvements' are considered as discouragements to the property investor, but at the same time do not deter tenants from

Figure 2.4: Plan of Ruhr Miners' Colony of Datteln-Beisenkamp

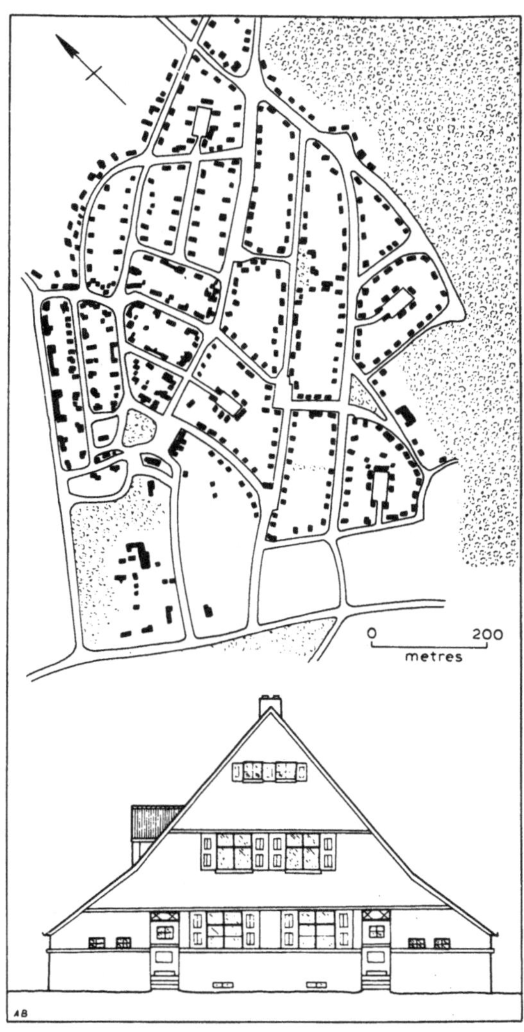

Note: The sketch shows the principal architectural features of one of Beisenkamp's miners' cottages.

Source: Based upon map and drawing in H. Strab, 'Einheitlichkeit und Recht und Freiheit: Reflexionen über einheitliche Gestalt am Beispiel der schönsten Arbeitersiedlungen des Ruhrgebietes, Arbeiterkolonie Beisenkamp, Datteln', *Baumeister*, vol. 78, no. 1 (1981), p. 23.

thinking in terms of becoming owner-occupiers. Indeed, with cheap loans and special mortgage terms now being available, the residents of Beisenkamp have been all too keen to purchase their own homes. In doing this they are protected from the competition of outsiders. Consequently, it has been possible to reach a situation under which owner-occupance can grow quickly, but without incurring social and residential displacement.

The Fourth Phase: New Perspectives and Problems in th 1980s

With its 'brutalist' architecture and limited concern with human values, civic design in West Germany during the 1950s and much of the 1960s had aimed at producing new shapes, dimensions and spatial relationships as ostensible challenges to the townscapes and urban structures created by previous generations. Fortunately, however, recent years have seen a widespread reaction to urban 'modernism'; they have also witnessed a fundamental shift in planning ideology in which, without doubt, the most outstanding feature is the growing desire to revitalise many of the environmental and physical qualities of prewar German cities.

The present-day concern for long-established street patterns, townscape ambiance and building-façades has taken root almost throughout urban West Germany, whether it be in towns and cities with strong pre-industrial traditions, or whether it be in communities whose origins belong primarily to the industrial revolution. But the question as to how far the present generation of West German planners have managed to achieve their objective of 'Schaffe eine menschliche Stadt' is still open to a variety of answers. Certainly, there have been some praiseworthy achievements over the last decade, each being closely related to the improvement of the urban quality-of-life. Yet, even when these are taken in total, they are a far cry from the type of utopia envisaged in some of the country's more enthusiastic planning reports of the late 1960s and early 1970s. Moreover, at a time now of spiralling costs, high interest rates and general tightening of public funds, an increasing number of West German cities are being forced to abandon or, at the best, modify the more enlightened objectives of their planning programmes.

There are other clouds on the horizon too, in particular the shortcomings of urban housing policy which have quickly emerged as major foci of West Germany's current social and political *Angst*. Indeed, the fact that during the first two decades of the 1980s more than 500 residential buildings, distributed collectively in 50 towns and cities, were taken over by squatters attests to certain underlying defects in urban management.[29] Whilst this phenomenon of urban squatting can to some extent be viewed as part of the general *Zeitgeist*, or 'spirit of the age', it does have specific causes. For one thing, the demand for low-cost accommodation still exceeds supply in several large cities, especially in West Berlin, Hamburg, Cologne, Frankfurt and Munich.[30] For another, there is a clear social polarisation of the housing problem, which is heavily orientated towards foreign immigrants, students, unemployed households and poor, large families.[31] During past decades these people drifted to the old apartment quarters of the inner cities where cheap, though often unfit, accommodation was once readily available. Recently, however, urban renewal schemes have had the effect of inflating property values and making certain inner-city neighbourhoods desirable for the middle classes; they have also meant that socially deprived households and families are having to face steep rises in monthly rental payments which, if unpaid, eventually result in evictions. These, and the tendency for renovated apartments and modern 'infill' housing to be left empty while awaiting a tenant who is affluent enough to afford the increased rent, have presented open provocations to *Initiative* groups with a grudge against society and an ideology to match.

The less favourable economic background, the more testing climate of urban politics and a growing awareness of the spatial connotations of social deprivation present challenges which must have positive responses if the record of physical progress experienced by West Germany's cities during the last generation is to continue during the 1980s and in future decades. For, despite its shortcomings, this progress in general terms has been quite remarkable by international standards. In many cases it has seen the transformation of towns and cities from what were largely heaps of rubble to a level of prosperity which could never have been foreseen thirty years ago. This, the West German 'urban miracle', has been achieved by a system of local and regional government which, despite its complexity, has shown to the world that it can adapt to (if not fully overcome) a wide range of quickly changing pressures and priorities. Some of these, notably the reconstruction of cities and the problems of providing for increasingly affluent and motorised urban communities, may now be considered as pressures of the past; but there are others, such as those arising from over-commercialisation, increased environmental concern and renewed interest in the historic urban fabric, which have yet to be resolved by a planning profession which today is finding itself more and more accountable to West German society.

Notes

1. R.E. Dickinson, *The West European City: a Geographical Interpretation*, 1st edn (Routledge & Kegan Paul, London, 1951).
2. Press and Information Office of the Government of the Federal Republic of Germany, *Facts about Germany* (Presse- und Informationsamt der Bundesregierung, Bonn, 1975), p. 211.
3. Bundesministerium für Raumordnung, Bauwesen und Städtebau, *Wohnungsbau und Stadtentwicklung: 10 Jahre Demonstrativbauvorhaben* (F. Fackler Verlag, Munich, 1967).
4. K. Friedrich, 'Funktionseignung und räumliche Bewertung neuer Wohnquartiere', *Darmstädter Geographische Studien*, vol. 1 (1978).
5. Gemeinnützige Wohnungsbaugesellschaft der Stadt Nürnberg, *Nürnberg-Langwasser, Stadtteil im Grünen* (H. Gröschner, Nuremberg, 1975), p. 39.
6. Ibid., p. 40.
7. H. Ludman, 'Innenstädte' in W. Pehnt (ed.), *Die Stadt in der Bundesrepublik* (Reclam, Stuttgart, 1974), pp. 166-80. The term *Innenstadt* (plural *Innenstädte*) should not be confused with 'inner city' (German, *Inner-City*) which excludes the central business district, but includes a much more extensive inner mixed-use and residential zone.
8. E. Giese, 'Der Einfluss der Bauleitplanung auf der wirtschaftliche Nutzung des Bodens sowie den Boden- und Baumarkt in Grossstädten der Bundesrepublik, dargestellt am Beispiel der Frankfurter Innenstadtplanung', *Geographische Zeitschrift*, vol. 65, no. 2 (1977), pp. 109-23.
9. Ibid., p. 113.
10. Ibid, p. 115.
11. F. Tamms and W. Wortmann, *Städtebau* (Habel Verlag, Darmstadt, 1973), p. 92.
12. M. Guther, R. Hillebrecht, H. Schmeissner and W. Schmidt, 'Ich kann mich nicht herausdenken aus dem Vorgang der Geschichte, in den ich eingebunden bin – Erinnerungen an den Wiederaufbau der Bundesrepublik: Hintergründe, Leitbilder, Planungen', *Stadtbauwelt*, vol. 72 (1981), pp. 368-70.
13. G. Albers, *Was wird aus der Stadt*?(Piper, Munich, 1972). H.P. Bahrdt, *Humaner Städtebau* (Nymphenburger Verlagshandlung, Munich, 1973).
14. J. Roth, *Zum Beispiel Frankfurt: Die Zerstörung einer Stadt* (Bertelsmann, Munich, 1975).
15. T. Ebert, 'Bürgerinitiativen' in W. Pehnt (ed.), *Die Stadt in der Bundesrepublik* (Reclam, Stuttgart, 1974), pp. 116-18.
16. R. Monheim, 'Fussgängerbereiche und Fussgängerverkehr in Stadtzentren in der Bundesrepublik Deutschland', *Bonner Geographische Abhandlungen*, vol. 64 (1980), pp. 270-1.
17. Ibid., pp. 88-9.
18. Deutscher Industrie- und Handelstag, *Einkaufs-Magnet Fussgängerzone* (DIH, Bonn, 1979), pp. 11-16.
19. Ibid., pp. 14-15.
20. Bundesministerium für Raumordnung, Bauwesen und Städtebau, 'Verkehrsberuhigte Zonen in Kernbereichen', *Schriftenreihe Städtebauliche*

Forschung, vol. 065 (1978).

21. G. Nieke, 'Bonner Sommer' in P. Peters (ed.), *Fussgängerstadt* (Callwey, Munich, 1977), pp. 160-3

22. Stadt Göttingen Planungsamt, Göttingen, 1977.

23. R. Bernhardt, 'Stadtplanung als Interessenkonflikt: das Für und Wider von Fussgängerzonen in Schwabisch Gemünd', unpublished thesis, Pädagogische Hochschule, Schwabisch Gemünd (Baden-Württemberg), 1975.

24. P. Breitling's paper was entitled 'Technical Problems' and was presented as Theme no. 2a in Symposium no. 4 at the Council of Europe's 1976 (Strasbourg) Conference on 'The Big European Cities and Change – a Future for their Past'.

25. A. Günther's paper was entitled 'Historic Towns and Population Structures' and was presented as Theme no. 1c in Symposium no. 4.

26. W. Dege, *Das Ruhrgebiet* (Ferdinand Hirt, Kiel, 1976), pp. 47-55.

27. Ibid., p. 49.

28. H. Strab, 'Einheitlichkeit und Recht und Freiheit: Reflexionen über einheitliche Gestalt am Beispiel der schönsten Arbeitersiedlungen des Ruhrgebietes, Arbeiterkolonie Beisenkamp, Dattlen', *Baumeister*, vol. 78, no. 1 (1981), pp. 23-7.

29. *Stuttgarter Zeitung*, 30 May 1981.

30. H. Meuter, 'Hintergründe der gegenwärtigen Wohnungsnot', *Geographische Rundschau*, vol. 33, no. 8 (1981), pp. 316-23.

31. H. Bucher, 'Die "neue Wohnungsnot", welche Regionen sind betroffen?', *Geographische Rundschau*, vol. 34, no. 1 (1982), pp. 13-18.

3 RESIDENTIAL ENVIRONMENTS IN WEST GERMAN INNER CITIES

Trevor Wild

Historical Framework

Although much has been altered by the successive shocks of wartime destruction, postwar rebuilding and recent forces of urban change, the physical fabric of the West German inner city today cannot be properly interpreted without first considering the historical background. In particular we need to turn our attention to certain important aspects of the character of urban development during the critical period of the German industrial revolution. Clearly identifiable as a formative age of burgeoning industrialisation and *intensive* city growth, this is considered by most writers to have commenced in force during the 1870s, and ended with the initiation of more extensive processes of urban expansion coinciding approximately with the outbreak of the First World War. Until the onset of the industrial revolution in Germany population growth, along with expanding economic, cultural and administrative functions, in most cities had of necessity always been tightly compressed inside the age-old morphological limits prescribed by encircling medieval, renaissance or baroque defences. Their massive walls, ramparts and ditches had for centuries acted as considerable obstacles in the path of urban extension. But there had also been two other major limiting factors: first, due to the prevailing conditions of long working days and very restricted daily travel-mobility, the necessity of maintaining rigid positional ties between place of residence and place of occupation; secondly, immediately outside the walls of many cities, the preservation of large tracts of extra-mural land as defensive 'firing zones', civic parks or public forests.

The second half of the nineteenth century witnessed a progressive easing of each of these three constraints. Those city walls and other defence lines which were still intact at the beginning of Germany's industrial revolution had to make way for wider arterial roads, new civic buildings and railway construction. Many fortification systems were demolished completely, their removal at last providing open access into the space beyond. Meanwhile, developments in passenger transport, and also releases of public land for building purposes, were widening the possibilities for residential location, while at the same time encouraging the first outwards spread of urban manufacturing. As a result of these changes most sizeable towns and cities experienced a quite sudden physical expansion which often assumed the form of regular frontal growth, but in some cases appeared as sharply differentiated suburban 'sectors'. Only rarely, however, did the rate of urban expansion during the industrial revolution match the pace of demographic increases. Indeed, during the four decades following the foundation of the Second German Empire, there were several large cities – for example, Cologne (129,233 inhabitants in 1871 and 516,540 in 1910), Nuremberg (83,214 and 333,142) and Mannheim (56,204 and 217,229) – where population growth was at least twice as fast as the rate of extension of the built-up areas.[1] One cause and effect of this was the continued crowding of people, particularly those representing the poorer social classes, into the old, pre-industrial housing quarters. An emphatic and well-documented case in point was the Altstadt district of Cologne. In 1850 this, the historic core of one of Germany's fastest growing cities, housed 95,500 people; sixty years later the number had increased to 162,900, and the population density had risen to the remarkable figure of 704 persons per ha of residential land use.[2]

The other reason why demographic increases in German cities during the industrial revolution commonly outstripped the pace of physical urban growth, rested in the perpetuation of traditions of high-density living in the first ring of suburbs surrounding the Altstadt cores. Not unusually, the working-class character of the 1850-1914 growth zone was relieved by the existence of sizeable middle-class quarters with their distinctive villa-type housing; but, these apart, the evolving residential landscape was dominated by apartment blocks. There is an awakening interest in the evolution of late nineteenth and early twentieth-century apartment designs in West Germany, where urban historians have noted how innovations in construction techniques and, at the same time, the application of less stringent regulations on height-levels, both served to encourage increasing scales and dimensions of new residential buildings. Turning again to the example of Cologne, we can see that the trend towards higher and larger units can be traced from this city's excellent collection of pre-Second World War housing surveys.[3] The earliest of these dates back to 1878, when only 19 per cent of Cologne's dwellings were reported to have been in residential buildings of four floors or more. By 1910, however, the proportional contribution of structures of this size had doubled to 38 per cent. Moreover, as much as 60 per cent of the city's housing in 1910 was reported to exist in apartment buildings of at least twelve dwellings: 28 per cent was to be found in units of more than twenty dwellings. By modern standards most homes were very small: 55 per cent consisted of no more than two rooms (usually a simple kitchen and a living room-cum-bedroom), while a similar proportion were without internal toilets and washing facilities. The statistical information for 1910 also highlights the extreme degree of overcrowding: only 10 per cent of land use within the built-up area was describable as open space, and less than one-third of Cologne's 119,000 houses had access to even the meanest form of garden.

In most parts of Germany the second decade of the twentieth century, despite the turmoils of the First World War, saw the beginnings of a much more open and socially inspired period of urban residential development. This was seen most ostensibly in the initiation of the 'middle-suburban ring' which, in marked contrast to what had gone before, was soon to be typified by its humanitarian housing designs, much lower population densities and careful separation of industrial sites from residential estates. The abrupt change in the character of urban growth was brought about by three interwoven influences. First of all, there were the 'freeing' effects of quickening advances in urban transport facilities, in particular the expansion of suburban railway services, the widespread introduction of electric-tramway networks and some small, but not insignificant, growth in personal car ownership. Secondly, borrowing heavily from the British 'model village' and 'garden suburb' approaches, but also embodying some of the stylistic details of the German *Heimatstil* movement, there was the implementation of new concepts of working-class housing provision. The third influence on change was the widening structure of building sponsorship in which housing associations, co-operatives and enlightened industrial patrons were collectively displacing the previous dominance of landowners and private speculators.

The most noticeable manifestation of the transformed urban growth process was the proliferation of company-housing communities (*Betriebskolonien*) and 'garden' estates (*Gartenvorstädte*). With their accents on spacious design and greenfield locations, these quickly appeared as common features in the new suburban landscapes of almost every large German town and city. They were also in the forefront of the first general departure from the apartment tradition and corresponding rise in the popularity of 'individual' varieties of dwellings. These two interconnected trends can be gauged by turning to the Federal Statistical Office's data on housing completions in Germany during the periods 1871-1918 and 1919-39.[4] The information for the earlier period shows apartments accounting for as much as 61 per cent of all housing construction within the German Reich; for the interwar years, however, their share for the equivalent territory was only 42 per cent, a proportion which indicated a drop of 19 percentage points. Moreover, a large amount of the heavily reduced apartment share consisted of greatly improved designs, and was positioned within new residential areas distinguished by their open layouts and attention to social needs.

So distinctive was the physical fabric of interwar suburban development that its initial appearance as a new element in the spatial evolution of German cities was bound to produce clearly differentiated lines of morphogenic, environmental and social discontinuity. Today, even after several decades of intensive internal urban change, the clarity of these lines – whichever criterion of identification is used – has not been eradicated. Furthermore, their relevance in West Germany as meaningful means of defining the outer limits of inner cities is enhanced by their normally close congruity with *Stadtdistrikt* (city 'district') boundaries and the ease by which they can be fitted into present-day frameworks of urban statistical areas.

Morphogenic Features

The Pre-1939 Building Fabric

The residual features from the formative age, and the sizeable quantity of infilling of buildings that continued during the interwar period, still survive as common ingredients of West German inner-city environments. Indeed, in some cities they still dominate the townscape of entire districts, as for example in Berlin-Kreuzberg, Nuremberg-Südstadt, Stuttgart-West and Elberfeld-Nordstadt. A small proportion of Elberfeld-Nordstadt is mapped out in detail in Figure 3.1, an exercise which highlights the typical crowding of old apartment buildings, the congested and outdated pattern of streets, the close mixing of housing and factories, the very small quantity of open space and the pervading atmosphere of physical obsolescence. The area selected consists of four streetblocks situated less than 1 km from central Elberfeld (the principal commercial focus of the Wuppertal conurbation) and overlooking the narrow industrialised valley of the river Wupper. Here, as is usually to be observed in the traditional working-class quarters of German inner cities, a stage-by-stage sequence of formative development can be recognised: first, the laying out of the streets and building-plots;

secondly, the construction of multi-floor apartment units along the street frontages; lastly, the construction of industrial and residential properties inside the *Blockkerne* (streetblock interiors).

In this sample area the first stage was undertaken during the early 1870s after blocks of land on what were then the northern outskirts of Elberfeld had been partitioned and sold to developers. A decade later building work along the street frontages had been completed, mainly in the form of apartment units of five floors and any number between eight and sixteen dwellings. Normally the owners, many of whom would also have been local shopkeepers or other small tradespersons, lived on the ground floors, leaving the rest of their property as tenanted accommodation. With support coming from their rental incomes and business profits, the more enterprising owners soon turned to the possibilities of building within the Blockkerne, which hitherto had functioned only as private backyards and gardens. As the map shows, this third stage of development assumed two forms. In some cases, as for example in the streetblock which adjoins Uellendahler Strasse, building plots were joined together to provide sufficient space for factories. In other cases, however, they were retained in their original state and used as sites for small workshops and *Hinterhäuser* ('rear' apartments). Representing nearly one-quarter of the housing within the sample area, the Hinterhäuser, unless they are substantially modernised, are invariably of a very poor quality, and this is irrespective of whether they appear as extensions of the 'parent' structure or whether they were built as separate units at the backs of the apartment curtilages. In every major West German city they feature as the very worst of residential accommodation, the large majority being flimsily built and having no direct street access. Lacking in some of the most basic of utilities, they also have problems of ventilation, sanitation, light, noise and fire-risk; for all too often these slums back directly onto each other and are hemmed in by unpleasant workshops and factories.

Some early diversity was given to prewar inner-city townscapes and social structures by the building of middle-class residential quarters. In German cities these tended to conform to the type of positioning and configuration outlined by Hoyt in his 'sector-model' of urban residential growth.[5] An interesting survival is Elberfeld's Nützenberg district, a small part of the Wuppertal conurbation where the earliest houses date from the 1860s, and represent the first of a series of outwards locational 'hops' by a wealthy merchant community which had formerly concentrated itself around the Neumarkt in Elberfeld-Altstadt.[6] The final quarter of the nineteenth century saw middle-class

Figure 3.1: Prewar Inner-city Housing Environments: Sample Areas in Elberfeld-Nordstadt and Elberfeld-Nützenberg

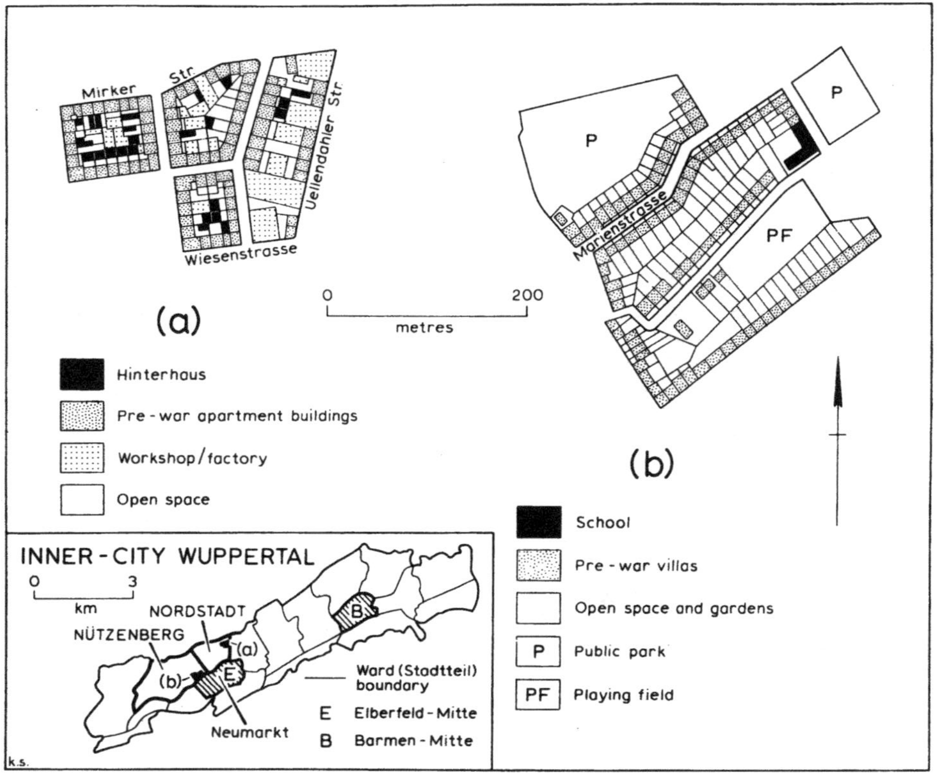

Mirker Str
Uellendahler Str
Wiesenstrasse
Marienstrasse
(a)
0 200
metres
P
P
PF
(b)
Hinterhaus
Pre-war apartment buildings
Workshop/factory
Open space
School
Pre-war villas
Open space and gardens
P Public park
PF Playing field
INNER-CITY WUPPERTAL
0 3
km
NORDSTADT
NÜTZENBERG
(a)
(b)
E
B
Neumarkt
Ward (Stadtteil) boundary
E Elberfeld-Mitte
B Barmen-Mitte
k.s.

Notes: (a) Represents a typical nineteenth-century, working-class apartment quarter in Elberfeld-Nordstadt.

(b) Represents a late-nineteenth-century, middle class housing area in Elberfeld-Nützenberg.

Source: Personal field-survey, conducted in October 1980 using 1972 editions of *Deutsche Grundkarte* (1:2,500 scale) as base maps.

residential development spreading up the tree-covered slopes on the northwest side of the city. Its morphological character is exemplified in the second sample area, showing the plan of four Nützenberg streetblocks of the period 1875-90 (Figure 3.1). Nearly all the dwellings here were built as fairly small but expensively designed villas and town houses, mostly forming secluded terraces set a few metres back from the pavements. Particularly noticeable on the plan is the informal layout and abundance of green open space. This accounts for as much as 67 per cent of the land use, and includes private gardens, two public parks and a large playing field. Also impressive, by urban standards, is the low housing density. Although several of the original villas have recently been converted into apartments, a large proportion of which are now bed-sitters occupied by students from the nearby *Gesamthochschule-Wuppertal*, the area still has only 37 dwellings per gross ha. This is less than one-sixth of the density calculated for the four Nordstadt streetblocks (Table 3.1).

Postwar Reconstruction

With the emphasis in suburban growth spreading futher and further outwards, the interwar period can be regarded as something of an interlude in the historical geography of West German inner cities; for apart from some further infilling of streetblock interiors and remaining patches of open space in working-class districts, there was little ostensible change in their general physical character. However, such apparent stability was broken dramatically by the Allied bombing offensives of the Second World War and the onslaught on German cities. At first the attacks were aimed specifically at the commercial centres, major industrial complexes and transport facilities; but owing to their close proximity to these targets, the crowded residential quarters of the inner cities also carried their share of the brunt. Later, when the Allied strategy intensified and turned to area-bombing, the inner cities were singled out as deliberate objectives and accordingly suffered widespread destruction.

As a general rule the amount of destruction within the inner cities varied in accordance with distance from the central areas, with the innermost parts being heavily devastated while further out there was only sporadic damage. But such a pattern was by no means even, for within the inner cities there were certain specially favoured targets. These are evident in Figure 3.2, which uses the example of Cologne-Alt Ehrenfeld as an illustration of the local distribution of wartime destruction. Occupying a portion of the northwest quadrant of the city,

Table 3.1: Sample Areas within Inner Cities

Sample area	1	2	3	4
Area in ha	3.0	6.3	4.4	9.6
Residential buildings	106	98	89	114
Hinterhäuser	25	0	6	0
All dwellings	687	235	582	1,095
Dwellings per residential building	6.5	2.4	6.5	9.6
Residential density (dwellings per ha)	229	37	132	114
% of area in open space (including gardens)	17	67	38	72
% of area occupied by non-residential buildings	36	3	30	5

Key to Sample Areas:

1 Prewar apartment area; Elberfeld-Nordstadt, part of Mirker Viertel (shown in Figure 3.1).

2 Prewar, middle-class housing area; Elberfeld-Nützenberg, Marienstrasse (shown in Figure 3.1).

3 Area of postwar reconstruction; Cologne-Alt Ehrenfeld, Gutenbergstrasse (shown in Figure 3.3).

4 Modern residential area; Cologne-Alt Ehrenfeld, Myliusstrasse (shown in Figure 3.3).

Source: Personal field-survey conducted in October 1980, using relevant sheets of 1: 2,500 *Deutsche Grundkarte* map series as the bases.

Alt Ehrenfeld suffered approximately the average for Cologne's inner-city 'girdle', losing nearly two-fifths of its housing stock and one-third of its factories and other non-residential buildings.[7] Thus, of the 82 streetblocks which made up the district in 1939, as many as 37 had more than one-half of their buildings destroyed or severely damaged; 31 others incurred losses amounting to at least one-quarter, and only 14 escaped with what may be described as moderate damage. Alt Ehrenfeld's nearest point to the city centre is the junction of Venloer Strasse and Innere-Kanal Strasse, just a few hundred metres outside the boundary of the Altstadt and central business district. In very broad terms the map does demonstrate some distance-decay effect as one proceeds outwards from this position, but this is greatly disturbed by some concentrations of heavy shading on either side of the Cologne-Düren-Aachen railway and alongside the arterial Venloer Strasse.

During the first few years after the war shortages of materials and restricted financial resources meant that the reconstruction of severely bombed suburbs like Alt Ehrenfeld could only proceed slowly, with provision of new housing often having to take lower priority than the rebuilding of factories and small businesses. At the time of the 1950 census, therefore, shortages of inner-city accommodation were still very

Figure 3.2: Distribution of Wartime Destruction in Cologne-Alt Ehrenfeld

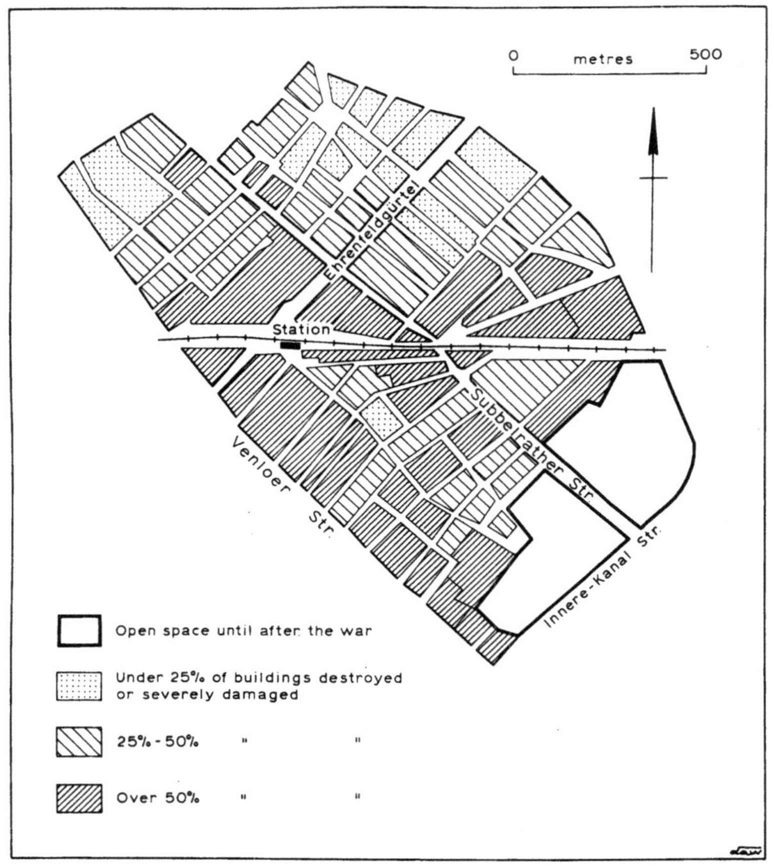

Source: Adapted from information in Statistisches Amt der Stadt Köln, *Leitplan der Stadt Köln*, vol. 2 (SASK, Cologne, 1970).

acute, and largely because of this many of the huge numbers of wartime evacuees were yet to return to their original urban abodes.[8] Some indication of the scale of population reductions between the census counts of 1939 and 1950 is provided in Table 3.2, where figures are presented for four of West Germany's largest inner-city areas. In Stuttgart the deficiency at the later date amounted to 18 per cent, in Munich 26 per cent, in Cologne 37 per cent and in Nuremberg 41 per cent.

Table 3.2: Populations of Selected Inner Cities,[a] 1939-79 (as Percentage of Total City Population in Parentheses)

Year	1939	1946	1950	1956	1961	1970	1975	1979
Cologne	575,692 (74.7)	290,139 (59.6)	364,640 (61.3)	439,176 (61.6)	479,458 (59.2)	454,129 (52.5)	415,308 (40.7)	391,417 (40.0)
Munich	399,994 (48.2)	n.a.	296,171 (35.6)	327,513 (34.0)	342,901 (31.6)	312,129 (24.1)	292,237 (22.0)	n.a.
Nuremberg	337,035 (79.7)	167,003 (53.5)	198,734 (54.8)	n.a.	279,549 (64.4)	261,354 (55.2)	240,449 (51.3)	229,670 (47.4)
Stuttgart	261,154 (52.6)	n.a.	215,292 (42.6)	n.a.	267,247 (41.9)	238,288 (37.6)	217,502 (35.5)	n.a.

Note: a. Comprising all statistical areas situated within the pre-1914 built-up limits of each respective city (including its Altstadt district).
Sources: Population tables in respective city statistical yearbooks (annual volumes).

Residential reconstruction did not get fully under way until after the Federal Housing Act of 1950. This important piece of legislation was designed primarily as an instrument for coping with the two very pressing needs of replenishing West Germany's estimated 2.5 million of wartime housing losses, and providing an even greater number of extra dwellings to accommodate the massive inflow of refugees and expellees. The central features of the Act and its various amendments and additions during the next three years were the extended inducements for the building of *Sozialwohnungen* (subsidised social housing). The new encouragements were mainly in the fields of tax concessions, cheap loans and direct money grants, all of which were made available for each principal type of building sponsor. During the first full year of the Act's operation federal and Land subsidies for social housing amounted to DM 1,700 million, or 38 per cent of the total money (public and private) spent on residential reconstruction. Five years later the annual social-housing budget reached DM 2,800 million, and in 1960 it exceeded DM 4,000 million.[9]

After a short delay the building industry responded vigorously to the Federal Housing Act, especially so in the inner cities. In 1949 dwelling completions in West Germany (including estimates for West Berlin and the Saarland) numbered less than 250,000; by 1952, however, the yearly rate had climbed to 460,800, and a year later it had passed the 500,000 mark.[10] As many as 5.3 million homes were constructed during the 1950s, of which 3.0 million were Sozialwohnungen. The acceleration in building activity varied from city to city; usually it was fastest in those which had suffered particularly heavy wartime destruction. In Nuremberg, for example, only 14,101 dwellings were built during the first five postwar years. From 1951 to 1956, however, completions here totalled 37,575, with more than three-quarters of this number carrying social-housing subsidies.[11] Corresponding counts are also available for Cologne, whose figures of 14,772 and 64,367 for the same two periods of time represent an extreme case.[12]

Only for special purposes, over the country at large never rising above 7 per cent of annual completions, did housing policy during the reconstruction period extend into the field of public ownership. But the release of subsidies was not without certain conditions. From the outset, assistance for social housing was normally only applicable for homes built for the rental market; then, as time progressed, city authorities were vested with the politically sensitive powers of rental control and priority allocation to the *Sozialschwache* (socially deprived) groups of West German citizens. Mention too should be made of the rigid building regulations which, for much of the 1950s, set an apartment with kitchen, living room, two small bedrooms and bathroom-cum-toilet as the basic standard for assisted dwellings. Until the easier prosperity of the following decade very few sponsors, large or small, saw fit to go beyond these rudimentary requirements. In this respect their caution was partly due to the urgency for speedy and cheap construction, but partly too because the postwar regulations did in fact represent some quite appreciable advance on average working-class housing quality.

While many local authorities were engaging themselves in the programmed reconstruction of their city centres, including several designs which have subsequently attracted much admiration from foreign observers, in marked contrast rebuilding within the inner cities was almost invariably performed with a lack of co-ordination and foresight. A typical example is illustrated in the part of Figure 3.3 which depicts the ground plan of one of the most war-ravaged portions of Cologne-Alt Ehrenfeld. Before the bombing this had consisted of a very characteristic mixture of old apartments, Hinterhäuser and industrial premises of various sizes and descriptions. About two-thirds of the buildings in these streetblocks were destroyed during the air raids, while few others escaped without some form of structural damage. At the end of the war, therefore, possibilities were presented for the more-or-less complete redesign of entire streetblocks (see those which are numbered 3 and 4 on Figure 3.3). But, as was usually the case outside the city centres, such opportunities were largely wasted as early redevelopment proceeded in a haphazard and generally uncontrolled fashion. More often than not it occurred in three overlapping stages:

first, the rebuilding *in situ* of demolished factories and small-business premises; secondly, the patching up of what was left of the prewar housing, often using materials painstakingly gathered from nearby piles of rubble; thirdly, residential reconstruction with a strong emphasis on social housing.

Figure 3.3: Postwar Inner-city Housing Environments: Sample Areas in Cologne-Alt Ehrenfeld

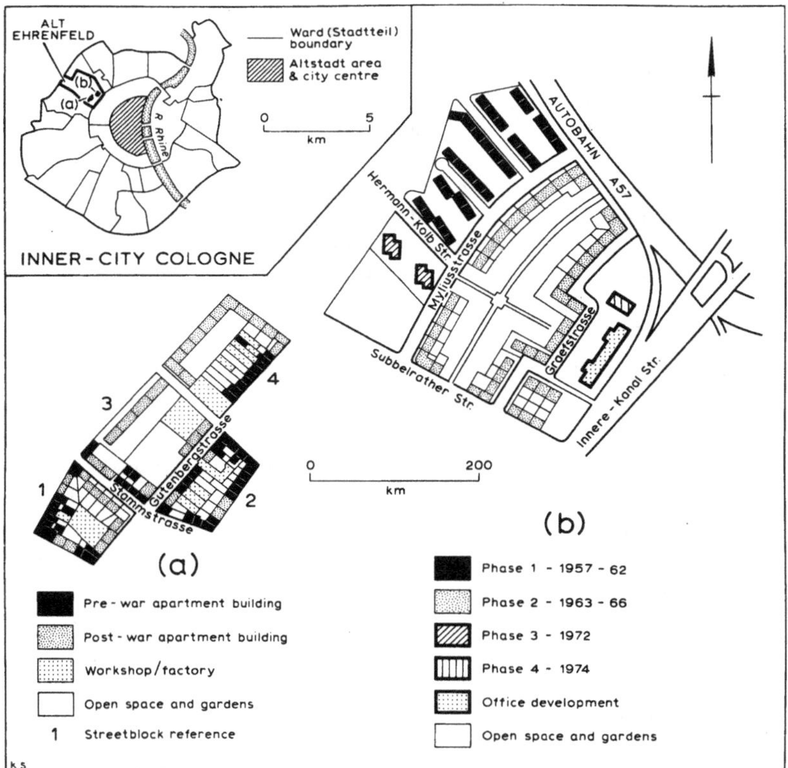

Notes: (a) Is an example of an area of mixed (prewar and postwar) apartment housing.

(b) Is an example of modern, inner-city housing development.

Source: Personal field-survey, conducted in August and September 1980 using 1972 editions of *Deutsche Grundkarte* (1: 2,500 scale) as base maps.

In the four streetblocks which constitute this third sample area, all save 15 of the 312 postwar dwellings were constructed with the help of public subsidies. About one-third were completed during the years 1950-5, a time when it was the normal practice for new buildings to be fitted onto individual sites within the original framework of property divisions. This type of development is noticeable in streetblocks 1 and 2, where postwar reconstruction can be seen to have done little to eradicate the worst features of prewar inner-city environments, especially the high densities of housing and the congested and irregular pattern of land uses. In the other two streetblocks, however, most of the rebuilding was delayed until the late 1950s. By then new laws and procedures for acquiring war-blighted land had been introduced, allowing the amalgamation of derelict plots and the building of less cramped and more regular residential layouts. Although it was still dominated by austere-looking social housing, this later phase of reconstruction was generally of a considerably better quality: not only were new apartments fitted with such extra domestic comforts as a third bedroom, rear balcony and toilet separate from bathroom, but also, wherever it was possible, parts of the Blockkerne were cleared to provide small areas of open space and recreational land.

Modern Housing Infill

By the mid 1960s residential reconstruction in the inner cities was virtually complete, although here and there the scars of war were still plainly visible in the occasional overgrown patch of wasteland and in the odd, unrestored building. By this time too, construction of new homes had shifted its locational emphasis to the outer suburbs and further afield into the spreading urban-rural fringes. The trend is clearly indicated in Cologne's annual sets of postwar housing statistics.[13] From 1948 to 1960 as many as 72 per cent of the city's remarkable figure of 127,089 completions were within the inner-city wards (including the Altstadt district), but from 1965 to 1978 these localities could account for only a modest 19 per cent of the total.

This dramatic change can be viewed as a clear reflection of the growing unpopularity of inner-city living which, in terms of demographic trends, first became apparent about the time of the 1961 census (Table 3.2). But within the inner cities there are some additional points of explanation: namely, the scarcity of vacant sites, the marked inflation of land prices,[14] and ever since the reconstruction period, the normal policy of city authorities favouring improvement and modernisation of substandard housing, rather than turning to programmes of comprehensive redevelopment. These influences have also meant that the much reduced quantity of housing construction that has taken place within inner cities during the last two decades has all too often had to be accomplished with little or no relief to the tradition of high residential densities. Moreover, it usually lacked in spatial contiguity, for most developments were forced to occupy small and scattered sites, such as the few remaining pieces of war-created waste or tracts of land made available through industrial dereliction. In only a small minority of inner-city districts were there any opportunities for large-scale schemes. Where they did occur these were mostly associated with the selling off of portions of public open space. An interesting example (the eastern corner of Alt Ehrenfeld) is shown in Figure 3.3. The land here had once been part of Cologne's 'Inner Green Girdle' – the semi-circle of public parks and playing fields which fill the former *glacis* and moat zone of the nineteenth-century Prussian fortification system. But housing on this extensive virgin site was never conceived as a planned and co-ordinated settlement; nor was it consciously intended to serve as a replacement for Alt Ehrenfeld's sizeable number of prewar slums. At present it accommodates 1,095 households and nearly 4,000 people; yet not even the most basic of service centres has been provided. Perhaps the most salient criticism, however, is the distinct lack of harmony between each of the four phases of building activity.

The first phase was completed during the early 1960s, and occupied the three small streetblocks lying to the east of Hermann-Kolb Strasse and west of Myliusstrasse. It consisted of tidy, but very drab, rows of standard social housing, behind which the streetblock interiors were left as open grassland and places for vehicle parking. The next phase of building occupied the space between Myliusstrasse and Graefstrasse. This too was partly financed from public subsidies, but compared with the previous social-housing scheme it was much larger in scale and more advanced in style. Finished in 1966, it comprised of 40 building units with height-levels ranging from four to six floors. In terms of facilities for good 'quality of life' this particular streetblock is arguably better equipped than any other part of the settlement. The 402 households living here not only each have a third bedroom, under-floor central heating and the option of a private lock-up garage, but they are also provided with a landscaped park in which special attention has been given to tree planting and childrens' play areas.

Rather unfortunately, the third and fourth phases came during the nationwide property boom of 1971-4, a time of unprecedented flows of investment into all major types of building speculation. In the field of residential development the end result was the so-called *Wohnungshalde* (housing mountain) of the mid-1970s. This attracted a wave of criticism, mostly directed at the seemingly poor judgement shown by large financial companies who ignored the growing preference for detached houses in 'green' environments, and instead concentrated their sponsorship into the building of high-rise flats.[15] Three such monuments to the housing mountain are represented in Figure 3.3. Two of them (both ten storeys high and accommodating 64 households each) were built on vacant land between Hermann-Kolb Strasse and the main Subbelratherstrasse. Other high-rise units were in fact envisaged for this streetblock, but in face of shrinking demand and mounting costs, no start has been made. Nevertheless, in 1974 such difficulties did not deter the *Allgemeine Kölner Wohnungsbaugenossenschaft* (AKW) from building the city's tallest residential structure within the streetblock facing the intersection of Innere-Kanalstrasse and the A 57 Cologne to Dusseldorf-Neuss Autobahn. This towering building is 32 storeys high and consists of 256 dwellings, more than two-thirds of which were still untenanted two years after their completion. Wisely, the AKW have cast aside ideas of constructing more high-rise housing on this valuable but noisy site. Instead, it decided to invest in a large, 13-floored office complex. Adjoining one of Cologne's busiest interior ring roads, this property is now occupied by a health-insurance firm which has recently purchased several of the nearby flats for the purpose of accommodating newly appointed managerial staff.

Intrusion of Commercial Buildings

During the industrial revolution the prime commercial functions of German cities, while expanding all the time, continued to be almost wholly concentrated within the confines of the Altstädte. Indeed, central business districts, with their near monopoly of finance, major public and professional services, civic administration and specialist retailing, could be precisely defined until well into the twentieth century; for in many cases their limits coincided exactly with fixation lines originally set by the positions of defensive walls and ramparts.

The first real indications of spatial extension of these functions came during the 1920s and 1930s, when increased passenger flows into and out from city centres encouraged the building of new commercial precincts just outside the congested Altstädte, and almost invariably focused around the main railway stations and tramway termini.[16] From these specific beginnings the outwards trend gathered in momentum after the Second World War, ostensibly as a response to steepening gradients of cost-difference within cities (especially prices of development land and property rentals) and planning policies aimed at protecting the morphological fabric of the historic and cultural cores. The underlying factor, however, has undoubtedly been the spatial pressures associated with the fundamental change in the economy of West German cities. Writers today often consider this change in terms of the emergent *Funktionsgesellschaft*, an expression which can be translated literally as 'the functional society', but is used really as a simplified description of the complex drift away from an urban society based mainly on manufacturing and production, to one which is becoming more and more committed to an increasing range of remunerative tertiary activities.

Nowhere in West Germany is this change more apparent than in the country's largest and most dynamic cities. Ever since the industry-dominated 'economic miracle' of the 1950s, these have each experienced spectacular growth in the tertiary sector, and with this a vigorous dispersal of new businesses away from the central area and into the surrounding residential districts. In the forefront of a spatial trend which involves both relative and literal movements are company offices and large-scale retail outlets, but new hotel, education, public administration and research buildings also play important parts. Recent years have seen increasing numbers of 'tertiary' investments turning to the outer suburbs and outlying dormitory towns in the urban-rural fringe; however, the heaviest degree of 'functional conversion' is still to be found within the inner cities. An extreme case in point is the commercialisation of Frankfurt-Westend, a large inner-city quarter which, with its interesting mixture of ornate apartments and bourgeois villas, was once almost wholly residential in character. In their joint research on the postwar development of Frankfurt-Westend, Kade and Vorlaufer have presented figures of annual amounts of building activity over the period 1949-72.[17] At first housing reconstruction prevailed, accounting for 63 per cent of total new floorspace during the years 1949-55. From the mid-1950s onwards, however, the contribution of commercial buildings increased dramatically, rising to 42 per cent of floorspace added from 1955 to 1959, and consistently exceeding 80 per cent each year after 1960. The full period saw the construction of 773,000 m^2 of office development within the Westend, more than half of this impressive figure coming after 1964, and nearly one-quarter being registered during the three years of 1970-2.

Figure 3.4 shows the locational pattern of new commercial buildings within suburban Cologne. Here the period in question is 1967-76, when a total of 1,126,372 m^2 of commercial floorspace was built in the city.[18] A quite substantial quantity appears in the outer suburbs, mostly in the form of small clusters of offices and trading premises, some close to the encircling Autobahn system, and others situated within certain of the peripheral 'industrial' estates. However, more striking to the observer are the large concentrations in the inner-city districts, notably those in Neustadt-Nord, Neustadt-Süd, Ehrenfeld, Lindenthal and Bayenthal in 'left bank' Cologne and Deutz, Poll and Mülheim on the other side of the Rhine.

Figure 3.4: Location of New Commercial Buildings in Suburban Cologne, 1967-76

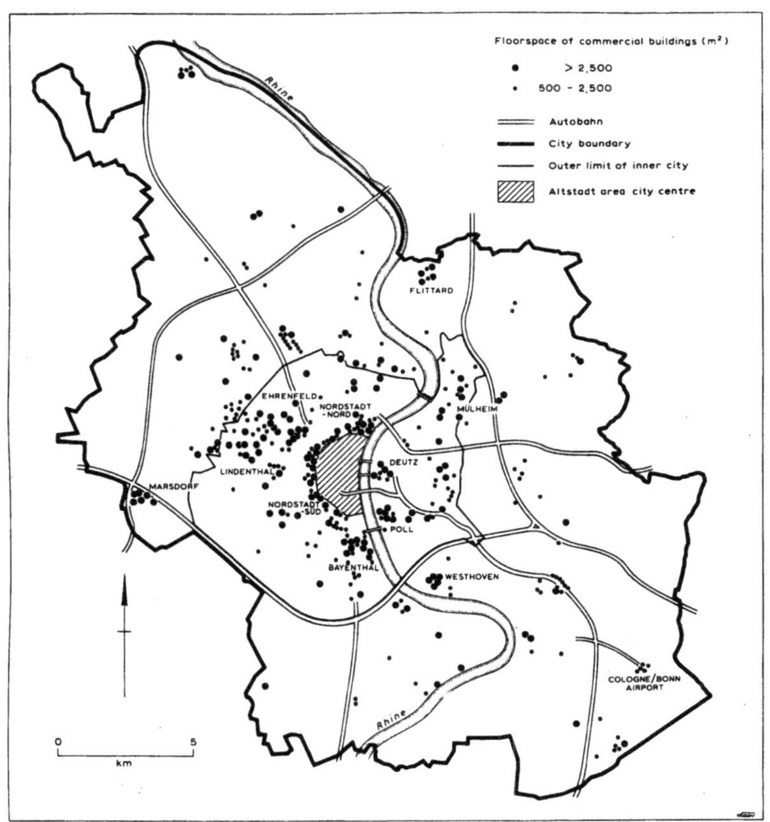

Source: Stadt Köln Dezernat für Stadtentwicklung, *Köln, Stadtentwicklungsplanung: Gesamtkonzept* (Stadt Köln, Cologne, 1978), section 6, pp. 30-43.

Inside these locations, positions close to arterial roads, suburban railway stations, *Stadtbahn* routes and *'U' Bahn* entrances exert a special attraction. This is clearly apparent in the next map, Figure 3.5, showing the distribution of large commercial buildings (over 1,000 m^2 floorspace) in Alt Ehrenfeld. Until the late 1950s the only tertiary activities here were the numerous small, family businesses – local shops, cafes and the ubiquitous *Kneipen* – all occupying the ground-floors of apartment buildings. They were scattered quite liberally throughout the residential area, but there were two prominent axial concentrations: one following Venloer Strasse and spreading into some of its side streets, the other aligning itself along Subbelrather Strasse and Landmann Strasse. Intrusion of larger-scale enterprises into Alt Ehrenfeld began in 1958, and has continued in growing strength to the present day. Three types of modern business activity are involved: first, company offices, the largest being the Cologne regional organisation and research branches of the multinational Siemens AG and Philips Ltd; secondly, discount stores and branches of retail multiples, mostly grouping themselves along the established shopping streets; thirdly, large hotels, three of which are equipped with conference facilities. Most of these developments, and also their adjoining car parks, occupy sites created by the demolition of residential buildings. The heaviest losses have been in the densely populated streetblocks facing Venloer Strasse which, with its direct tramway link to the city centre, its nearness to Ehrenfeld railway station and recent proposals for a 'U' Bahn route, has emerged today as one of Cologne's largest 'district centres'. Since 1965 approximately 750 homes (some of prewar vintage and substandard, but also including many average-quality dwellings of the 1945-55 period) have been pulled down to make way for commercial buildings.[19] As has happened elsewhere in inner-city Cologne, such destruction has done much to hasten local population decline. In Alt Ehrenfeld the number of inhabitants has fallen sharply from a postwar peak of 41,282 in 1961 to 32,362 at the latest reckoning in 1979, with more than two-thirds of this decrease coming after 1970.[20] Understandably, demolition of housing, which city authorities appear to oppose openly only in cases where there are threats on buildings of historic and architectural merit, has caused deep resentment amongst the shrinking community. Recently feelings in Alt Ehrenfeld have come to a head with the formation of a very active *Bürgerinitiative* (Residents' Action Group) which, like those of several other similarly threatened inner-city communities, is militantly opposed to any further commercial intrusion. Over the last few years this opposition has been channelled into various courses of action, ranging from involvement in squatting demonstrations to organised protest at planners' and developers' 'participation' meetings.

Figure 3.5: Intrusion of Commercial Buildings in Cologne-Alt Ehrenfeld

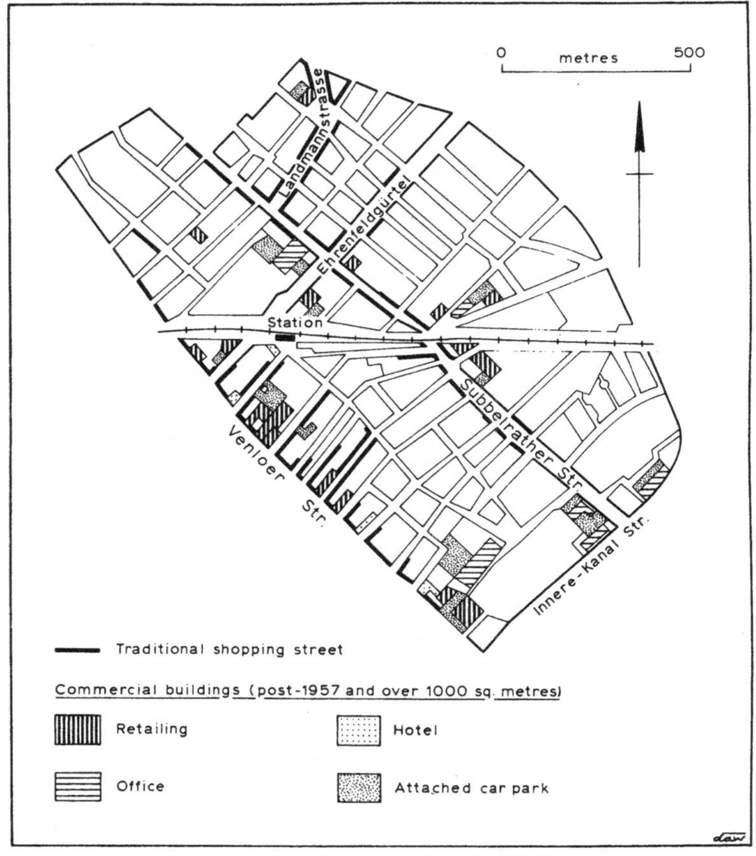

Source: Personal field-survey, conducted in August and September 1980 using 1972 editions of *Deutsche Grundkarte* (1 : 2,500 scale) as base maps.

Residential Improvement Policy

The residential environments of West German inner cities pose severe, if highly localised, problems of urban living. The issue of housing standards is of paramount concern, but this is followed by a lengthy catalogue of environmental and social disadvantages all contradicting the optimistic government declaration in 1965 to achieve 'healthy living and working conditions, as well as balanced economic, social and cultural opportunities, in all parts of the Federal Republic'.[21]

Improvement versus Comprehensive Redevelopment

With remarkably few exceptions, West German approaches towards bettering the amenities and infrastructure for 'quality of life' in inner cities, since postwar reconstruction, have not sought to emulate the drastic strategy of large-scale redevelopment so popular in British planning during the 1960s and early 1970s. There are three reasons for this.

First of all, importance must be attached to the special fondness of the West German public for historic buildings and the traditional physical fabric of their diverse towns and cities. During the postwar period this feeling was first expressed in changing approaches to the rebuilding of city centres; for example, the Altstadt cores of cities like Münster, Nuremberg, Würzburg and Mainz where original schemes for more-or-less completely new, traffic-dominated layouts were soon put aside and replaced by policies of 'adaptation' which aimed at a humanistic balance between modernisation and preservation.[22] Throughout the 1950s active interest in urban conservation remained firmly within the historic city centres, partly because these places were subject to particularly heavy threats from developers, and partly owing to the fact that they included so much of the country's 'pre-industrial' cultural and architectural heritage. By the mid-1960s, however, interest was beginning to turn to the *Nostalgie* townscapes of the industrial revolution, especially the old apartment quarters of the inner cities. At the time these were seen to be under the dual pressures of destruction for commercial development and sporadic erosion in face of traffic planning. So great was the tide of of public opinion against these two environmental attacks that it became an important issue during the campaigning for the 1969 federal election. The incoming SDP–FDP (Socialist-liberal) coalition was sympathetic to conservationist interests whilst also wishing to improve urban living conditions. Accordingly, a series of federal acts was passed, culminating in the first *Städtebauförderungsgesetz* of 1971. The main feature of this 'Act to Promote Urban Development' was the introduction of the principle of inner-city improvement areas (*städtische Sanierungsgebiete*), and the encouragement given to city authorities to submit applications for their designation. After designation, these improvement areas qualified for special federal funding in the fields of housing modernisation, infrastructure investments and provision of recreation facilities. The first annual budget was just under DM 100 million, and as the number of designations increased it rose in successive stages to DM 144 million in 1974, DM 182 million in 1979 and DM 239 million in 1980.[23] Two other relevant outcomes of the 1969-71 phase of planning legislation were the increased influence of regional conservation departments and the greater powers for city authorities to intervene against private demolitions of vernacular buildings.

The second reason for the rarity of comprehensive redevelopment on anything approaching the British scale rests in the very small incidence of public ownership of residential property. This has been a consistent feature of West German cities throughout the postwar period, even during the reconstruction years when large amounts of government money were poured into subsidising housing provision. Moreover, despite some early recognition of the residential problems of inner cities and the need for adequate planning instruments to deal with the worst cases, progress in the critical field of compulsory purchase has been belated and insufficient. Indeed, apart from the special context of acquiring land for new road and transport schemes, authorities were unable to intervene positively in the urban property market until the late 1960s; even then, insufficient financial backing meant that little extensive progress could be made. The amounts of public funding which were made available for such purposes as compensation and legal fees were eventually increased to something near realistic levels in 1976 with the introduction of the second Städtebauförderungsgesetz. Yet this Act, and the related *Wohnungsmodernisierungsgesetz* of the following year, still leaves major obstacles in the path of compulsory purchase. For one thing, the onus continues to lie with the municipality to prove individual buildings as 'totally unfit for habitation', a procedure which can be easily prolonged for several years, and which in the meantime may be easily pre-empted by owners or tenants bringing in their own improvements. For another, it is obligatory for local housing authorities to pay at the current market value when acquiring residential properties. This stipulation, of course, is fair in principle, but it has quickly become a major source of controversy, for in several localities experience has already shown that prices of housing, however poor its standard may be, tend to be pushed up steeply as soon as public intervention is rumoured. Not surprisingly, where it has succeeded in acquiring properties, the city is usually much happier to renovate rather than reconstruct:

the latter course of action usually adds substantially to the already heavily inflated expense, while it also has the disadvantage of a longer lapse of time before the eventual inflow of rental income.

The third reason is the striking degree of diversity within West German inner cities, not only from district to district but also at the narrowest local level. Quite commonly, the full spectrum of inner-city environments and housing conditions, ranging from the poorest to those which pose little or nothing in the way of residential problems, can be seen compressed together within the confines of one small locality. A revealing example of this characteristic is shown in the composite map of Alt Ehrenfeld, Figure 3.6. Here, within an area of not more than 1.5 km^2, all five environmental types are all well represented: first, a typically scattered pattern of streetblocks with frontages still dominated by nineteenth-century, working-class apartments, and with interiors still filled with factories, workshops and Hinterhäuser; secondly (also surviving the Second World War), a small enclave of attractive, early twentieth-century villas centred around the tree-lined section of the Ehrenfeldgürtel; thirdly, a very haphazard distribution of streetblocks containing a fairly even mixture of old apartment buildings and postwar social housing; fourthly, streetblocks dominated by postwar reconstruction, each faithfully depicting the locales of heaviest wartime bombing and, whichever yardstick is used, coming above the margins of present-day acceptability; lastly, the various forms of modern residential development already described in some detail with reference to Figure 3.3.

The Case of Elberfeld-Nordstadt

The real need for the type of planning intervention envisaged under the terms of the first Städtebauförderungsgesetz is only acute in places where there is a prevalence of substandard and mostly prewar housing. But, as epitomised in Cologne-Alt Ehrenfeld, such places commonly exist today in the form of scattered streetblocks intermingled amongst others of variously better residential quality. Indeed, it is only in a minority of West Germany's inner-city districts that there are slum quarters extensive and homogeneous enough to merit large-scale improvement schemes.

One such area is Elberfeld-Nordstadt (Figure 3.7), a large inner-city ward which, unlike other parts of the Wuppertal conurbation, not only managed to come out of the Second World War with remarkably little destruction, but has also been able to escape commercial intrusion. As much as 84 per cent of its housing is prewar, most of it dating back

Figure 3.6: Environmental Types in Cologne-Alt Ehrenfeld

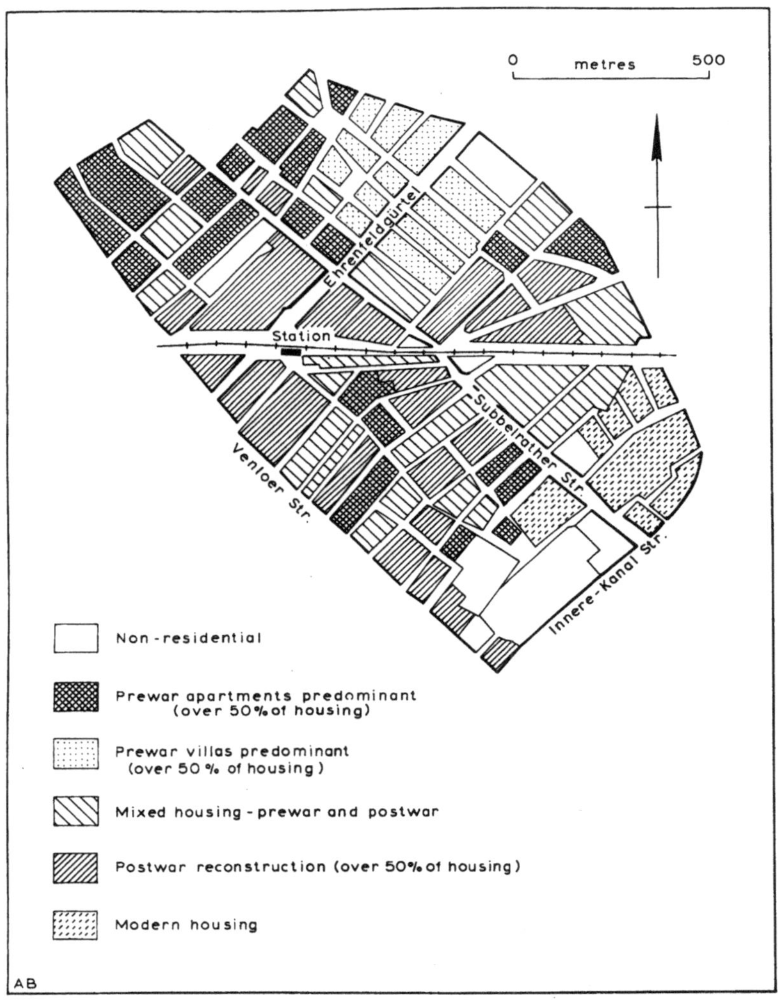

Source: Personal field-survey, conducted in August and September 1980 using 1972 editions of *Deutsche Grundkarte* (1:2,500 scale) as base maps.

to the period 1845-90. Before submitting its application for the Nordstadt to be designated as an urban improvement area, the city of Wuppertal contracted the Swiss research company Prognos AG to undertake a detailed survey of the whole district. Completed in 1971 under the title of *Sanierung Elberfeld-Nord*,[24] their report highlighted the notoriously poor housing and environmental conditions. As many as 9,308 dwellings were counted, but only 562 of these were considered to have modern standards of comfort. More than half the total had major defects: 29 per cent had no interior toilets; 27 per cent were without baths; 31 per cent consisted of fewer than three rooms, and 24 per cent (most of pre-1870 vintage) were of timber construction. Moreover, nearly one-fifth of the residential buildings were Hinterhäuser without any direct access to the street. The population density of 241 persons per ha, rising to more than 500 in some streetblocks, was the highest in the conurbation, and over ten times the Wuppertal mean. Bearing in mind that the Nordstadt also included a large amount of industrial land use, much of it being occupied by obsolete textile factories and finishing works, there was hardly any open space and recreation land. At the time of the Prognos survey, this amounted to only 1.4 ha; a paltry 0.6 m^2 for each inhabitant.

For information on the local demographic characteristics one can turn to the annual volumes of *Wuppertaler Statistik, Jahresbericht* compiled by the City Office for Urban Research and Development.[25] These reports indicate three significant trends in Elberfeld-Nordstadt, each of which is common to most inner-city districts: first, the rapid rate of population decline, with the number of inhabitants falling from 30,867 in 1961 to 24,867 in 1971 and 20,915 in 1978; secondly, the pronounced ageing of the demographic structure to the extent that 59 per cent of household heads are older than 60 years, and 40 per cent are pensioners; thirdly, the growing proportion of Gastarbeiter and their families among the local community. The rapid build-up of the immigrant population (6.4 per cent of all inhabitants in 1970 but thereafter increasing to 23.2 per cent in 1978) is of particular interest. As in many other West German cities, it is very much a reflection of the incomers' high reliance on the poorest sectors of the urban housing market – in other words, the oldest and cheapest types of rental accommodation. To add to this point, it is worth noting in the Nordstadt that all save 11 per cent of dwellings are occupied under tenancy agreements, and prior to the main phase of housing improvement during the late 1970s rents were running at less than half the city average.[26]

For more than a decade the city of Wuppertal has been following the example of other local authorities in providing money to encourage private initiative in housing improvement. At first, however, allocations of general improvement grants and 'incentive' prizes were made outside the realm of planning strategy. All too often funds were given to owners of far sounder properties than those which predominated in districts like the Nordstadt. In fact, most went into subsidising an apparently random distribution of façade painting and heating insulation in the affluent Nützenberg quarter and outlying industrial and dormitory communities on the northern and southern fringes of Wuppertal's elongated built-up area. Suddenly, the initial policy of spatially uncontrolled improvements was changed in 1972. For this was the year when the city housing department was given powers to concentrate grant allocations into the more needful parts of the conurbation, while at the same time Elberfeld-Nordstadt earned the distinction of becoming the country's first designated Städtisches Sanierungsgebiet.

The area is divided by the arterial Hochstrasse into two fairly equal-sized parts; the Hombücheler Viertel in the west with 4,123 dwellings in 1971, and the Mirker Viertel in the east with 5,185 (Figure 3.7). It is in the Mirker Viertel where the worst conditions prevail, and where by far the largest amount of improvement activity has taken place. With financial assistance now being available from both city and federal sources, 180 residential buildings have been treated here, to date, out of a total of 963. Public funds have also helped the construction of several new apartment units, mostly adopting traditional styles of architectural design and making use of derelict industrial sites. Of the improvements themselves, the majority have been sponsored by private individuals, and have usually followed the standard modern format of external decorating, insulation, installation of central heating and, where necessary, provision of toilets and bathrooms. However, in certain cases (mostly within the core area) the municipality has intervened directly, taking advantage of government grants and preferential loans to buy up old apartment units and see to their complete renovation. So far, 40 residential buildings in the Mirker Viertel have been subject to this operation, each undergoing the total gutting and rebuilding of its interior (*Durchbau*) with only the outside walls being left in their original state.[27]

There are some interesting features to observe in the spatial distribution of these housing improvements and renovations (Figure 3.7). One is the existence of small clusters of treated buildings, which are particularly noticeable along Ludwigstrasse, Friedrichstrasse and Wiesenstrasse. They have emerged as a result of neighbours being encouraged to reduce costs by combining together and having the work

Figure 3.7: Housing Improvements and Renovations in the Mirker Viertel of Elberfeld-Nordstadt, 1972-80

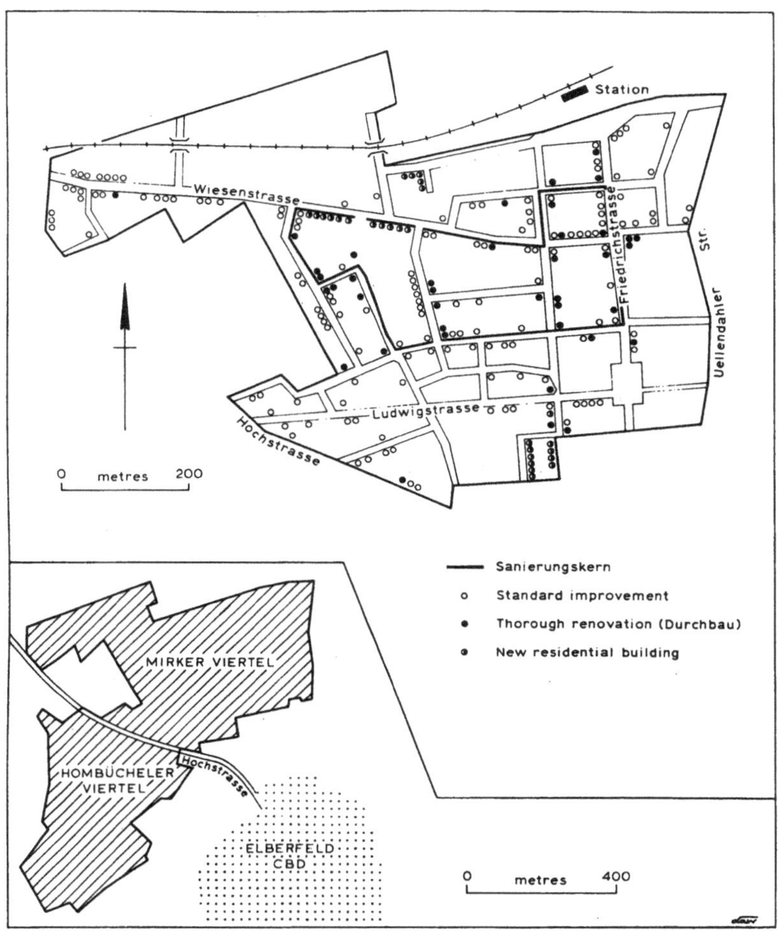

Source: Personal field-survey, conducted in October 1980 using 1972 editions of *Deutsche Grundkarte* (1:2,500 scale) as base maps. Advice on this survey was kindly given by H. Klammer and other officers of the Sanierungsbüro Elberfeld-Nordstadt, Wiesenstrasse, Wuppertal-Elberfeld.

performed under joint contracts. A second feature is the importance which is attached to corner positions: these account for as many as 29 per cent of post-1972 grant allocations in the Mirker Viertel. Prominent here are the *Geschäftswohnungen* (apartment buildings with ground-floor retail, catering or other small-business activity) whose owners are especially eager to modernise.

The Sanierungskern. The third point which arises from Figure 3.7 is the special significance of the *Sanierungskern* (improvement-area core) in the centre of the Mirker Viertel. A decade ago the six streetblocks which constitute this small locality represented the most run-down part of Elberfeld-Nordstadt. All except 9 per cent of the residential buildings were prewar, and only 7 per cent were reported to have been without at least one major defect.[28] Indeed, housing conditions here were so poor that in 1974 it was decided that the only worthwhile planning solution was to go beyond normal West German practice and undertake a programme not very far removed from comprehensive redevelopment. Through further concentration of financial resources, the initial plan in fact envisaged creating for the nation at large a prototype showpiece of how an obsolete inner-city precinct could be converted into a 'model' urban neighbourhood.[29]

As far as the streetblock interiors were concerned, it was possible to embark on the programme straightaway without having to invoke the tedious and often inconclusive machinery of compulsory purchase. Depression in the staple textile trade had already enforced several factory closures, while surviving firms were only too willing to accept offers of assisted relocation to Wuppertal's Autobahn-orientated industrial estates. Moreover, in a part of the conurbation where there was virtually no market for commercial development, it was quite easy for the city to aquire most of the dilapidated workshops and Hinterhäuser, whose owners understandably preferred not to delay the process of selling. Thus, within two years following the initiation of the *Bebauungsplan Nordstadt-Sanierungskern*, the first Blockkern was ready for clearance and land-use conversion. By 1980 aquisition of properties (internal and frontage) had been completed in three other streetblocks.

The conversion work itself, which has now been finished in streetblocks A, B, and C (Figure 3.8), begins with excavations for the construction of underground car parks and the laying of new drainage and sewerage piping. Three discreetly placed underground car parks have now been installed within the Sanierungskern, and two more are planned for the near future. Their use, however, is restricted to local residents, who had previously been given no other choice than to leave their vehicles on the street verges. Whilst providing a much needed type

Figure 3.8: Elberfeld-Nordstadt; Land-use, Buildings and Residential Change in the *Sanierungskern*, 1971-80

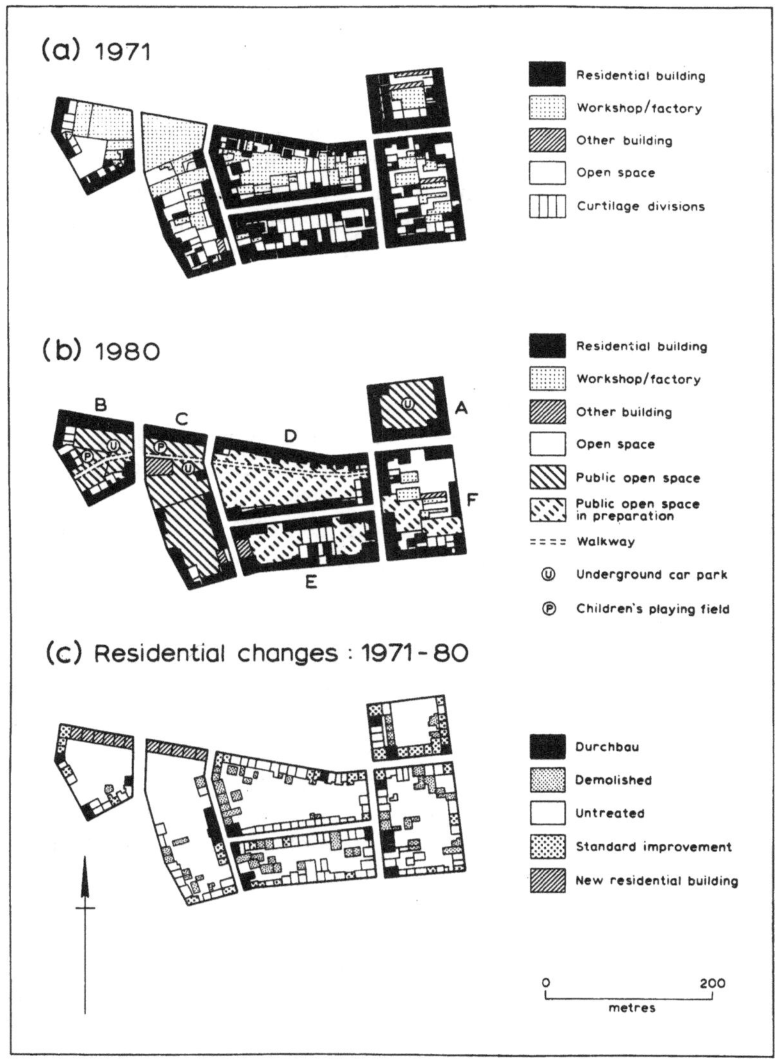

Source: Personal field-survey, conducted in October 1980 using 1972 editions of *Deutsche Grundkarte* (1: 2,500 scale) as base maps. I am indebted to H. Klammer of the Sanierungsbüro Elberfeld-Nordstadt for advice on this survey.

of infrastructure facility, these expensive investments can also be regarded as an important part of the general emphasis on environmental improvement, for they relieve congestion along the narrow thoroughfares and also help reduce the risk of pedestrian accidents. Once this time-consuming stage of the conversion sequence is finished, the next step is to cover the workings with new soil and to landscape the surface. Apart from the provision of a new primary school in streetblock C, all the cleared land has been developed as communal open space, mostly as small secluded parks with tidy flower beds and shrubberies, but also including pedestrian ways and children's play areas.

As well as initiating this costly sequence of environmental improvement, the plan for the Sanierungskern also instituted a programme of extensive housing renovation. In its original format the scheme anticipated an achievement well beyond the scope of private initiative and improvement grants, and accordingly it was intended that all uncleared residential properties in the locality would be fully modernised under public sponsorship. As an immediate priority, eleven new residential buildings (80 new dwellings), all qualifying for social-housing subsidies, were constructed along the frontages of two abandoned industrial sites in streetblocks B and C. These, however, have gone only a small way towards compensating for the 280 homes which have been lost through the demolition of Hinterhäuser and other old apartment units (Figure 3.8). The insufficient number of 'compensatory' new dwellings is an obvious shortcoming of the housing programme in the improvement-area core, and has aroused considerable local discontent. But serious too is the extent to which modernisation of old properties has fallen behind schedule. So far the city housing department, faced with the four pitfalls of compulsory purchase procedure, widening competition between cities for a share of federal support, opposition from conservation bodies and costs now reaching DM 60,000 per dwelling,[30] has managed to renovate only 22 apartment buildings here out of a target figure of 156. In recognition of this failure there is now a turning away from the idea of bringing all the housing into municipal ownership and then treating each unfit structure to systematic Durchbau. In its place, additional encouragements are being offered for private improvements which, despite their limited scope and tendency in the past to be accompanied by steep rent increases, do find favour amongst many tenants. One reason for their acceptability is that their retention of the interior building structures and their relatively quick completions means there does not have to be any period of residential displacement for the occupants. Moreover, the noise and disturbance caused by the work lasts only a matter of a few months, just a fraction of the time which is usually taken for municipal renovations. One final point to consider, and one which may well prove to be further justification for the change in policy, is the possibility in future years that new legislation will be introduced to strengthen the penalties for 'unfair' rent increases and to make rental control (at present still almost wholly confined to social housing) a necessary concomitant of receiving improvement grants.

Notes

1. The figures for Cologne are taken from historical data contained in Statistisches Amt der Stadt Köln, *Leitplan der Stadt Köln*, vol. 2 (SASK, Köln, 1970); those for Nuremberg are from Stadt Nürnberg Amt für Stadtforschung und Statistik, *Statistisches Handbuch der Stadt Nürnberg*, 1972 edn (SNASS, Nuremberg, 1973); those for Mannheim are from an analysis in H. Friedmann, 'Alt Mannheim im Wandel seiner Physiognomie, Struktur und Funktionen, 1606-1965', published thesis presented in Bundesanstalt für Landeskunde und Raumforschung, *Forschungen zur deutschen Landeskunde* (BfLR, Bad Godesberg, 1968), vol. 168.

2. These figures have been calculated from data in F. Schumacher, *Köln, Entwicklungsfragen einer Grossstadt*, 1st edn (Saaleck Verlag, Cologne, 1923), pp. 120-6.

3. For an early analysis of this information see L. Lenz, 'Die Mietkaserne in Köln' in K. Schroeder Verlag, *Bonner Staatswissenschaftliche Untersuchungen* (K. Schroeder Verlag, Leipzig, 1930), vol. 14; for a modern interpretation see Henriette Meynen, *Die Wohnbauten im nordwestlichen Vorortsektor Kölns mit Ehrenfeld als Mittelpunkt* (L. Röhrschied Verlag, Bonn, 1978).

4. Statistisches Bundesamt, *Fachserie E: Gebäude- und Wohnungszählung* (SB, Wiesbaden, 1968).

5. H. Hoyt, *The Structure and Growth of Residential Neighborhoods in American Cities* (Federal Housing Administration, Washington DC, 1939), pp. 112-22.

6. G. Werner, W. Köllmann and H.W. Schürmann, *Heimatchronik der Stadt Wuppertal* (Archiv für Deutsche Heimatpflege, Cologne, 1958), pp. 78-81.

7. Data for each city district are listed in Stadt Köln Vermessungsamt, *100 Jahre stadtkölnisches Vermessungs- und Liegenschaftswesen* (Stadt Köln Vermessungsamt, Cologne, 1975). Far worse than the housing losses in Alt Ehrenfeld were those recorded in Altstadt–Süd (89.5 per cent), Altstadt–Nord (81.7 per cent), Kalk (71.7 per cent), Mülheim (68.9 per cent) and Deutz (59.6 per cent).

8. M.T. Wild, *West Germany, a Geography of its People* (William Dawson, Folkestone, 1979 and Longman Group, Harlow, 1981), pp. 199-201.

9. D. Häring, 'Zur Geschichte und Wirkung staatlicher Interventionen im Wohnungssektor' in D. Häring (ed.) *Gesellschaftliche und Sozialpolitische Aspekte der Wohnungspolitik in Deutschland* (Hammonia Verlag, Hamburg, 1974).

10. Statistisches Bundesamt, *Fachserie, E*, annual volumes.

11. Early-postwar figures of annual dwelling completions within the city of Nuremberg are given retrospectively in the tables of *Bau- und Wohnungswesen* in Stadt Nürnberg Amt für Stadtforschung und Statistik, *Statistisches Handbuch der*

Stadt Nürnberg, 1965 edn (SNASS, Nuremberg, 1966).

12. Statistisches Amt der Stadt Köln, *Leitplan*, vol. 1, pp. 14-16.

13. Statistisches Amt der Stadt Köln, *Statistisches Jahrbuch der Stadt Köln* (SASK, Cologne, annually).

14. T. Polensky, 'Die Bodenpreise in Stadt und Region München', *Mitteilungen der geographischen Gesellschaft in München*, vol. 10 (1974).

15. G. Hallett, *Housing and Land Policies in West Germany and Britain* (Macmillan Press, London, 1977), pp. 12-14.

16. G. Gad, 'Büros im Stadtzentrum von Nürnberg', *Erlanger Geographische Arbeiten*, vol. 23 (1968), pp. 133-341.

17. G. Kade and K. Vorlaufer, 'Grundstucksmobilität und Bauaktivität im Prozess des Strukturwandels citynaher Wohngebiete; Beispiel Frankfurt-Westend', *Frankfurter Wirtschafts- und Sozialgeographische Schriften*, vol. 16 (1974), p. 24.

18. Stadt Köln Dezernat für Stadtentwicklung, *Köln, Stadtentwicklungs-Planung: Gesamtkonzept* (Stadt Köln Dezernat für Stadtentwicklung, Cologne, 1978), section 6, pp. 30-43.

19. Ibid., pp. 22-9.

20. SASK, *Statistisches Handbuch*, 1980 edn, table on *Einwohnerzahlen*.

21. This statement is a personal translation from the preamble to the *Bundesraumordnungsgesetz* 1965.

22. A particularly interesting study of the approaches to the rebuilding of historic city centres is contained in E. Mulzer, 'Die Wiederaufbau der Altstadt von Nürnberg; 1945 bis 1970', *Erlanger Geographische Arbeiten*, vol. 31 (1972), pp. 1-225.

23. Press- und Informationsamt der Bundesregierung, *Gesellschaftliche Daten 1979* (Press- und Informationsamt der Bundesregierung, Bonn, 1979), pp. 311-19.

24. Prognos AG, *Sanierung Elberfeld-Nord*, (Prognos AG, Basle, 1971).

25. Stadt Wuppertal Amt für Stadtentwicklung und Stadtforschung, *Wuppertaler Statistik, Jahresbericht* (SWASS, Wuppertal, annually).

26. Stadtplanungsamt Wuppertal, *Sanierung in der Elberfeld-Nordstadt* (Stadtplanungsamt Wuppertal, Wuppertal, 1980), pp. 3-5.

27. Ibid., p. 7.

28. Prognos AG, *Sanierung Elberfeld-Nord*, p. 36.

29. Stadtplanungsamt Wuppertal, *Bebauungsplan Nordstadt-Sanierungskern* (Stadtplanungsamt Wuppertal, Wuppertal, 1974).

30. I am indebted to H. Klammer of the Sanierungsbüro Elberfeld-Nordstadt for kindly answering this and other questions relating to the Sanierungskern development project. The figure of DM 60,000 for the costs of renovating an old apartment building is for October 1980.

4 GUESTWORKERS AND THEIR SPATIAL DISTRIBUTION

Philip Jones

> They are people too. We forget that they would not have left the 'country of origin' had it offered work, and that, disruptive as the emigrants may be, the 'host country' tolerates them, even seeks them, because it needs them.[1]

The migration of individuals and families from one country to another is a profound human experience; it generates an enormous variety of human situations and responses which remain hidden beneath econometric analyses or sophisticated mathematical models. West Germany has more than four million persons of foreign (non-German) origin, representing almost 7 per cent of its total population.[2] Yet they live in an uneasy relationship with the host population, largely because West German society cannot reconcile itself to their presence, and denies the majority even the most elementary of political rights.[3] The ensuing dilemma has been posed by Rist, who states,

> The present economy of the Federal Republic of Germany cannot sustain itself without foreign labour. At the same time, however, the issue remains unsolved as to whether this indispensable group of guestworkers should be understood as an additional transitory source of manpower or as new immigrants into society.[4]

Evolution of the Foreign Population

The influx of guestworkers into West Germany since the end of the 1950s forms part of a wider transference of labour from the backward regions of southeastern and Mediterranean Europe to the industrial countries of northwest Europe.[5] By 1975 there were approximately 5.3 million foreign workers employed in Austria, Belgium, France, West Germany, the Netherlands, Sweden and Switzerland, constituting between 5.5 per cent and 19.8 per cent of the employed population.[6] Almost three-quarters of this huge army of labour originated in Portugal,

Spain, Italy, Yugoslavia, Greece and Turkey.[7]

West Germany became an important destination only after 1960, because hitherto the labour requirements of the 'economic miracle' had been largely satisfied from the enormous pool of refugees inherited from Potsdam and replenished by the constant, if depleting, stream from East Germany.[8] But the inflow of refugees eventually ceased as a result of the building of the Berlin Wall in 1961. This necessitated a reappraisal of labour sources for the West German economy, with attention turning abruptly to the possibilities of recruiting from foreign countries. Subsequently, as Figure 4.1 shows, the evolution of the foreign labour force has progressed through four clearly defined stages: first, a period of uninterrupted expansion lasting until 1966; secondly, a short-lived retrogression during the years 1967 and 1968; thirdly, a phase of renewed expansion culminating in the peak total of 1973; lastly, the rather indeterminate trend since 1973, starting with a steep decline but subsequently showing indications of a small recovery after 1978.

This uneven progression closely reflects temporal trends in 'unsatisfied' labour demand above that which could be met from the numbers and preferences of German citizens.[9] Until 1973 the need for cheap labour, especially in unskilled and unattractive occupations, was insatiable. Accordingly, the recruitment of foreign labour on temporary one-year contracts appeared to offer a means of matching cyclic fluctuations in demand without sustaining inflationary wage pressures.[10] Bi-lateral agreements were signed with Greece, Portugal, Spain, Yugoslavia and Turkey in the 1960s, and recruitment offices were set up by the *Bundesamt für Arbeit* (Federal Office for Employment).[11] But the introduction of foreign labour represented something more than just a straightforward response to economic expansion. Between 1960 and 1970 West Germany's working population declined by 800,000 as a consequence of normal ageing; meanwhile, the upward mobility of a better-educated indigenous workforce created further job opportunities.[12]

Broken only by the recession of 1966-8, the expansionary years came to a sudden halt with the imposition of the *Anwerbestopp* (ban on new recruitment) in November 1973, in the wake of the poor economic trends accompanying the oil crisis. The recruitment ban has continued to be enforced and, although applying only to source areas outside the EEC, resulted in a 21.4 per cent decline in foreign workers between 1974 and 1977.[13] However, evidence of a small but distinct rise after 1978 demonstrates that guestworkers still play a vital role in the West German economy, because, as Kayser stresses within a wider west European context, 'they are in jobs which others do not want'.[14] Furthermore, through the process of natural demographic increase, the resident foreign population will generate a large proportion of West Germany's labour force in future years even if there is no further immigration.[15]

Figure 4.1: West Germany: Evolution of Foreign Employed Population, 1960-80

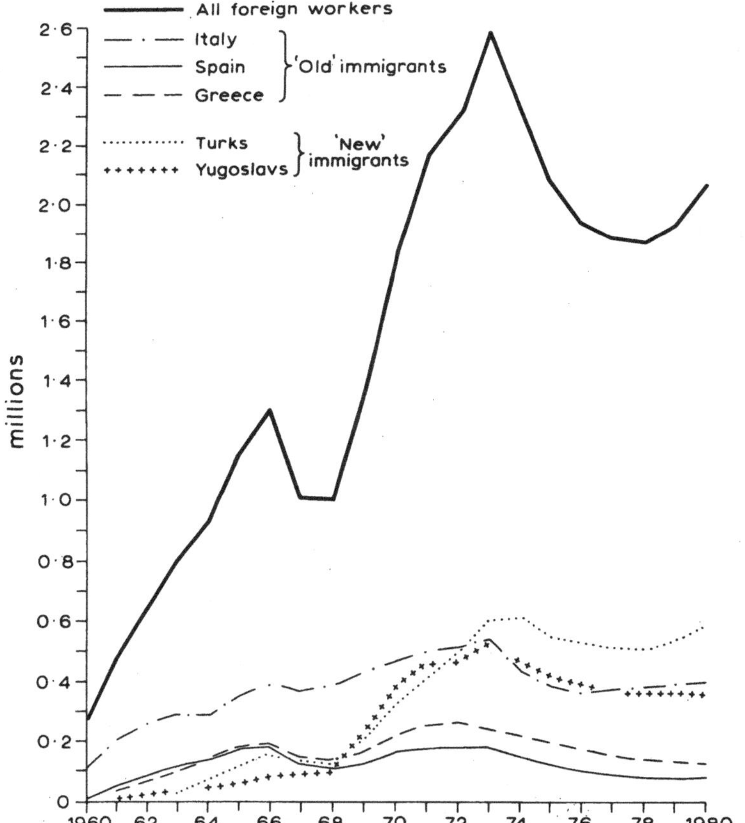

Source: Data presented in H. Werner, 'Freedom of Movement and Migration of Workers in the Countries of the European Community' (English version), *Mitteilungen aus der Arbeitsmarkt- und Berufsforschung*, vol. 4 (1973), pp. 326-71, Table 1; also Statistisches Bundesamt, *Statistisches Jahrbuch*, annual volumes, 1974-80.

Guestworkers and their Origins

Figure 4.1 shows that the numerical contribution of the major countries of origin has fluctuated through time. In the early years, prior to the 1966-8 recession, Italian, Spanish and Greek workers dominated. After 1968, however, Yugoslavs and Turks proved increasingly attractive on account of their reputation for cheapness and docility.[16] The recruitment ban in 1973, coupled with the impact of generally worsening economic conditions, has stimulated a substantial but unevenly distributed fall in numbers of foreign workers. Table 4.1 illustrates that the decline in Spanish and Greek workers has been very steep. As far as these two groups are concerned, it is worth noting Kayser's claim that their return migration was already in progress before the Anwerbestopp, and until then was largely in response to improving conditions at home.[17] There has been a smaller, though still quite substantial, percentage decline in numbers of workers from the 'late' countries of Yugoslavia and Portugal, whilst Italians have been relatively little affected on account of their EEC status. Most striking, however, is the minimal decline in Turkish workers who, as Clout and Salt emphasise, have little incentive to return to a desperately poor Third World background.[18] Consequently, the foreign labour force has become less diversified during the 1970s, and the Turks have rapidly assumed the leading position in the guestworker component. Although Table 4.1 indicates that the 'other countries' category (primarily EEC countries with the exclusion of Italy, and neighbours such as Austria) has expanded to form one-quarter of the total, these populations are not categorised nor indeed even perceived as *Gastarbeiter*.[19]

Guestworkers in the Labour Force

The 2,072,000 (1980) figure) socially insured foreign workers represent approximately 10 per cent of all active persons in West Germany; but the ratio is considerably higher in manufacturing and construction, which account for more than two-thirds of the total Gastarbeiter employment (Table 4.2). Within the manufacturing sector there is a clear tendency for foreigners to be concentrated in trades which are monotonous, dirty and undemanding of skill. This can be seen, for example, by contrasting their ratios in industries like metal foundries (27.7 per cent of employees), motor vehicles (17.7 per cent) and textiles (20.0 per cent) with those in activities involving a higher technical and skill content, such as aircraft production (6.5 per cent) and publishing 7.7 per cent).[20] It is this pronounced weighting of their occupational profile towards menial and low-status jobs that underlies

Kolodny's view that guestworkers constitute a special 'underclass' within which any small deviations are to be considered as mere nuances.[21]

Table 4.1: West Germany: Changes in the Composition of the Foreign Labour Force, June 1974-June 1980

Country of origin	1980 employment		% change
	Number	% of total	1974-80
Turkey	590,623	28.5	– 4.4
Yugoslavia	357,427	17.3	– 24.5
Italy	309,226	14.3	– 9.3
Greece	132,980	6.4	– 43.3
Spain	86,547	4.2	– 45.5
Portugal	58,780	2.8	– 28.7
Other countries	536,075	25.9	+ 26.6
All employed foreigners	2,071,658	100,0	– 11.1

Source: Bundesanstalt für Arbeit, *Sozialversicherungspflichtig Beschäftige im Bundesgebiet am 30 Juni 1980* (BfA, Nuremberg, 1981), Table 7.

Table 4.2: West Germany: Foreign Employees by Economic Activity

Economic activity	1980 employment			
	Number	% of employment in each activity	% of total foreign labour force	1974-80 % change in foreign employees
Manufacturing	1,191,366	13,8	57.5	– 18.2
Construction	218,247	12.9	10.5	– 26.3
All foreign employment	2,071,658	9.9	100.0	– 11.1
Energy and mining	34,966	7.3	1.7	n.a.
Farming, forestry and fishing	18,682	8.5	0.9	– 18.3
Retailing and wholesale	135,344	4.6	6.5	+ 11.3
Transport & communications	76,395	7.7	3.7	– 5.1
Finance	15,088	2.0	0.7	+ 17.3
Services	315,011	8.9	15.2	+ 17.6
Domestic service	14,866	4.2	0.7	+ 26.9
Local authority work	50,536	3.8	2.4	+ 3.6

Sources: Bundesanstalt für Arbeit, *Sozialversicherungspflichtig Beschäftige im Bundesgebiet am 30 Juni 1980* (BfA, Nuremberg, 1981), Table 6; and *Sonderdruck Sozialversicherungspflichtig Beschäftige Arbeitnehmer Ende Juni 1980* (BfA, Nuremberg, 1981), Table 1.50, pp. 394-5.

Nevertheless, guestworkers are taking part, if only to a limited degree, in West Germany's recent shift of labour resources from the secondary to the tertiary economic sector. Table 4.2 indicates that the most rapid declines in foreign labour since 1974 have occurred in manufacturing industries and construction, whereas increases have taken place in most major tertiary activities. Despite this trend, however, the proportion of foreign labour which is engaged in the latter group of occupations remains far below the national average.[22]

Demographic Change and Composition of the Foreign Population

Although there is a rough similarity between the national composition of the *guestworker labour force* and that of the total *guestworker population* (see 'A Note on Terminology', on p. 107), the latter also reflects the intercession of social and demographic factors. This is amply illustrated in the post-1973 period when, in spite of the decline in numbers of foreign workers, the overall immigrant population managed to increase by 4.5 per cent (Table 4.3). The single most dramatic change was again the 'explosion' in the Turkish component, which by 1979 had come to represent almost one-third of all foreign persons resident in West Germany. All other guestworker populations declined; marginally so as far as the Italians and Portuguese were concerned, but precipitously so in the cases of the Spanish and Greeks.

Table 4.3: West Germany: Changes in the Composition of the Foreign Population, 1973-9

Country of origin	1973		1979		1973-9
	Number	%	Number	%	% change
Turkey	966,200	22.5	1,268,300	30.6	+ 41.9
Yugoslavia	673,300	17.0	620,600	15.0	– 7.8
Italy	622,000	15.7	594,400	14.3	– 4.4
Greece	399,200	10.1	296,800	7.2	– 25.7
Spain	286,100	7.2	182,200	4.4	– 36.3
Portugal	111,700	2.8	109,800	2.7	– 1.7
All 'guestworker' countries	2,985,900	75.3	3,072,100	74.1	+ 2.9
All foreign population	3,966,200	100.0	4,143,800	100.0	+ 4.5

Source: Statistisches Bundesamt, *Statistisches Jahrbuch für die Bundesrepublik Deutschland*, 1974 and 1980 eds (W. Kohlhammer Verlag, Stuttgart and Mainz, 1974 and 1980).

This recent transformation in the composition of the guestworker population has been accompanied by important social and demographic changes. In his life-cycle model of migration, Böhning showed how an initial migration stream of adult male workers would eventually evolve into a family movement.[23] He stressed that this would come after some individuals found themselves able to adapt to new circumstances, stay longer and, ultimately, send for their dependants. An initial, transient adult labour force would thus develop into a settled population of mainly young families; it would follow, therefore, that in general terms the demographic composition of any migrant group will reflect the length of its presence in West Germany.[24] The 1973 recruitment ban, combined with the introduction of policies designed to encourage family reunification and stabilisation of guestworkers already resident in the Federal Republic, has accelerated this temporal process among nationalities who were at early stages in the migration cycle.[25]

Social Consequences

Contemporary West Germany contains a diverse foreign population which differs in important respects from that at the peak of immigration in the early 1970s. The large majority, the guestworkers and their dependants, originate from the most backward regions within their respective countries, and are predominantly from conservative, agrarian-based societies.[26] The enormous increase in the importance of the Turks is especially significant, because social surveys indicate that the indigenous German population ranks them lowest in a scale of 'social acceptability'.[27] Consequently, the guestworkers and their families have become increasingly strange in a cultural and social sense. But they have also become a population of longer-term settlement, in which a high proportion have been resident in West Germany for over six years (Table 4.4). Furthermore, in 1976 foreign births formed over 30 per cent of all live births registered in as many as 18 of West Germany's major cities.[28]

The impact of the guestworker population on everyday life in West Germany has inevitably risen above the levels experienced during the earlier years of an initially male-dominated immigration. The heavy pressure on educational and health facilities, together with the urgency for residential accommodation, have brought many problems for local and national government. But, despite their lengthening sojourn, the incomers appear to have achieved very little in their efforts to integrate socially with the host population. Undoubtedly, the formidable barriers of language and culture are partly to blame; but unfortunately West

Table 4.4: West Germany: Guestworker Population, Selected Demographic Indices, 1973 and 1979

Country of origin	Children under 15 years		% of total population resident in W. Germany for more than 6 years	
	1973	1979	1973	1979
Turkey	158,500	419,700	15.7	57.2
Yugoslavia	62,200	118,600	14.2	79.1
Italy	116,000	128,300	36.2	70.9
Greece	79,000	76,100	35.5	75.6
Spain	45,800	39,100	36.6	85.2
Portugal	14,300	27,300	16.1	69.3

Source: As for Table 4.3.

German society has shown little sympathy for, or understanding of, the newcomers. Indeed, it has reacted strongly at various levels against suggestions that West Germany might develop into a multi-cultural society.[29] Furthermore, foreigners from outside the EEC still live in an atmosphere of insecurity concerning their legal status and rights of residence; they also face much discrimination in various important fields, including housing and employment.[30] Yet, as aliens, they lack any direct political means of redressing these grievances, since they cannot participate in elections. Perhaps the most depressing signs of their deprivation in West Germany are those which indicate that patterns of inequality and discrimination are being transmitted to the second generation. These children of guestworkers, born or at least raised in West Germany, feel their disadvantages more acutely. As minority children they fare badly in an educational system which has been parsimonious in its allocation of resources to accommodate their special needs; in consequence they emerge with few formal qualifications, and this means that they quickly become handicapped in what is now a highly competitive labour market.[31] Accordingly, as soon as they leave school they experience very high unemployment rates, and even when work can be obtained they are virtually condemned to filling unskilled jobs.[32]

West Germany's guestworker population finds itself in what may be described as a 'social no man's land' in which it is socially ignored and unwanted, but economically essential. According to Rist, their inferiority has been institutionalised into a status of 'social marginality'.[33] Yet, notwithstanding the potentially serious undertones of this situation, it is the foreigners' concentrated spatial distribution, often in very poor living conditions, which is seen by Kreuzaler to present not only the more obvious perceived threat to the German population, but also the possibility of forming the targets of any future phase of 'social aggression'.[34] Consequently, it is to the facts of this distribution that we must now turn.

The Geographical Distribution of Guestworkers in West Germany

Regional Perspectives

The regional importance of foreign labour in 1980 is illustrated in Figure 4.2, which depicts foreign workers as a percentage of all socially insured employees within each of West Germany's 142 *Arbeitsamts-bezirke* (Abz), or labour-market areas.[35] The distribution pattern is very uneven, and the national average has little relevance locally since in territorial terms the majority of the country falls into the lowest two classes in the statistical distribution. Areas of high values form a limited number of compact areal concentrations. We can discern, however, a general 'tilt' from higher values in the south and west to lower values in the northern and eastern regions. Indeed, an imaginary line from near Duisburg in the Ruhr, and stretching southeastwards to Munich, bisects the country into two broad zones of dissimilar utilisation of foreign labour. Four nodes of intense dependence on foreign labour can be identified, in which immigrant ratios exceed 14.5 per cent. The most prominent is the Stuttgart-Middle Neckar region, which constitutes the sole geographical grouping of Abz in the highest shaded category. Secondly, there is a linear zone embracing the urban agglomerations of the Rhine-Main and Rhine-Neckar regions, and including such major cities as Frankfurt and Mannheim. The third node consists of the isolated Munich Abz. The fourth node, and the only one which is situated in the northern half of the country, is less intense and more geographically diffuse: it extends from Cologne in the Rhineland eastwards into Wuppertal and other industrial cities in the Sauerland. All other Abz with over 12 per cent foreign labour quotients are to be found in southwest Germany: these include such expanding manufacturing centres as Karlsruhe, Pforzheim and Villingen.

Most of northern, central and eastern West Germany fall into categories which are broadly below the national average. Occasionally, as can be seen in the northern part of the Frankfurt area, the juxtaposition of very low values with a high concentration node is abrupt. Some large cities lie above the prevailing low-surface of this general

Figure 4.2: West Germany: Foreign Workers as Percentage of Insured Employees, 1980

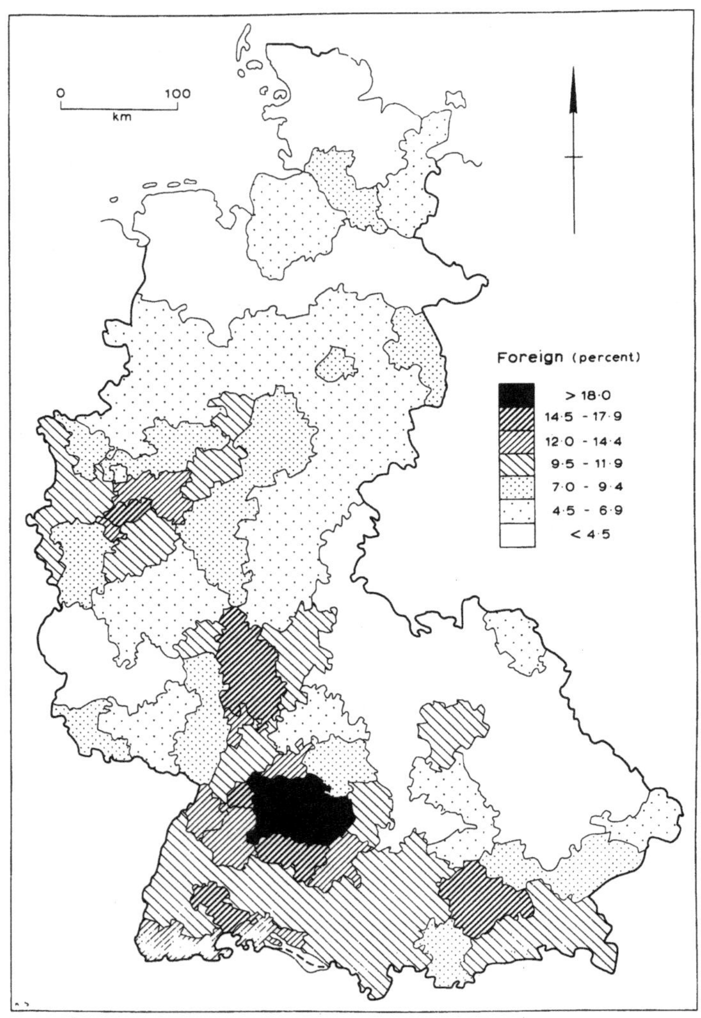

Note: The data are for ***Arbeitsamtsbezirke***; boundaries between areas falling in the same shading category have been omitted for clarity. The data exclude a minor proportion of economically-active foreigners who are self-employed.
Source: Bundesanstalt für Arbeit, ***Sozialversicherungspflichtig Beschäftigte Arbeitnehmer Ender März 1980*** (Bfa, Nuremberg, 1981), Table 1.62, pp. 1716-19.

zone, for example Nuremberg, Hanover and Hamburg. On the other hand, most of the Ruhr and all of the Saarland do not, despite being heavy industrial regions *par excellence*. Before attempting to explain this very uneven pattern, therefore, a further perspective on the spatial distribution is needed.

The Urban Dimension

The prominent regional concentrations of guestworkers are mostly major urban regions. In 1978, when 6.5 per cent of the total population was foreign, this proportion was exceeded in all *Gemeinde* of more than 50,000 inhabitants: the highest foreign ratios were in Gemeinde exceeding 500,000 inhabitants.[36] Consequently, large towns and cities form the prime foci of foreign settlement, although it is worth pointing out that the metropolitan bias is less developed than it is among Great Britain's ethnic minorities.[37] Figure 4.3 in effect represents the pressure points of the foreign population in West Germany, since it maps out all cities with over 100,000 inhabitants and a foreign quotient of at least 10 per cent. Moreover, in view of the especially difficult problems of its social integration, it highlights the Turkish component.

Two particularly dense concentrations of urban centres present themselves. The first is the large group of cities within the triangle with Cologne, Duisburg and Dortmund at its apexes. The second is the constellation of cities which stretches southwards from Wiesbaden and Frankfurt, through Mannheim, to Stuttgart and the Middle Neckar. Some other important concentrations of urban populations occur as individual cities, especially in northern Germany where the cities of Hamburg, Hanover and Bremen are in fairly close proximity to each other. It is significant, however, that these appeared less noticeable on the preceding map; on the other hand, certain regions of predominantly 'small-town' industrial settlement structures do not feature in Figure 4.3 despite their prominence in Figure 4.2. Amongst such areas are southern Baden and the outer margins of the Stuttgart region. Another interesting point to observe is that the inter-urban distribution of the foreign population does not conform in detail to the national ranking of city sizes. The former is headed (in rank order) by Munich, West Berlin and Cologne, whereas the latter places these cities respectively in third, first and fourth positions. Generally speaking, urban centres in the north tend to rank lower on foreign population than do those in the south and along the Rhine axis, although there are some important exceptions such as Wolfsburg and Bielefeld.

Apart from the normal high showing of the Turkish immigrants, the

Figure 4.3: West Germany: Distribution of Foreign Population in Urban Centres with more than 100,000 Inhabitants

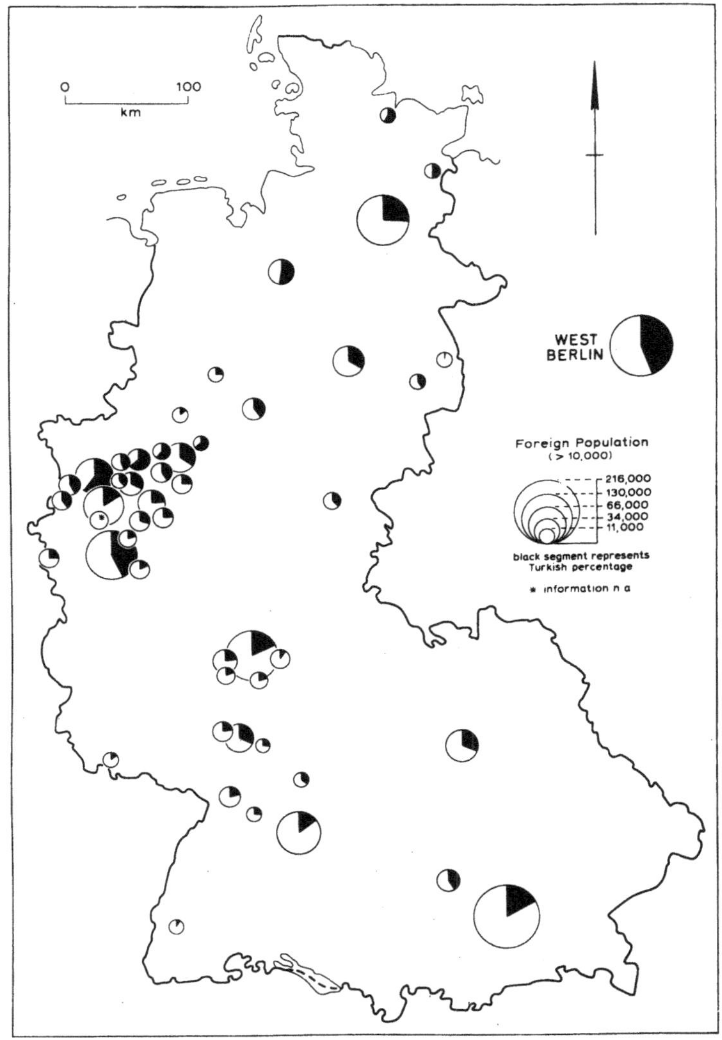

Note: The total foreign population (including dependants) is shown for all cities with a foreign ratio of 10% and above.
Source: Constructed from data presented in Deutsche Städtetag, 'Statistische Materielen zur Ausländer Frage', *Deutsche Städtetag zur Statistike und Stadtforschung*, vol. 19, Reihe H (1980), pp. 44-7.

nationality composition of the foreign population is very diverse in most cities: few have more than one-quarter of their foreigners coming from any single country of origin other than Turkey. In proportionate terms Turks are particularly prominent in West Berlin, the Rhine-Ruhr cities (except Dusseldorf and centres in the Sauerland) and northern West Germany in general; but they feature less strongly in the majority of southern cities (Figure 4.3). Once again, Wolfsburg, with its extraordinary Italian preponderance,[38] represents an exception to the rule. Italians also figure well in the Rhineland and the Saarland, forming more than one-third of all foreigners in the cities of Solingen and Saarbrücken. Yugoslavs account for over one-quarter of the foreign population in only one city, Stuttgart, although this proportion is approached closely in certain other large urban centres of the south, including Munich, Frankfurt and Karlsruhe. Geographical accessibility would appear to be an important factor in both the Italian and Yugoslav cases, but the main impression remains as one of remarkable diversity in the guestworker communities of all save a small minority of West German cities.

Regional Distribution: the Explanatory Framework

Any explanation of the uneven distribution of foreign workers must allocate a prominent role to regional variations in labour demand which, if unmet from local sources, creates a pool of unfilled vacancies and provides a propitious environment for the engagement of foreign workers. In an analysis of regional employment trends in West Germany since 1945, Wild has drawn attention to 'the continuing concentrations of net additions in job opportunities along the Rhine axis and throughout all but the most peripheral parts of southern Germany'.[39] These spatial inequalities in employment availability were rooted in contrasts in the manufacturing sector, particularly the localisation of growth industries, such as vehicles, chemicals and electrical engineering, along the Rhine valley south of Dusseldorf and over much of southern Germany. This propulsive industrial expansion stimulated further growth in construction and services through the operation of 'multiplier' effects. The coincidence of Arbeitsamtsbezirke with high foreign ratios (Figure 4.2) and regions with 'strong' industrial structures according to a classification devised by the *Bundesanstalt für Arbeit* in 1961 (and subsequently mapped by Wild), is indicative of the strength and persistence of this relationship.[40] In regions with 'weak' industrial structures, such as the Ruhr, or with locational disadvantages, as for example is to be found in the areas which adjoin the East German border, labour demand was far less buoyant, and foreign workers, therefore, are still weakly represented. The demand for labour was also below average in most rural regions, especially those lying beyond easy commuting distance to large towns. High unemployment rates are also indicative of a lack of buoyancy in labour demand of all types. Giese has demonstrated how in 1976 there existed a strong inverse correlation ($r = -0.61$) between the percentage of foreign labour in an Abz and its unemployment level.[41] If further amplification of the relationship is needed one can turn again to Figure 4.2, in which areas identified by Giese as having exceptionally severe unemployment rates by West German standards (for example, Upper Franconia, Lower Bavaria and Rhineland-Palatinate) almost invariably have very low foreigner ratios.

Whilst the variable factor of labour demand plays a crucial role as an explanatory factor, we must not neglect the contribution made by the migration process itself. Each individual's migration behaviour is influenced by information received and contacts acquired at a personal level, often taking the form of a more direct sponsorship for a job or accommodation, or both. Using a sample of 148 Yugoslavs in Hanover, Franzen found that as many as 90 had received personal information relevant to their migration behaviour in West Germany, and 50 admitted to being directly influenced by this information.[42] Salt suggests that this typical 'chain migration' process was strengthened by the official recruiting mechanism, which allowed 'satisfactory' guestworkers to nominate a potential migrant, who thus acquired a priority status for entry.[43] In this way individual firms, including major companies such as Ford or Mercedes, have established distinctive national emphases in their recruitment programmes. Furthermore, many resultant strong linkages have been identified between specific West German cities and particular localities in the countries of origin. This feature is exemplified in Kolodny's study of the guestworker community of Stuttgart, where as many as three-quarters of the Greek immigrants originated from the two provinces of Thrace and Macedonia, and a large number came from the single administrative district of Hevros.[44]

In a seminal contribution, Giese has interpreted the distribution of foreign labour in West Germany within the dynamic framework of diffusion theory, thereby adding a temporal dimension to the causal nexus.[45] Figure 4.4 attempts to synthesise the essence of Giese's interpretation of the vital first phase of foreigners' arrivals between 1961 and 1965. The earliest 'innovation centres' (identified as Abz with a foreign ratio of at least 4 per cent in 1961) are found in the southwest corner of the country adjacent to Switzerland, where the use of immigrant labour on a temporary basis was already well established. At a later stage innovation centres appear progressively northwards, running in a sequence from Stuttgart via Frankfurt to Cologne. This spatial sequence, leapfrogging intervening territory, illustrates that the early adoption of the innovation of foreign labour had proceeded in an hierarchical manner from one major to city to another and befitting their pre-eminence in the exchange of ideas. After a further lapse of time the use of guestworkers diffused outwards into the hinterlands of the primary innovation centres, largely because of local contacts and the exchange of information about employment opportunities among established guestworkers. By 1964 the majority of Abz along the Rhine axis, and in southwest Germany generally, exceeded the 4 per cent threshold: the 'Duisburg-Munich line' was discernible, and the 'tilt' of values was already in evidence. During the second major phase of immigration, between 1968 and 1973, the neighbourhood effect of the localised infiltration of foreign workers extended to other areas of West Germany as deficits in labour supply were increasingly met by recruiting guestworkers. Nevertheless, the major innovation centres such as Stuttgart and Frankfurt, with their combination of labour shortages and already large foreign populations, also exerted a powerful attraction on the newcomers. The net result is seen in the gradient profiles in Figure 4.4, where the early peaks of foreign-labour use in 1961 experienced the most pronounced advance by 1972, whilst the initial regional tilt was also maintained. Both trends testify to the strength of the factors which acted as progenitors of the distribution pattern.

Leib and Mertins have criticised this emphasis on diffusion, pointing in particular to the geographical stability of the spatial distribution of Spanish guestworkers at successive dates between 1961 and 1976.[46] They attribute this stability to the consolidation of initial recruitment patterns of Spanish workers, who were mainly used in unskilled work in metal manufacturing. Moreover, until as late as the mid-1970s, there appears little evidence of any secondary dispersal of individual guestworkers within the country.[47] It is also unlikely that the shortlived and largely ineffectual 'overburdened settlement area' restrictions on the movement and residence of guestworkers[48] had any major impact in discouraging the internal redistribution of the foreign population. In fairness, it must be emphasised that Giese's primary concern lay in the pattern of aggregate foreign labour and its spatial evolution, which was amenable to analysis within a statistical framework. In this respect his

Figure 4.4: West Germany: Spatial Evolution of Foreign-labour Utilisation, 1961-72

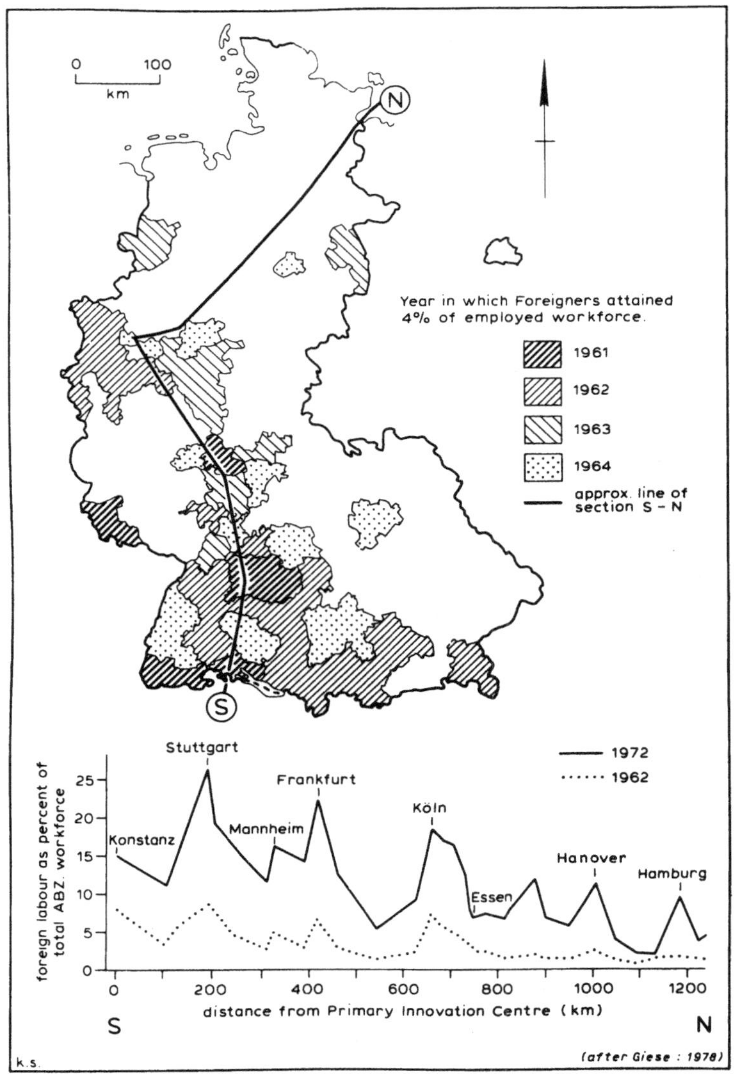

Source: Adapted from E. Giese, 'Raumliche Diffusion ausländerischer Arbeitnehmer in der Bundesrepublik Deutschland; 1960-76', *Die Erde*, vol. 109 (1978), pp. 92-110.

work adds a valuable dynamic insight into the shaping of the present-day distribution of guestworkers in West Germany.

The Residential Distribution of Guestworkers in the West German City

The crucial interface between guestworkers and their hosts exists within the geographic context of cities. In the major components of their spatial distribution within the city structure, in their degree of segregation from the host population, and in the dynamics of their internal population changes, there are encapsulated many indications of the place allocated to guestworkers in West German society, and some which form pointers to the future. Nuremberg is used extensively as a case study in this section, but the results are amplified or extended with reference to other studies undertaken in other cities.

Spatial Distribution and Concentration

The spatial distribution of Nuremberg's foreign population in 1979 is shown in Figure 4.5. The statistical areas on which this map is based are the city's *Stadtdistrikte* (henceforth to be referred to as SDs): each of these consists of a small group of streetblocks, and is somewhat larger than the enumeration districts of the British census.[49] Nuremberg (484,184 inhabitants in 1979) is in many respects a useful representative of a large, West German city. It is essentially 'free-standing', and has a comparatively uncomplicated urban morphology. The 52,132 resident foreigners represent 10.8 per cent of the total population, and in terms of the size of its foreigner ratio Nuremberg is placed in the middle ranks of West German cities. Three-quarters of this immigrant community originated from acknowledged 'guestworker countries', whilst the city's 'mix' of guestworkers comes close to the national average.[50]

Many of Nuremberg's SDs are far from being residential in function: as a corrective, those with fewer than 26 inhabitants have been left completely blank, while in others only the residential portion has been shaded using information published by the city's *Amt für Stadtforschung und Statistik*.[51] The disparity between the foreign population mean (10.8 per cent) and median (6.5 per cent) demonstrates the skewness of the data set, and thus the highly uneven spatial distribution of the immigrant community. Consequently, a simple quartile system of class intervals has been used, in which the shading scheme emphasises the areas with high ratios of foreigners.

Figure 4.5: Nuremberg: Distribution of Foreign Population, 1979

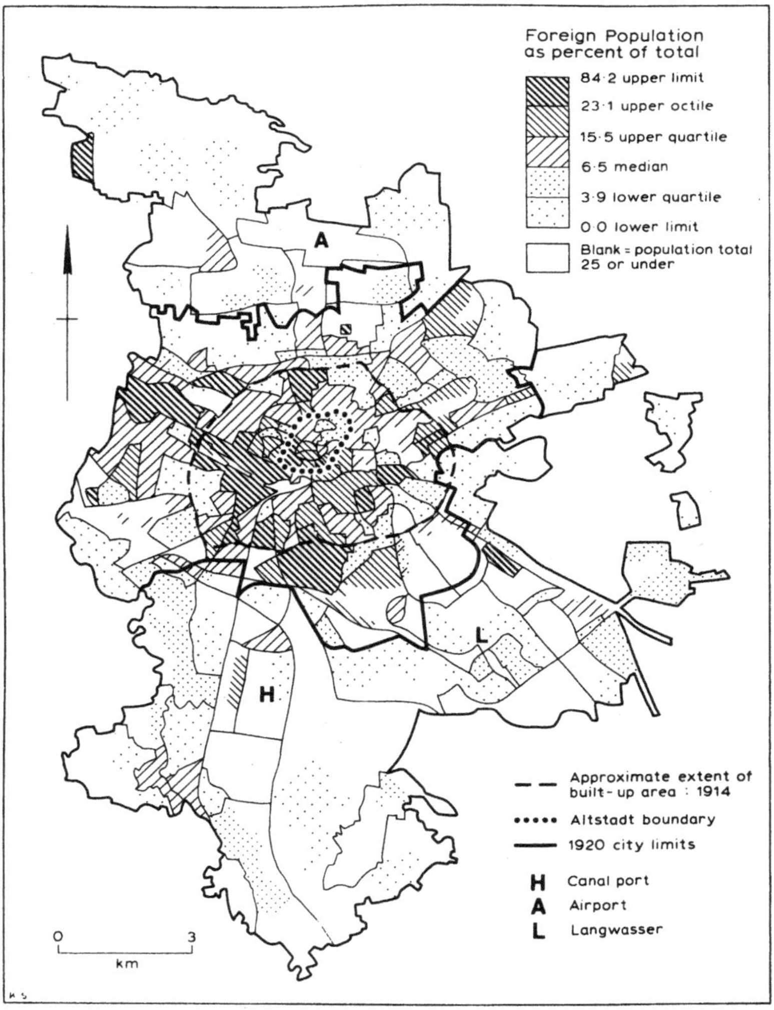

Note: The data are for *Stadtdistrikte*: boundaries between those districts falling in the same shading category have been omitted for clarity.

Source: Constructed from statistical tabulations in Stadt Nürnberg Amt für Stadtforschung und Statistik, *Statistisches Jahrbuch der Stadt Nürnberg 1980* (SNASS, Nuremberg, 1980), pp. 114-25.

The outstanding feature is the concentration of the foreign population in the inner parts of Nuremberg, and a generally sparce representation in the outer suburbs. To assist the interpretation of this 'inner city-outer city' dichotomy, three key urban boundaries have been drawn in Figure 4.5. First, the Altstadt boundary is used to define the historic and commercial core which, nevertheless, still includes a quite considerable residential function. The next boundary, that of the area which had already been built up by 1914, is based upon a combination of cartographic evidence, and forms a fair approximation of the outer limits of the inner city.[52] Between this line and the city's far-flung administrative boundary of 1920 are contained most of the interwar urban extensions, in which not only does the style and density of residential development differ markedly from the previous zone, but also there are contained many of the largest industrial concentrations. Beyond the 1920 administrative boundary the land, with the exception of old village cores, has been essentially taken into urban uses only during the post-1950 period, and even today much is still under agriculture.

The largest contiguous concentration of SDs with high foreign ratios lies astride the important axis of Fürtherstrasse, which leads northwestwards from the centre of Nuremberg to the neighbouring industrial city of Fürth. This area falls mainly within the inner-city zone of old, high-density apartment housing intermixed with industrial and commercial land uses. Here, streetblock cores are commonly infilled with buildings, often in the form of Hinterhäuser. Housing standards are generally extremely poor, while the residential environment is made even more unattractive on account of the major railway constructions, extensive traffic blight, minimal green space and large manufacturing plants such as AEG. Another extensive area of high foreign concentration lies in the Südstadt quarter of the inner city, immediately to the south of the Altstadt. Here, the rapid alternation of high and low foreign percentages from one district to another reflects the more diverse residential fabric of a part of the city where several streetblocks had been subject to devastation during the Second World War, and had subsequently experienced postwar reconstruction. Significantly too, the Südstadt quarter at its southern extremity adjoins a vast complex of manufacturing industry (for example, MAN and Siemens AG) and transportation at Gibitsenhof.

High foreign ratios also characterise the Lorenz portion of the Altstadt, where pockets of poor housing still remain. This is in marked contrast to the low ratios in the more northerly Seebalds quarter of the historic and commercial core. Here, the sparse distribution of foreigners is to be seen in the light of the large proportion of reconstructed dwellings and their predominantly middle-class clientele.[53]

In general, the northern and eastern sectors of Nuremberg's inner city consist of good quality nineteenth and early twentieth-century housing which has retained much of its original high social status. In these areas pockets of substantial foreign ratios are fragmentary, and mostly lie along the northern axis of Bucherstrasse or around small industrial nuclei in the Pegnitz valley to the northeast. The outer city, beyond the 1920 civic limits, contains only occasional high-value districts. These are coincident with outlying industrial concentrations, the two most notable examples being the SD which contains the Grundig factories and the one (marked by the letter H in Figure 4.5) which includes the industrial estate of the Europa-Canal port. Elsewhere in the 'outer city' foreign ratios are mostly well below the median, whether in former village cores, mushrooming private-housing estates, or the planned satellite town of Langwasser (L) with its high proportion of social housing.

Table 4.5: Nuremberg: Summary Data for Clusters of Foreign Population, 1979

Cluster	Total population	Foreign population Number	% of pop. in cluster	% of all Nuremberg foreigners
Fürtherstrasse	35,103	11,319	32.3	21.7
Südstadt	48,274	10,108	20.9	19.4
Altstadt	4,309	1,045	24.3	2.0
Pegnitz	6,150	1,510	24.6	2.9
Nordstadt	7,607	1,834	24.1	3.5
Total	101,443	25,816	25.5 (av.)	49.5 (av.)

Source: Calculated from tabulations in Stadt Nürnberg Amt für Stadtforschung und Statistik, *Statistisches Jahrbuch der Stadt Nürnberg*, 1980 edn (SNASS, Nuremberg, 1980), pp. 114-25.

Using the upper-quartile value of 15.5 per cent as the basis for differentiation, five main 'clusters' of concentrated foreign population can be identified in Nuremberg: these are indicated in Figure 4.6. Because of the strict contiguity constraint in this schema, there are certain departures in detail from the *Schwerpunkte* (concentration points) of foreign population as recognised in the 1974 *Nürnberg Plan.*[54]

Figure 4.6: Nuremberg: Foreign-population Changes, 1974-9

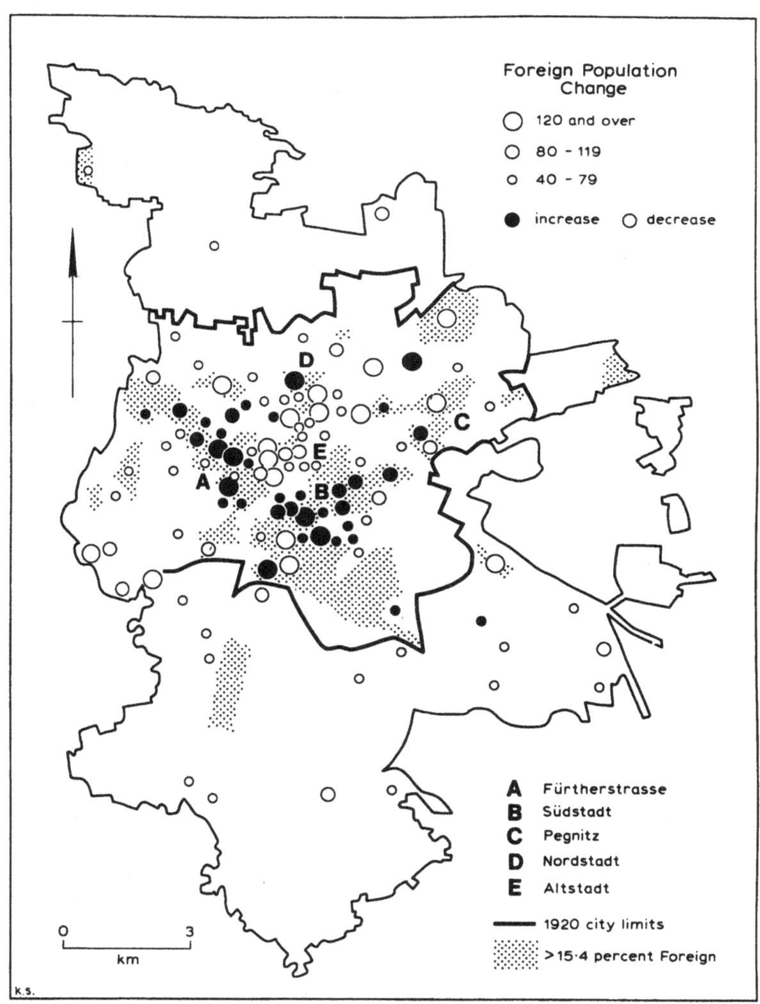

Note: The locations of the 'clusters' of foreign population are shown.

Source: Constructed from data presented in Stadt Nürnberg Amt für Stadtforschung und Statistik, *Nürnberg in Zahlen, 1972-75* (SNASS, Nuremberg, 1976), pp. 146-55; also, ibid., *Statistisches Jahrbuch der Stadt Nürnberg 1980* (SNASS, Nuremberg, 1980), pp. 114-25.

However, both classifications are in broad agreement on the major features, especially the cardinal role played by the Fürtherstrasse area, in which one-fifth of the city's foreign population live, and where about one-third of all residents are foreign (Table 4.5).

The predominantly inner-city orientation of the foreign population, coupled with spasmodic and small concentrations in the outer areas, has been observed in other West German cities. In Stuttgart the basic model is disturbed by the presence of old industrial suburbs such as Cannstadt and Untertürkheim, which form important subsidiary centres of attraction.[55] Furthermore, in the widely dispersed settlement system of the Stuttgart city-region, guestworkers are also commonly to be found in the interiors of erstwhile agricultural villages which have been engulfed by the very rapid postwar suburbanisation process.[56] Two other cities which have received detailed attention are Hanover and Cologne: the former has an above-average degree of concentration within the inner city,[57] whereas the latter additionally has a well-developed outer belt of high foreign ratios at between 4 and 6 km from the commercial core.[58] Lastly, after an analysis based on the mapping of population data for Bremen, Dusseldorf, Frankfurt and Stuttgart, O'Loughlin concluded that 'the spatial distribution of foreigners in German cities displays two consistencies – concentration near the city centre and near industrial areas'.[59] There is, therefore, a concensus concerning the salient characteristics of the spatial distribution of the foreign population in the 'average' West German city, and it is necessary now to examine the degree of segregation which this involves.

Residential Segregation and the Scale Factor

Figures 4.5 and 4.6 demonstrate a type of geographical unevenness that is the hallmark of a spatially segregated population. Nevertheless, at the 'ecological' level of analysis (using aggregate data either for SDs or for the smaller *Stadtteile*), the segregation of the minority population in West German cities appears much lower than in urban Britain. In Nuremberg, for example, there are only 7 SDs in which foreigners account for more than 40 per cent of the inhabitants. Yet as long ago as 1971 in Birmingham, England, 80 enumeration districts had a coloured *majority* and collectively contained one-quarter of this city's total coloured population.[60] Typically, foreigners represent above 20 per cent, but rarely more than 40 per cent, of residents in those parts of West German inner cities where they are concentrated. This relatively modest degree of spatial segregation is accompanied by a limited level of separation of national groups at the SD scale. An analysis by the *Nürnberg Plan* in the mid-1970s demonstrated that only in the Fürtherstrasse area was there a noticeable tendency for any of the immigrant nationalities (in this case the Greeks) to form an 'ethnic' enclave.[61] Table 4.6 substantiates the weakness of ethnic separation within the foreign clusters. Very few SDs had a majority of guestworkers from any one national group, although in 19 cases either Greeks or Turks comprised between one-third and one-half. But the districts in question accommodated a relatively minor proportion of the respective national population living within the city as a whole. Even in the Fürtherstrasse cluster, previously identified as an embryonic Greek neighbourhood, the number of Greek residents was less than 40 per cent of the city total. At a broader *Bezirk* (city ward) level in Stuttgart, Kolodny graphically describes the characteristic mixed pattern as a 'cohabitation' of the various nationalities.[62]

Table 4.6: Nuremberg: Ethnic Separation at *Stadtdistrikt* Level within the Five Foreign-population Clusters[a] in 1974

	Country of origin				
	Turkey	Greece	Italy	Yugoslavia	Spain
Numbers of SDs in which national group forms 50% or more of local guestworkers	2	3	1	2	nil
Guestworker population of above locations	94	706	18	120	nil
Numbers of SDs in which national group forms 33-49% of local guestworkers	12	7	2	3	nil
Guestworker population of above location	2,645	2,266	259	206	nil
Contribution of all five clusters to total Nuremberg foreigners	2,739	2,272	277	326	nil
% contribution of all five clusters to total Nuremberg foreigners	18.5	21.1	3.3	3.0	nil

Note: a. Excludes one SD for which information is not available.

Source: Derived from tabulations in Stadt Nürnberg Arbeitsgruppe Nürnberg-Plan, *Ausländer in Nürnberg*, edn E, vol. 11 (Stadt Nürnberg Beitrage zum Nürnberg-Plan, Nuremberg, 1975), Table 18, pp. 75-7.

Concluding the analysis at this juncture would, however, omit an important element in the pattern of nationality segregation in West

German cities, and one which is associated with the country's most distinctive type of urban housing – the rented apartment or *Mietwohnung*. Apartment buildings, typically of four, five or six floors, with each dwelling leading off from a common stairway and entrance hall, are fundamental social units of West German urban life.[63] Clark has stressed that 'the public stairway is very important to German apartment dwellers. Behaviour there is carefully regulated.'[64] Factors such as noise and cleanliness (especially in older, unmodernised apartment blocks which have shared sanitation) depend on cultural norms of acceptable behaviour, and it is not surprising that the reluctance of national groups to 'share' social space is most pronounced at this micro-scale. Of the Turkish population in Clark's Altstadt-Nord survey of inner Cologne, 72 per cent were living in fewer than 3 per cent of the district's residential buildings, a situation which he describes as 'the single-building ghetto'.[65] An examination of the ethnic composition of 149 apartment houses in Dusseldorf-Oberblick revealed that 'the range of the dissimilarity indexes, from 71.6 to 100.0, indicates almost total segregation among the groups. Foreigners in each apartment building are predominantly, or exclusively, of one group.'[66] At the streetblock scale, segregation is still more intense than appears at the SD level, because ethnic groups tend to congregate along particular street frontages. Thus, in the Dusseldorf–Oberblick study, indices of dissimilarity between the major guestworker nationalities and the German population were uniformly high, ranging from 61.9 to 70.4; moreover, it is significant that the indices between the guestworker nationalities themselves were almost as high, varying from 54.0 to a maximum of 66.3.[67]

As a result of its urban morphology, the geographical expression of ethnic segregation in the typical West German city is very distinctive. In the inner-city districts high levels of segregation exist at the 'micro-scale' of individual apartment buildings and streetblocks. Such intensity of segregation is not maintained at the 'ecological' scale of even the smallest statistical areas. Nevertheless, as later evidence reveals, the spatial separation of the foreign population has certainly been intensifying at the Stadtdistrikt level during the 1970s, a trend which has obvious implications for urban planning.

Residential Segregation: the Causal Processes

Guestworkers in West German cities are concentrated mainly in the inner residential areas, where housing is older and the environment is most deficient in those qualities of openness, greenery and quietude that are eagerly sought by contemporary urban dwellers. This inner-area concentration largely results from the interaction between, first, constraints operating in the housing market, and secondly, social factors stemming from the incomers' migrant status. This broad division is not mutually exclusive, especially as the responses of individual guestworkers tend to change over time. However, the fundamental dilemma facing the migrants, to strike a balance between their present requirements and envisaged future demands, remains. Cornelisen remarks that,

> Two solutions are available: scrimp on life and save every coin, no matter how small, or spend moderately, enjoy a better place to live, have some comfort, and save. Neither way is irrefutably right. Whichever is chosen, the principle of saving is sacrosanct.[68]

Within the context of his or her migration goal, each individual, therefore, makes a 'trade-off' between consumption and accumulation. This inevitably means that migrants evaluate their housing needs differently from the German population; a simple proposition which in turn renders it impossible for any single 'universal' explanation of the residential distribution of guestworkers to suffice.

The Housing Market. The company dormitory (*Betriebswohnheim*), which provides hostel-type accommodation for unaccompanied male workers, is a very important source of housing supply. German employers in fact are obliged to guarantee the availablility of accommodation of a minimum, basic standard.[69] In 1971 over 40 per cent of Turkish workers in Cologne resided in dormitory hostels, and a similar ratio was found in Stuttgart in 1975.[70] Since the major providers of these Betriebswohnheime tend to be the major manufacturing and construction firms, their spatial distribution reflects the general suburban bias of large industrial plants. Thus, the spasmodic high concentrations of foreign population in outer Nuremberg, as seen in Figure 4.5, relate to the important spatial symbiosis between key foci of modern industry and *in situ* dormitory provision. Smaller hostels are occasionally found in inner-city areas, whilst some public employers such as Deutsche Bundesbahn often operate centrally located hostels out of necessity.[71] Company hostels form reception centres for a large proportion of new immigrants, a role which is cemented by the highly regulated recruitment process. However, once they have established themselves in this initial foothold, most guestworkers have tended to seek accommodation that is either less institutionalised or is suitable for accommodating wife and children. In this way Franzen found that the *Wohnheime* of Hanover's major industrial companies, like Continental Gummiwerke, were common 'first addresses' for his Yugoslavian sample.[72]

The majority of guestworkers today, including all those with dependants in Germany, are to be found in private rented accommodation. This varies from 'lodging houses', whereby apartment buildings are filled to bursting point with (usually) male lodgers, to rented flats. In most cases the common denominators are that the buildings are old, the facilities inadequate and the standards poor.[73] The Nuremberg planners emphasise that guestworkers are willing to rent accommodation of a quality which is increasingly unacceptable to the rising residential aspirations of the German population, and they attribute this to the combination of low incomes and a reluctance to spend more than a limited proportion of this money on housing.[74] However, the German property owners are satisfied, because they can make a substantial return without the expensive outlays which would be necessary to improve their dwellings to a standard attractive enough for a German clientele. Indeed, the poor environmental conditions of many inner-city districts mean that the risks of the latter option are considerable.[75] In many respects, therefore, the presence of guestworkers becomes associated with a cyclic process of lack of investment and property deterioration.

Despite this situation, subsidised social housing appears to play a minor role in the housing of guestworkers. Remarkably, only 200 guestworkers families were resident in social housing in Nuremberg in 1972, mostly in older properties which had been refurbished by the city authorities.[76] In certain other West German cities, as Spengel notes in his study of social differentiation in Hanover,[77] there are some reports of guestworkers obtaining accommodation in new housing projects via the route of compulsory slum-clearance. However, the widespread cutbacks in these programmes during recent years mean that this remains a highly restricted avenue.

In summary, what German geographers term the *Bausubstanz* – the age, type and quality of the built-up residential environment – is obviously crucial to our understanding of the spatial distribution of guestworkers. In general, it can be seen that guestworkers usually occupy the poorest types of accommodation and most notably the unmodernised, pre-1914 apartment houses. Even so, to condemn this outright is to ignore the influence of social factors in the residential equation.

Social Factors. Because most guestworkers entered West Germany with the prime intention of accumulating capital, and for various reasons remain uncertain about their length of stay, they tend to look for housing which satisfies their basic needs as cheaply as possible. Apart from the company dormitories, this is mostly found in the inner cities, within which their residential search is often conditioned by a desire to maintain proximity with their compatriots. Spatial proximity presents the opportunity of replicating some of the ambience of their homeland, not only through patronage of local shops and cafés, but also through the use of the mother tongue. It also forms something of a defence against the low degree of social acceptance which they experience from the host population. Indeed, many immigrants are introduced to these areas by personal contacts. Although homogenous enclaves of any great extent have not developed, the heterogenous ethnic composition of the guestworkers adds an exotic vitality to certain sectors of the larger cities, which otherwise would undoubtedly be declining in population.

Population Succession in Nuremberg

During the 1960s and 1970s Nuremberg, in common with most large west European cities, lost large numbers of population through outwards migration to settlements beyond its administrative boundaries. Despite three boundary extensions in 1966, 1969 and 1972, the city's population in 1979 was little different from what it had been in 1961 within the equivalent area.[78] Consequently, the immigration of guestworkers and their families into Nuremberg can be viewed as a countercurrent to the more general process of change. Since the city achieved its present administrative extent in 1972, its population has declined from a peak of 514,981 inhabitants to 484,184 (1979 figure); but this decline has been due entirely to a fall in the German population (Table 4.7). The foreign population in 1979 was in fact 6,000 higher than in 1972, despite having in the interim experienced a sharp fall immediately following the recruitment ban of 1973. It is important, therefore, to appreciate that, far from declining in any consistent manner, Nuremberg's foreign population has stabilised at somewhere near its peak level; moreover, the proportion of foreigners in the total population reached an all-time high in 1979. It is clear, therefore, that, whatever the original circumstances and intentions surrounding the 1973 Anwerbestopp, guestworkers and their dependants have subsequently become even more significant in the social geography of this typical West German city.

Table 4.7: Nuremberg: Annual Population Statistics, 1972-9

Year	Total	German	Foreign	% foreign
1972	514,981	469,213	45,763	8.9
1973	514,666	462,647	52,010	10.1
1974	509,813	456,649	53,164	10.4
1975	499,060	451,183	47,877	9.6
1976	492,447	446,756	45,691	9.3
1977	488,755	442,180	46,575	9.5
1978	485,801	437,213	48,588	10.0
1979	484,184	432,052	52,132	10.8

Sources: Stadt Nürnberg Amt für Stadtforschung und Statistik, *Nürnberg in Zahlen 1972-5* (SNASS, Nuremberg, 1978), p. 9; and Stadt Nürnberg Amt für Stadtforschung und Statistik, *Statistisches Jahrbuch der Stadt Nürnberg*, 1978 and 1980 eds (SNASS, Nuremberg, 1978 and 1980), p. 12 (1978) and Table 1.6, pp. 40-1 (1980).

This is not simply because of the crude numerical situation. As Table 4.8 illustrates, the net migration balance has passed from a record gain in 1973, through a phase of post-Anwerbestopp losses, and then back to modest rises in 1978 and 1979. The enormous drop in the quantity of in-migration between 1973 and 1975 has been arrested because of the growing emphasis on family reunion among the guest-worker population; in the meantime, the amount of out-migration of foreigners has continued to diminish.

Table 4.8: Nuremberg: Components of Foreign-population Changes, 1973-9

Year	Out-migration	In-migration	Migration balance	Natural increase	Birth-rate per 1,000
1973	12,269	17,321	+5,052	n.a.	n.a.
1974	13,140	12,822	−318	n.a	n.a.
1975	13,684	7.062	−6,622	+1,355	28.3
1976	10,073	6,759	−3,314	+1,128	26.1
1977	7,886	7,800	−86	+970	22.5
1978	7,300	8,444	+1,144	+861	20.2
1979	7,151	9,865	+2,714	+830	18.3

Sources: Stadt Nürnberg Amt für Stadtforschung und Statistik, *Nürnberg in Zaheln, 1972-5* (SNASS, Nuremberg, 1976), Table 22, pp. 24-5 and Table 5, p. 14; also Stadt Nürnberg Amt für Stadtforschung und Statistik, *Statistisches Jahrbuch der Stadt Nürnberg*, 1980 edn (SNASS, Nuremberg, 1980), Table 2.1, p. 46.

The growing significance of foreigners in the social sphere also owes much to their high rate of natural demographic increase. The guestworkers and their wives represent a predominantly youthful group of people. Thus, although the foreign birth-rate is now declining rapidly, it still remains three to four times higher than that of the indigenous German population. Consequently, between one-quarter and one-third of live births in Nuremberg are to foreign mothers.[79] Indeed, by 1979 almost 30 per cent of Nuremberg's immigrant community was under 15 years of age, compared to only 16.5 per cent in 1970.[80] There was a corresponding degree of stabilisation of the adult immigrants, so that by the end of the 1970s a majority of all the national populations had been resident within the city for at least five years.[81]

Spatial Pattern of Foreign Population Changes, 1974-9

The stabilisation of the foreign population of Nuremberg during the 1970s, and its associated process of maturing, has been accompanied by some significant geographical change. Figure 4.6 illustrates that the majority of increases in numbers of foreigners have occurred within, or immediately adjacent to, the Fürtherstrasse and Südstadt clusters. This confirms that these inner-city quarters have acted as the major nodes of attraction, despite sustaining some localised outwards movement occasioned by housing demolitions close to the edge of the Altstadt. Elsewhere in inner-city Nuremberg the prevailing pattern is one of foreign population decline, although there are exceptions in a few SDs in the northern sector. Figure 4.6 also shows a pattern of fairly uniform decline in the outer city, both within the interwar and the postwar portions. In the latter it is worth noting that several of the largest absolute decreases are in SDs containing industrial dormitories. Essentially these spatial trends reflect underlying social processes. For example, the rapid fall in primary foreign-labour recruitment after 1973 has severely affected numbers in the outer-city dormitories; at the same time, however, the search for private rented accommodation, so essential for family reunion, has accentuated pressures in those parts of the inner city where the foreign population was already most heavily concentrated.

Population changes are summarised in Table 4.9 for these critical quarters of inner Nuremberg. Here, there is evidence of a substantial population turnover, with a particularly prominent fall in the numbers of German residents. The foreign population, on the other hand, has increased in all clusters except the rather untypical Altstadt and Pegnitz areas, although nowhere do these gains come close to offsetting the scale of the German exodus.

Table 4.9: Nuremberg: Population Change in the Five Foreign Clusters, 1974-9

Cluster	German population change		Foreign population change	
	Number	%	Number	%
Fürtherstrasse	−3,369	−12.4	+104	+0.9
Südstadt	−5,007	−11.6	+646	+6.8
Altstadt	−572	−14.9	−404	−27.9
Pegnitz	−2,289	−33.0	−114	−7.0
Nordstadt	−947	−14.1	+160	+9.6
Total	−12,184	−13.9	+392	+1.5

Sources: Derived from *Stadtdistrikte* tabulations in Stadt Nürnberg Amt für Stadtforschung und Statistik, *Nürnberg in Zahlen 1972-5* (SNASS, Nuremberg, 1976), pp. 146-55; and Stadt Nürnberg Amt für Stadtforschung und Statistik, *Statistisches Jahrbuch der Stadt Nürnberg*, 1980 edn (SNASS, Nuremberg, 1980), pp. 114-25.

This process of population succession is not new, neither is it unique to Nuremberg. Spengel has observed a similar succession in inner Hanover where he describes it as an 'inner-city concentration process'.[82] In Nuremberg it was found that the correlation between German decline and foreign increase in each SD during the years 1972-4 was $r = 0.63$, indicating that the departure of Germans was accelerating the trend by releasing further residential space.[83] In certain circumstances, however, the same trend can be reversed by the physical refurbishment of apartment blocks, which can lead to the displacement of the pre-rehabilitation guestworker tenants by affluent Germans.[84] But such programmes are expensive, locationally selective and unlikely to halt the general direction of demographic and social change, although they may have the effect of further directing the impact towards the least desirable districts. Certainly, spatial trends in Nuremberg lend support to those who identify the increasing concentration of the foreign population in the inner city as a formidable obstacle to their integration. O'Loughlin states that inner cities in West Germany 'are losing population, particularly young and middle-aged Germans. Inner-city neighbourhoods are increasingly composed of old, childless German families and young foreign workers.'[85] Undoubtedly, the social implications of the guestworker phenomenon cannot be concealed, and.by and large, will not willingly depart.

These inner-city concentrations of foreign populations certainly leaven the sober German townscape with their imprint, and the crowded kindergartens and children's play spaces bear witness to their demographic vitality. Nevertheless, real concern is felt at local levels regarding the common association of guestworkers with aspects of deprivation, under-investment and neighbourhood deterioration.[86] Whilst agreeing with O'Loughlin that ethnic neighbourhood concentrations in West German cities are in many important respects socially dissimilar from the black ghettos of North American cities, I feel that he does seem to understate the extent of social and physical deprivation experienced by the guestworkers and their families.[87] Local initiatives, such as the establishment of an *Ausländerbeirat* (Foreigners' Advisory Board) in Nuremberg, to assist in breaking down the social isolation of guestworkers and also the implementation of much needed environmental improvements in areas of high immigrant concentration, are ultimately only palliatives.[88] Permanent progress towards resolving the problems facing the guestworker population can only occur when federal policy firmly and unambiguously recasts their social and political status to accord with the realities of the situation.

Conclusion

The cruel paradox facing the guestworker population in West Germany is that the federal government, in the face of all the evidence, bases its policies on the belief that the incomers are temporary workers, each anxious to return 'home' at the first opportunity. Yet, as we have seen, the great majority of guestworkers, particularly those from non-EEC countries, constitute in Cornelisen's phrase, 'the survivors'. They have experienced many hardships and disturbances, and their lives have been profoundly changed; but the evidence suggests that most have ambitions for their children's future within West Germany. Despite many obstacles, petty discriminations and frustrations, a high proportion of guestworkers and their families will never return to their home countries unless they are forcibly repatriated – although most still retain a sentimental vision of an eventual homecoming. Federal policies, so strict and correct in the work sphere, remain ambivalent and contradictory when it comes to social matters. Moreover, threats in the form of political references to repatriation and deportation for petty offences add greatly to the foreigners' feelings of insecurity. The politically expedient myth that West Germany is *not* a country of foreign settlement, which figures at various levels of government,[89] has to be discarded while the uncertainties surrounding settlement rights must be removed before any meaningful assault can be made on the multifarious problems of housing, education and employment. The 1980 Conference of German Lawyers has boldy advocated the granting of full citizenship for those guestworkers who desire it, a policy directive which is fully in line with current European Community thinking.[90] The example of the United Kingdom, with its panoply of race-relations legislation, should serve as an ample warning that even this step would not, of itself, remove all manifestations of marginality suffered by guestworkers in West German society. However, it would dismantle the superstructure of the institutionalised partitioning of the resident population of an advanced industrial country into a superior and an inferior group. Furthermore, it would pave the way for ensuring a greater access to the resources which are urgently needed to equip the guestworkers more adequately for survival in a rich but highly competitive society.

Notes

1. A. Cornelisen, *Flight from Torregreca*, (Macmillan, London, 1980), p.2.
2. Statistisches Bundesamt, *Statistisches Jahrbuch für die Bundesrepublik Deutschland*, 1980 edn (Kohlhammer Verlag, Stuttgart and Mainz, 1980), p. 66. In 1979 only 3.7 per cent of the population of the United Kingdom were of New Commonwealth ethnic origin, according to Office of Population Censuses and Survey, *OPCS Monitor Reference PPI 81/1* (OPCS, London, 1981).
3. B.E. Schmitter, 'Immigrants and Associations: their role in the socio-political process of immigrant workers integration in West Germany and Switzerland', *International Migration Review*, vol. 14 (1980), pp. 179-92.
4. R.C. Rist, *Guestworkers in Germany – the Prospects for Pluralism* (Praeger, New York, 1978), p. 133.
5. On the movement of guestworkers to other West European countries see J. Salt and H. Clout, *Migration in Post-War Europe* (Oxford University Press, Oxford, 1976), chs 4 and 5.
6. H. Werner, 'Some current topics of labour migration in Europe', *International Migration*, vol. 15 (1977), p. 301. Statistics can be taken only as an approximation in view of wide national differences in recording, illegal entrants etc.
7. R. Lohrmann, 'European Migration – recent developments and future prospects', *International Migration*, vol. 14 (1977), p. 231.
8. E.G. Drettakis, 'Changes in the composition and sectoral distribution of migrant workers in West Germany 1960-72', *International Migration*, vol. 11 (1973), p. 192. He points out that the numbers of foreign workers in West Germany were a mere 167,000 in 1959; this was fewer than 1 per cent of the total employed population.
9. Lohrmann, 'European Migration', p. 230.

10. G.E. Volker, 'Labour Migration: Aid to the West German economy?' in R.E. Kane (ed.), *Manpower Mobility across Cultural Boundaries: Social, Economic and Legal Aspects* (E.J. Brill, Leiden, 1975), pp. 7-45, presents a full discussion of the advantages and disadvantages, but considers that evidence is not conclusive either way. S. Paine, *Exporting Workers – the Turkish case* (Cambridge University Press, Cambridge, 1974), pp. 9-22, contends that the weight of evidence suggests that West Germany had gained on balance, at least up until 1973.

11. H. Werner, 'Freedom of movement and migration of workers in the countries of the European Community' (English version), *Mitteilungen aus der Arbeitsmarkt- und Berufsforschung*, vol. 4 (1973), pp. 326-71. He defines 'countries of recruitment' as Greece, Yugoslavia, Portugal, Spain and Turkey.

12. Volker in Krane, *Manpower Mobility across Cultural Boundaries*, pp. 13-14.

13. Bundesanstalt für Arbeit, *Sozialversicherungspflichtig Beschäftige im Bundesgebiet am 30 Juni 1980* (BfA, Nuremberg, 1981), Table 3. This indicates that the lowest point was 1,833,464 in December 1977. For details of the operation of the labour-recruitment ban, see Rist, *Guestworkers in Germany*, pp. 76-8.

14. B. Kayser, 'European Migrations: the New Patterns', *International Migration Review*, vol. 11 (1977), p. 236.

15. Ibid., p. 235.

16. Cornelisen, *Flight from Torregreca*, pp. 180-1, describes German employers' mounting dissatisfaction with Italian labour, and their increasing preference for 'docile' Yugoslavs and Turks.

17. Kayser, 'European Migrations', p. 233.

18. See, for example, Paine, 'Exporting Workers', pp. 27-35.

19. Drettakis, 'Changes in the composition and sectoral distribution of migrant workers', pp. 199-202, demonstrates that workers from northwest European countries were less orientated towards mining, manufacturing and construction. Werner, 'Freedom of movement and migration of workers', p. 15, observes that 'the main impact of the introduction of free movement (of EEC nationals) seems to have been an increase in the number of frontier workers', who constituted approximately half the total from France, Belgium and the Netherlands.

20. Bundesanstalt für Arbeit, *Sonderdruck Sozialversicherungspflichtig beschäftige Arbeitnehmer ende June 1980* (BfA, Nuremberg, 1981), Table 1.47, pp. 360-1.

21. E. Kolodny, *Les étrangers à Stuttgart* (Centre Nationale de la Recherche Scientifique, Paris, 1977), Recherche co-operative sur la programme no. 397, p. 218.

22. This generalisation, of course, does not apply to all branches of service activity: in June almost one-quarter of workers in hotels and restaurants were foreign (data source as for Table 4.2).

23. W.R. Böhning, *The Migration of Workers in the United Kingdom and the European Community* (Oxford University Press, London, 1972), pp. 54-71.

24. Anomalies do occur, however, and the strong male dominance of Italians in Stuttgart did not reflect their very long presence in this city, but rather their habit of leaving wives and children in Italy: see Kolodny, *Les étrangers à Stuttgart*, pp. 182-90.

25. C. Wilpert, 'Children of foreign workers in the BRD', *International Migration Review*, vol. 11 (1977), pp. 473-85.

26. J. Leib and G. Mertins, 'Die Abwanderung Spanischen Arbeitnehmer in die Bundesrepublik Deutschland', *Erdkunde*, vol. 34 (1980), pp. 197-202. On the other hand, Kolodny maintains that no general model of migration origins can be postulated, citing as just one instance the feeble levels of migration from

desparately poor rural areas such as eastern Anatolia and southern Yugoslavia: see Kolodny, *Les étrangers à Stuttgart*, pp. 36-48.

27. S. Castles and G. Kosach, *Immigrant Workers and Class Structure in Western Europe* (Oxford University Press, London, 1973), ch. 10. The authors of this work examine the scale of acceptability, and stress that the pattern varies from country to country within west Europe.

28. E. Kreuzaler, 'The Federal Republic of Germany as Host Country to Foreign Guestworkers and their Dependants', *International Migration*, vol. 15 (1977), p. 142.

29. Thus, at a 1981 congress held near Frankfurt on 'Aliens Policy', the secretary-general of the German Red Cross came out in favour of a repatriation programme for some of the foreign resident population: *German Tribune*, issue no. 982, March 1981, p. 12.

30. Rist, *Guestworkers in Germany*, chs 5, 6 and 7.

31. Guestworkers' children also have to grow up in a bilingual fashion, and face formidable communications problems as a consequence. Research conducted by the University of Saarbrücken has identified their variety of spoken German as 'Gastarbeiterdeutsch', which is certainly not standard German: *German Tribune*, issue no. 980, March, 1981.

32. A survey of foreign youths conducted by the Bavarian Social Ministry in the three cities of Munich, Nuremberg and Augsburg in 1980, showed that 30 per cent were unemployed, and only 20 per cent held an apprenticeship: *Kölner-Stadt Anzeiger*, 22 July 1980.

33. R.C. Rist, 'Guestworkers in Germany: public policies as the legitimation of marginality', *Ethnic and Racial Studies*, vol. 2 (1979), pp. 401-15.

34. Kreuzaler, 'The Federal Republic as Host Country', pp. 141-2. According to Kreuzaler, the 'social aggression' would result from a reaction by the Germans against a feeling of 'imminent inundation' by foreigners.

35. Class intervals were selected after inspection of a scattergram of values: the shading scheme was chosen to create a visual 'break' at 9.5 per cent, which approximates the national average.

36. Deutsche Städtetag, 'Statistische Materielen zur Ausländerfrage', *Beiträge zur Statistike und Stadtforschung*, vol. 19 (1980), p. 41.

37. P.N. Jones, 'The distribution and diffusion of the coloured population in England and Wales, 1961-71', *Transactions of the Institute of British Geographers*, vol. 3, New Series (1978), pp. 515-32.

38. This is directly related to the continued preference shown by Volkswagen AG for Italian labour recruitment.

39. M.T. Wild, *West Germany: a Geography of its People* (William Dawson, Folkestone, 1979), p. 92.

40. Ibid., p. 70.

41. E. Giese, 'Arbeitslosigkeit und Gastarbeiterbeschäftigung in BRD', *Geographische Rundschau*, vol. 30 (1978), pp. 427-32. Referring to this correlation of $r = -0.61$, Giese considers that part of the unexplained residual can be attributed to the time-lag of guestworkers' contracts and the inclusion of many 'long-stay' guestworkers on the unemployed registers.

42. J. Franzen, *Gastarbeiter – Raumrelevante Verhaltensweisen: Migrationsmodell und empirische Studie am Beispiel jugoslawischer Arbeitskräfte in Hannover* (Geographische Gesellschaft zu Hannover, Hanover, 1978), p. 113.

43. Salt and Clout, *Migration in Post-War Europe*, pp. 110-12. Kolodny, *Les étrangers à Stuttgart*, p. 220, comments on the Greek predominance at Mercedes's factories, whilst J.R. Clark, 'Residential patterns and Social Integration of Turks in Cologne' in Krane, *Manpower Mobility across Cultural Boundaries*, p. 67, refers to Ford's reliance on Turkish workers.

44. Kolodny, *Les étrangers à Stuttgart*, p. 45.

45. E. Giese, 'Räumliche Diffusion ausländischer Arbeitnehmer in der Bundesrepublik Deutschland 1960-76', *Die Erde*, vol. 109 (1978), pp. 92-110.

46. Leib and Mertins, 'Die Abwanderung Spanischen Arbeitnehmer', p. 204.

47. Kolodny, *Les étrangers à Stuttgart*, p. 176. Kolodny does, however, stress the very high degree of residential mobility of foreigners within the Stuttgart agglomeration.

48. For the initiation of this policy, see Rist, *Guestworkers in Germany*, pp. 78-82. Rist sees the policy as yet another example of insensitive official thinking which perceives the foreign population as a social problem incurring social costs, which might be reduced by deconcentration measures regardless of implications for the foreign population. More than one-half of the foreign labour force was exempt from the regulations anyway, and the policy was discontinued at the end of 1976 (personal communication from the Federal Ministry of the Interior, Bonn, 1982).

49. The *Stadtdistrikte* are multi-purpose administrative districts, and not simply census units; this accounts for some being virtually devoid of population. At the time of writing, only the *aggregate* foreign population figures were available for 1979.

50. The percentage breakdown of the foreign population of Nuremberg in 1979 was as follows: Turks, 30.8; Yugoslavs, 17.3; Greeks, 15.3; Italians, 14.8; Spanish, 5.1; Portuguese, 0.8. These figures should be compared with Table 4.3. Nuremberg did, however, record a sizeable representation from Central European states such as Austria and Czechoslovakia. Stadt Nürnberg Amt für Stadtforschung und Statistik, *Statistisches Jahrbuch der Stadt Nürnberg* (SNASS, Nuremberg, 1980), pp. 42-3.

51. Ibid., map entitled 'Der Anteil der Ausländer an der Wohnbevölkerung in den Distrikten', following p. 125.

52. K. Baedeker, *Southern Germany*, (Karl Baedeker, Leipzig, 1910), pp. 150-1. The outer limits of *Stadtteile* 1 and 2 circumscribe the '*Innenstadt*' of official statistics for Nuremberg.

53. P. Rohrseitz, 'Die Anderung der Bevölkerungsstruktur ins Nürnberger Burgviertel zwischen 1970 und 1977', *Mitteilungen der fränkischen geographischen Gesellschaft*, vol. 27 (1980), pp. 102-14.

54. Stadt Nürnberg Arbeitsgruppe Nürnberg-Plan, *Ausländer in Nürnberg*, edn E, vol. 11 (Stadt Nürnberg Beitrage zum Nürnberg-Plan, Nuremberg, 1975), p. 39, outlines the *Schwerpunkte* of the foreign population. Two notable departures from the author's scheme are, first, that the southern protuberance from the Fürtherstrasse axis is separately identified as St Leonhard, and secondly, that there is a more widely spread St Johannis-Maxfeld zone which extends over the area of the Nordstadt cluster.

55. Kolodny, *Les étrangers à Stuttgart*, pp. 116-22.

56. F. Geiger, 'Zur Konzentration von Gastarbeitern in Alte Dorfkernen: Fallstudie aus dem Verdichtungrsaum Stuttgart', *Geographische Rundschau*, vol. 27 (1975), pp. 61-71.

57. U. Spengel, 'Zur sozialräumlichen Differenzierung Hannovers – eine Skisse auf statistischer Grundlage' in W. Erikson and A. Arnold, *Hannover und sein Umland* (Geographische Gesellschaft zur Hannover, Hanover, 1978), pp. 140-5.

58. Clark in Krane, *Manpower Mobility across Cultural Boundaries*, p. 63.

59. J. O'Loughlin, 'Distribution and migration of foreigners in German cities', *Geographical Review*, vol. 70 (1980), p. 259.

60. P.N. Jones, 'Ethnic areas in British cities' in D.T. Herbert and D.M. Smith (eds), *Social Problems and the Cities: Geographical Perspectives* (Oxford University Press, Oxford, 1979), p. 170. It should be remembered, however, that enumeration

districts are a smaller areal unit than the *Stadtdistrikte*. Nevertheless, it is also remarkable that the average coloured population in Birmingham in 1971 was 9.9 per cent – a proportion which was considerably *lower* than the foreign average in Nuremberg.

61. Stadt Nürnberg Arbeitsgruppe Nürnberg-Plan, *Ausländer in Nürnberg*, pp. 43-51.

62. Kolodny, *Les étrangers à Stuttgart*, p. 162.

63. For a general analysis of the diffusion and urban-geographical importance of the apartment house, see E. Lichtenberger, 'The nature of European urbanism', *Geoforum*, vol. 4 (1970), pp. 45-62.

64. Clark in Krane, *Manpower Mobility across Cultural Boundaries*, p. 68.

65. Ibid., p. 69. Note that Clark is referring here to the physical structure: each residential building would contain multiple units of accommodation.

66. O'Loughlin, 'Distribution and migration of foreigners in German cities', p. 268. The segregation index and its companion dissimilarity index, are calculated on the basis of a postulated *pro rata* allocation of two populations within a set of subareas: departures from the overall breakdown indicate a rising level of segregation (of one population from the total) or increasing dissimilarity (of two subpopulations) on a scale from zero (absence of segregation–integration) to 100 (total segregation or dissimilarity). For a thorough appraisal of its calculation and its sensitivity to scale effects, see R.I. Woods, 'Aspects of the Scale Problem in the Calculation of Segregation Indices', *Tijdschrift voor Economische en Sociale Geographie*, vol. 67 (1976), pp. 169-74.

67. O'Loughlin, 'Distribution and migration of foreigners in German cities', p. 267.

68. Cornelisen, *Flight from Torregreca*, p. 229.

69. Castles and Kosack, *Immigrant Workers and Class Structure*, pp. 259-62, demonstrate just how *basic* this minimum-standard accommodation can be, claiming that in some cases hutments built for foreign labourers during the Second World War were still in use.

70. Clark in Krane, '*Manpower Mobility across Cultural Boundaries*', p. 65: also, Kolodny, *Les étrangers à Stuttgart*, pp. 125-30.

71. Franzen, *Gastarbeiter – Räumrelevante Verhaltensweisen*, p. 129.

72. Ibid., p. 114.

73. Ibid., pp. 130-1. Franzen shows that in the Linden district of Hanover, which he describes as 'ein Getto der Gastarbeiter', between 58 per cent and 64 per cent of residential buildings were pre-1918, and between one-third and 45 per cent had no exclusive WC.

74. Stadt Nürnberg Arbeitsgruppe Nürnberg-Plan, *Ausländer in Nürnberg*, p. 49.

75. Geiger, 'Zur Konzentration von Gastarbeitern in Altern Dorfkernen', p. 63.

76 Stadt Nürnberg Arbeitsgruppe Nürnberg-Plan, *Ausländer in Nürnberg*, p. 46.

77. Spengel, 'Zur sozialräumlichen Differenzierung Hannovers', p. 144.

78. Stadt Nürnberg Amt für Stadtforschung und Statistik, *Statistisches Jahrbuch der Stadt Nürnberg*, 1980 edn, pp. 36-9.

79. Ibid., Table 2.3, p. 48. In 1979 there were 943 live births in the city.

80. Ibid., Table 1.6, pp. 40-1.

81. Ibid., Table 1.7, p. 42.

82. Spengel, 'Zur sozialräumlichen Differenzierung Hannovers', p. 141.

83. Stadt Nürnberg Arbeitsgruppe Nürnberg-Plan, *Ausländer in Nürnberg*, p. 43.

84. Spengel, 'Zur sozialräumlichen Differenzierung Hannovers', p. 145. In

Bezirk no. 103 the renovation of blocks of houses without regulation of subsequent rents resulted in a drop in the foreign population before the '*Sanierungsprozess*' to just 24 after completion.

85. O'Loughlin, 'Distribution and migration of foreigners', p. 257.

86. Stadt Nürnberg Arbeitsgruppe Nürnberg-Plan, *Ausländer in Nürnberg*, p. 37, describes the major concentrations of guestworkers as '*städtebauliche Problemzone mit verfallender Bausubstanz*'.

87. O'Loughlin, 'Distribution and migration of foreigners', pp. 264-5, states, 'Although some individual immigrant concentrations coincide with redevelopment areas and are characterised by poor quality of life, most are not.'

88. Stadt Nürnberg Arbeitsgruppe Nürnberg-Plan, *Ausländer in Nürnberg*, pp. 64-7.

89. Kreuzaler, 'The Federal Republic of Germany as Host Country', p. 139, repeats this viewpoint. At the time of writing Dr Kreuzaler is First Secretary at the Federal Ministry of Labour and Social Affairs.

90. *German Tribune*, issue no. 959, October 1980, p. 4.

A Note on Terminology

The focus of attention is the great bulk of foreign workers who originate in either the 'countries of recruitment', such as Yugoslavia and Turkey, or in Italy. For this whole group of workers the term 'guestworkers' (for *Gastarbeiter*) is in general usage. Although there are important differences in legal status between Italian workers (as EEC citizens) and all others, Italian migrants, nevertheless, exhibit the essential social and economic characteristics of other guestworkers. Within the text I have used the term 'guestworker' whenever possible, and where the constraints imposed by data sources permit. In essence this means either when the nature of the discussion is general, or when the data specifically refer only to national groups belonging strictly to the guestworker category. Where the information refers to all foreign workers I have attempted to be consistent and use terms such as 'foreign workers' or 'foreign labour', even though the great bulk of these are, strictly speaking, guestworkers. In fact, whilst evidence exists which points to clear social and occupational differences between the 'guestworker' and 'other' subsets of the total foreign workforce, the latter are such a small and generally very localised part of the whole that many authorities have used 'foreign', 'immigrant' and 'guestworkers' as synonymous descriptions.

5 TRENDS IN CONSUMER BEHAVIOUR AND RETAILING

Gareth Shaw

Since the 1950s changes in methods of retailing in West Germany have been on such a scale that not only have they transformed the distributive sector of the economy, but have also exerted far-reaching influences on its spatial distribution. The new methodology has stemmed from a virtual revolution in retail technology and organisation. This was fostered by the interaction of several general economic and social trends, each helping to create new conditions and new directions of consumer demand. However, the relationships between consumer demand, retail technology and business response have never been completely freed from conservative influences. Paramount amongst these is the interventionist effect of public policy.

Intervention in the Retailing Field

West Germany, like most other west European countries, does not have a clearly defined public policy and attitude towards retailing, but rather a complex set of mechanisms that to different degrees intervene in the distributive sector. This lack of a coherent approach can be accounted for by the fact that past efforts have mainly gone into exercising control over the primary and secondary sectors of the economy, with much less regard being given to major tertiary activities. However, with the changing-balance of employment in what is now a post-industrial society, the tertiary sector has become pre-eminently important. The recognition of this new status means that more thought is now being directed to the formulation of effective retail policies. It is appropriate to view this development by paying attention to the temporal perspective, and from the outset to the importance in the immediate postwar years of the creation of the West German version of the market economy.

The replacement of the Third Reich's centrally planned economy by the postwar ideals of a 'socially responsible market economy' (*Sozial-markt-Wirtschaft*), with its dualistic emphasis on competition and social justice, heralded a new political climate for retailing and the prospect of a harmonious balance between the aspirations of shop owners and the interests of West German consumers.[1] The early years of the Federal Republic saw the declaration of two fundamental and, in theory, lasting objectives of retailing policy.[2] The first was the development of a consumer-orientated retail system based on the shopping preferences of the general public, and in particular the guarantee of wide ranges of choice in the three critical spheres of retail location, methods of selling and types of outlets. The second objective of policy was the protection of the vast numbers of small, family businesses, especially those which were most likely to suffer from the full force of unregulated competition. To a large extent this particular directive came in response to the once very high standing of small-scale independent firms within the structure of German retailing. At the time of the 1950 federal census, in several major West German cities, these businesses provided work opportunities for more than 10 per cent of the active population, while for the country as a whole their contribution to employment amounted to approximately one out of every twenty workplaces.[3] At the time due recognition was given to this important job-providing function. In addition, however, these small-scale retail enterprises were also highly valued for their facility to stimulate entrepreneural activity, particularly amongst the incoming refugee population.

The two principles of maintaining consumer choice and protecting small, specialised retail concerns soon showed themselves to be in open conflict with a general direction of organisational change which favoured larger and more capitalised selling outlets. Moreover, most attempts to preserve the traditional retail structure, especially those measures which were designed to restrict the expansion and proliferation of department stores, floundered on account of legal difficulties, and were 'kept alive' only by informal compromises between the firms involved.

Some early progress, however, was made through department stores, in consultation with local authorities, initiating their own voluntary limitations on business expansion. For example, some firms agreed not to open stores in certain 'protected' towns; others, for just a few years during the 1950s, restricted new investment to cities with more than 50,000 inhabitants.[4] In theory these voluntary concessions were intended to allow small-scale retailers time to reorganise and improve their efficiency; in practice, however, they had little apparent value and did little to delay the growing momentum of change.

Since the late 1950s direct government intervention, both at federal and *Land* levels of jurisdiction, has placed increasing controls on retailing activity. To date, most of the policies which have been initiated are still of a restrictive nature, although in recent years there have been some moderately successful attempts to induce a more positive approach towards encouraging the survival of small retail businesses. The federal and Land governments now provide a range of financial help for independent shop owners. This takes the form of grants and loans at favourable rates of interest, which are available both for new firms and for assistance in the modernisation of traditional outlets. In addition, various programmes of technical instruction have been provided for small retailers, while, depending largely on the size of trading turnover, these firms can also benefit from a sliding scale of state subsidies on advisory services.[5]

As far as the assistance from Land governments is concerned, there is considerable regional diversity. The federal states of Baden-Württemberg, North Rhine-Westphalia and Rhineland-Palatinate provide special loans for retailers locating in new housing estates, urban improvement areas and depressed areas.[6] Land assistance for small businesses to reorganise and adapt to new techniques is also limited in geographical availability, in this case to Baden-Württemberg, Lower Saxony, Hamburg and Bremen. However, even within these favoured parts of the country traditional retailing has been unable to stave off the effects of increasing competition. Not even the growing intervention of local authorities and their increasing restrictions on the granting of planning permission for new, large-scale retail outlets have been able to reduce the pace of change. Their attempts to stem the tide have concentrated mainly on combating the impact of new stores on traditional shopping structures. In endeavouring to accomplish this difficult feat, city planners are now able to call upon a complex system of zoning and building-usage regulations which in an ideal world can be used to control all new retail developments within the locales of individual municipalities. However, all too often the operation of planning restrictions is severely weakened by matters of political and economic expediency.

Changes in Demand and Consumer Behaviour

The prosperity of contemporary West German society is evidenced by the huge rise in disposable incomes, especially during the 1960s and the first half of the 1970s, when rates of increase averaged as much as 8 per cent each year. But even more significant in the sphere of retail consumption has been the social diffusion of purchasing power amongst a rapidly growing number of middle-class households.[7]

Demographic trends too have played an important role in the advance of postwar consumerism. During the period from 1946 to 1970 the population of West Germany (including West Berlin and the Saarland) rose by a massive 14.4 millions, which in effect represented a 31 per cent increase in the consumer market. In 1974, however, the population peaked at 62.1 millions, and since then has declined as a result of the birth-rate falling below the death-rate. By 1990 it is expected that West Germany's population figure will shrink to less than 59 millions, and in so doing will adjust itself to the 1965 level.[8] Yet the effect of this trend, and also that of demographic ageing on consumer demand will undoubtedly be offset by a continued (if slower) rise in total spending power through further additions to average household incomes.

A standard method of measuring regional variations in consumer demand is to combine the two general indicators of gross domestic product and population density. This is undertaken in Figure 5.1, in which most areas of above-average market potential can be seen occupying the elongated stretch of territory that runs from Bremen in the north, through the industrial regions of North Rhine-Westphalia, and thence southeastwards along the Rhine axis and into southern Bavaria. This part of West Germany, with the addition of the shaded outlier of Hamburg, includes the majority of the country's major manufacturing regions and nearly all of its major cities and urban agglomerations.

At a more local level, the distribution of consumer demand is undergoing significant geographical changes, associated with large outwards movements of population from urban centres to their surrounding urban-rural fringes. In some cases these centrifugal shifts are exerting a forceful impact on the hinterlands of cities at distances as far away as 30, 40 or even 50 km from urban administrative limits.[9] Accordingly, while there is some continued concentration of retail investment within the shaded regions of Figure 5.1, substantial intra-regional changes are also taking place. The most ostensible of these has been the recent proliferation of 'out-of-town' shopping complexes, some of which now include free-standing hypermarkets and superstores. The underlying change, however, has been a general decentralisation of the retail function, initially as a relative trend, but during the last few years also involving literal relocations of businesses.

The spatial changes in consumer demand have been accompanied by important behavioural responses. In particular, there has been a

Figure 5.1: West Germany: Regional Variations in Consumer Demand

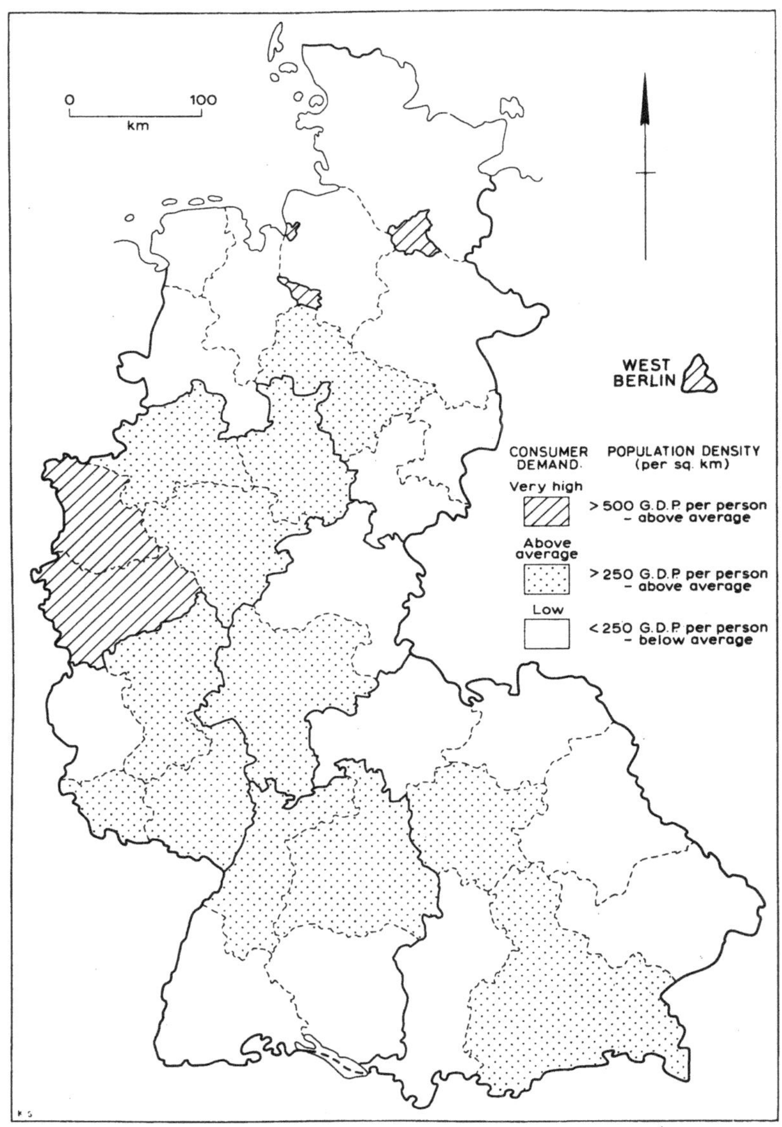

Source: Adapted from data in Bundesforschungsanstalt für Landeskunde und Raumordnung, *Untersuchung Kundenverkehr 1976* (BfLR, Bonn, 1977).

Table 5.1: West Germany: Modes of Consumer Travel and Percentage Variations According to Size of Urban Centres, 1971-6

	Saturday		Thursday	
	1971	1976	1971	1976
Urban centres with populations less than 50,000				
Foot or cycle	35.1	27.8	39.9	33.7
Public transport	12.3	10.7	23.3	21.3
Private motor car	51.8	60.8	36.1	44.7
Urban centres with populations between 50,000 and 100,000				
Foot or cycle	31.3	25.3	34.0	30.2
Public transport	23.0	15.6	34.1	27.3
Private motor car	45.1	58.9	31.1	42.0
Urban centres with populations between 100,000 and 250,000				
Foot or cycle	25.8	21.3	28.9	25.1
Public transport	27.3	23.1	40.1	35.9
Private motor car	46.1	55.3	30.3	38.6
Urban centres with populations between 250,000 and 500,000				
Foot or cycle	21.9	20.8	27.9	26.3
Public transport	25.2	23.6	36.6	36.2
Private motor car	52.2	55.1	34.5	37.8
Urban centres with populations over 500,000				
Foot or cycle	21.3	18.4	23.9	20.7
Public transport	32.4	29.1	46.4	42.2
Private motor car	44.9	50.1	27.9	33.9

Source: Bundesforschungsanstalt für Landeskunde und Raumordnung, *Untersuchung Kundenverkehr 1976* (BfLR, Bonn, 1977).

substantial increase in the proportion of consumer trips which are made by private motor car. By 1976 these were accounting for as many as 56 per cent of all Saturday shopping visits, compared with 48 per cent only five years previously.[10] The same consumer survey, however, showed considerable variations in degree of car usage according to size of urban centre (Table 5.1). As a general rule, the smaller the town or city the greater is the reliance on motorisation. There are three main reasons why this is the case: first, more often than not the smaller urban centres serve a scattering or rural and semi-rural settlements in which consumers are heavily dependent on car travel; secondly, many of these centres, particularly those which are situated within easy car journeys from major cities, have become prime locations for vehicle-orientated, retail investments; thirdly, in contrast to the metropolitan centres, they mostly command a limited range and frequency of public-transport services.

Changes in Retail Organisation

One of the most significant trends affecting the retail system in West Germany has been the increasing degree of organisational concentration. This has mainly come about through the expansion of 'multiple' firms and the widespread development of voluntary retail associations. These changes are primarily responsible for the sharp decline in numbers of traditional shops, in which losses amounted to 90,000 outlets from 1961 to 1971, and a further 50,000 during the next seven years. The decline is very much associated with closures of small businesses which have been unable to keep abreast with modernisation and increasing competition.[11] Thus, during the period from 1962 to 1978 the proportion of retailers with yearly turnovers below DM 50,000 (at a constant 1978 money value) fell from 28.3 per cent to 12.8 per cent. Table 5.2 shows that during the same period the proportion of medium-size firms, whose turnovers lay within the DM 50,000-250,000 range, declined less sharply from a dominating 56.0 per cent to 40.8 per cent, while the figure for the largest category of retail enterprises (businesses with annual turnovers greater than DM 250,000) rose steeply from a modest 15.7 per cent to as much as 46.4 per cent.

Table 5.2: West Germany: Changes in the Proportion of Retailers in Three Categories of Turnover-size, 1962-78

Value of annual turnover[a]	Percentage of retailers		
	1962	1974	1978
Under DM 50,000	28.3	14.0	12.8
DM 50,000-250,000	56.0	45.6	40.8
Over DM 250,000	15.7	40.4	46.4

Note: a. These are constant 1978 money values.

Source: Statistisches Bundesamt, ***Statistisches Jahrbuch für die Bundesrepublik Deutschland***, 1964, 1976 and 1978 edns (Kohlhammer Verlag, Stuttgart and Mainz, 1964, 1976 and 1978).

The rapid upsurge in the importance of large-scale retail concerns has affected all major branches of distributive selling. They are mostly represented as one of three types of modern trading organisation – multiples, retail buying groups and voluntary wholesale chains. Since the early 1970s the multiples have experienced only marginal growth, and their share of total turnover has remained fairly static. Traditionally, West Germany's multiples operated as regionally organised businesses, but, with a special emphasis on food selling, the trend today is towards much wider scales of organisation, including six firms which now operate a nationwide trading network. These concerns, especially the Tenglemann-Kaiser and Deutscher Supermärkte companies, have played a leading role in the implementation of retailing innovations, particularly in the field of self-service methods.

Voluntary wholesale chains were first introduced into West Germany from the Netherlands during the early 1950s, and quickly made inroads into a wide range of retail trades. By 1962 they had captured about one-sixth of the market, with the greatest successes being achieved in food selling. At present the wholesale sector in West Germany is dominated by two major enterprises; CMG (Centrale Marketing) with around 14,000 members and Deutsche Spar-Zentrale with approximately 10,000. Both organisations have been important innovators in the development of superstores and hypermarkets, with Deutsche Spar-Zentrale already having direct selling interests in 50 large-scale outlets by the beginning of the 1970s. This thrust towards store and hypermarket selling has cast voluntary wholesale chains in a new light, since they are no longer seen as a saviour and protector of small independents. However, rather surprisingly and despite heavy rationalisation, voluntary wholesalers have had a declining share of West German retail turnover since 1970, and have suffered particularly badly from the general fall-off in trade during recent economic recessions.

Under present-day trading conditions the most successful mode of large-scale retail organisation is proving to be that of retail buying groups, in which individual enterprises combine together to effect scale-economies. This idea originated in Germany during the later stages of the industrial revolution, and has survived the tests of two world wars and the intervening political upheavals and economic depressions. In postwar West Germany the retail buying groups have involved themselves in all sectors of retailing, and, unlike the multiples and wholesale chains, have continued to increase their share of turnover right up to the present day. In food selling alone the number of retailers who are members of buying groups exceeds 100,000, including as many as 33,000 who are linked to the two largest organisations of Edeka and REWE. The Edeka group operates as a collection of affiliated regional associations which run their own food-processing factories and warehousing facilities, in addition to controlling several large stores. These integrated functions are exemplified in the case of Edeka's *Minden-Osnabrück Verein*. This regional association has 644 members, and controls 30 bakeries, four large cash-and-carry stores, a meat-products factory and a centralised deep-freeze plant.[12]

Innovative Change in Retailing

Mainly through the introduction of new techniques of selling, developments in the organisational operation of retail firms have had a decisive influence on the structure and form of shopping in West Germany. Indeed, three major, overlapping phases of retail innovation can be identified: first, the introduction of self-service selling within small shops; secondly, the proliferation of fully fledged supermarkets; thirdly, the creation of superstores and hypermarkets. These developments are closely interrelated, although each has its own locational requirements, and has occasioned special sets of problems for surviving traditional retail businesses.

The idea of self-service retailing was first firmly established in West Germany in the mid 1950s, and was quickly accepted in the food trades. By 1960 one out of every ten small-scale, food shops had converted to this method of selling; a decade later, the proportion had risen to around 50 per cent.[13] The fastest pace of proliferation of self-service shops came during the 1960s, when their numbers increased at an average yearly rate of 24 per cent (Figure 5.2). However, since 1971 the trend has been reversed, mainly in response to a redirection of investment to the construction of supermarkets, superstores and hypermarkets.

The second phase of innovation, the proliferation of supermarkets, necessitated substantial increases in the size of new, and also converted, retail outlets. In West Germany the minimum-size definition of a supermarket is 400 m^2 of selling floorspace: this is more than six times the average dimension of 'traditional' self-service shops. By 1965 there were about 1,300 supermarkets in the country, but, as shown in Figure 5.2, the fastest increase in numbers did not come until the years 1970-6, when the total suddenly rose from just over 2,000 to nearly 5,000.

The third phase, the creation of superstores and hypermarkets, belongs almost wholly to the period since 1968. On account of their efficient economies of operation these large-scale retail concerns are well advantaged by their ability to overcome indivisibilities in labour, management and capital equipment. However, there is no consensus as to what is the most rational scale of operation, and because of this both superstores and hypermarkets vary greatly in size and conception. This diversity leads us on to the problem of the absence of any commonly accepted definitions, either from the consumer or from the planning points of view. In West Germany most large stores with selling floor-spaces exceeding 1,000 m^2 are known as *Verbrauchermärkte*, a description which translates literally as 'consumer markets', and as such does nothing to remove the confusion.

Figure 5.2: West Germany: Phases of Retail Innovation, 1960-80

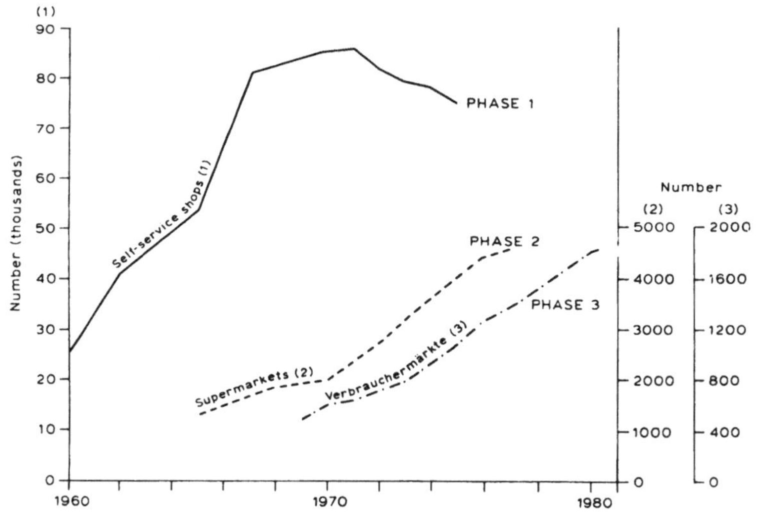

Note: A different numerical scale is employed for each graph in order to facilitate comparison.
Source: Drawn from data in Bundesforschungsanstalt für Landeskunde und Raumordnung, *Untersuchung Kundenverkehr 1976* (BfLR, Bonn, 1977).

The German terminology is unfortunately further complicated, since Verbrauchermärkte also include the larger varieties of discount stores and self-service warehouses. Apart from their undefined 'giant' scale of operation and their wide range of consumer products, the only common features are their extensions of self-service to non-food items, their relatively low investments in the basic building structure and, lastly, the out-of-town and low-cost locations.

The development of Verbrauchermärkte has been very rapid since their introduction to West Germany in the late 1960s. In 1970 they numbered 590, of which almost one-third exceeded 6,000 m^2 of floorspace. By 1976 there were more than 1,200, altogether accounting for 10.6 per cent of West German retail turnover.[14] In spite of a generally deteriorating economic climate since the mid 1970s, their increase has continued during recent years and their number is now approaching the 2,000 mark. The Verbrauchermärkte are financed not only by major retailing companies, but also in a number of cases from capital provided by industry. The latter direction of investment flow has particular significance within the Ruhr industrial region, where high consumer demand, availability of derelict land and special inducements for the expansion of tertiary activities have combined to provide a specially favourable background for large-scale retailing.

Regional variations in the distribution of Verbrauchermärkte are reflective of the influences of demand and differences in the application of planning controls. The highest frequency of superstores and hypermarkets is to be found in Land North Rhine-Westphalia, which in 1975 accounted for nearly one-quarter of the West German total. However, it is worth noting that their proliferation within this part of the country, especially in the Ruhr and around the Rhineland cities, came several years earlier than elsewhere. This explains why the size of most Verbrauchermärkte in North Rhine-Westphalia is somewhat smaller than average, with 73 per cent of the premises having floorspaces of less than 5,000 m^2, and only 9 per cent having areas of more than 10,000 m^2.[15] By way of contrast, regions where more recent developments dominate have a sparcer distribution but, at the same time, a greater proportion of 'giant' outlets. For example, in Schleswig-Holstein, a federal state which had very few superstores and hypermarkets until the early 1970s, the proportion of premises with floorspaces greater than 10,000 m^2 is nearly twice as high.[16]

The impact of these three phases of innovation on the traditional structure of retailing has been cumulative, with small, family enterprises (especially those concerned with food selling) having to withstand most of the pressure. The introduction of self-service initiated a sequence of changes with which many independent retailers were unable to cope. Those who were able to adapt to the new competition all too often found that they lacked the necessary capital resources to enlarge their turnovers and increase their profitability. The advent of supermarkets, followed in turn by the introduction of Verbrauchermärkte, greatly aggravated the problems accruing from changing consumer behaviour.

Not surprisingly, therefore, the 1960s and the 1970s were decades of widespread failures of small retail businesses.

Planning Control and Verbrauchermarkt Developments

Until very recently the main debate on the impact of Verbrauchermarkt developments focused on their potentially damaging effects on existing retailers. However, public concern today is widening to cover such associated issues as traffic congestion, environmental problems and broader questions relating to the need to ensure adequate provision of retail facilities to all sectors of society. For example, many people in West Germany are now arguing that the small shop plays a vital role in the servicing of scattered communities in remote rural areas. Even more pertinent to the growing criticism of 'consumer markets', however, is their inaccessibility and lack of appeal to immobile customers, especially among the elderly population.[17]

Despite the increasing concern over the escalation of Verbrauchermarkt retailing, local planning authorities have found it extremely difficult to exert proper controls. The reason for this lies in the ineffective nature of planning mechanisms. During the 1950s the federal government took very little part in a framework of town-and-country planning jurisdiction that operated under a variety of inadequate local laws and agreements, including some which predated the Second World War. The situation was partly rectified in the early 1960s with the appearance of the first of a series of Federal Building Acts. This was primarily designed to consolidate the nature of the existing decision-making system and to unify the planning of urban areas.[18] A two-tier method of development control was introduced, with local *Gemeinden* having to work in conjunction with their respective Land ministries. The First Federal Building Act also made it obligatory for all urban planning departments to draw up two types of empirical plans; a general land-use plan (*Flächennutzungsplan*) and a building plan, or *Bebauungsplan*.[19] The former designates the zonation of land uses at the local level, and provides Gemeinde authorities with the necessary guidelines for a phased land-use policy. It is the Bebauungsplan, however, that contains the various legal mechanisms of planning control. In theory this control was extended into the fields of densities, scales, location and visual appearance of all new building projects; but, as far as retail developments are concerned, experience shows that, even today, it is still quite possible to find loopholes in the legislation.

Until the redrawing of Gemeinde boundaries after 1969, there were in West Germany more than 24,000 communities (Gemeinden) with individual responsibilities for local planning. Very often the lack of direct co-operation between one authority and another in the preparation of plans and formulation of objectives allowed retail developers a considerable latitude of locational and siting choice. Retail investments which, for good reasons, were 'zoned-out' by one Gemeinde, could well be accepted by a neighbouring authority. This state of affairs is typified within and around the Nuremberg conurbation. Here, the Nuremberg planning department successfully controlled further growth of Verbrauchermärkte after 1974 by withholding planning certificates for any new superstores and hypermarkets within the administrative limits of the city.[20] However, as was the experience in many other urbanised regions of West Germany, unfortunately no such control was exercised within the adjoining local authority areas. Investors, therefore, simply turned their interest to the most accessible part of Nuremberg's urban-rural fringe and the neighbouring cities of Fürth and Erlangen. As a result, the mid-1970s saw a sudden upsurge in Verbrauchermärkte within these locations, and near enough to Nuremberg's boundary to have a deprecatory effect on this city's established retail structure.

Retail Patterns within Urban Areas

Within most large West German cities it is possible to identify a three-tier hierarchy of retail centres based on the amount of shopping floor-space, the types of retail outlets and an approximation of the number of people living within the catchment area. At the top of the hierarchy is the 'regional centre' which, commonly represented as the central business districts of cities, usually account for more than 75 per cent of a city's turnover in durable sales, compared with only about 30 per cent of the trading in convenience products. The intermediate level of centres is represented by what are rather ambiguously described as 'community centres', which have a potential customer catchment of between 15,000 and 30,000 persons. Lastly come the 'neighbourhood centres', or *Nachbarschafts-Zentren*, usually having less than 20 retail businesses which serve a very local population of less than 6,000 consumers. Many of the 'community centres' and 'neighbourhood centres' have appeared as features in the urban scene since the end of the Second World War, and more specifically since the late 1950s. These were usually purpose-built, in some cases modelled on North American lines. Moreover, as far as the postwar versions are concerned, the large majority are to be found in the outermost ring of residential suburbs, in accordance with current trends in intra-urban population distribution. Numerous too, however, are the suburban retail centres which have evolved from prewar concentrations of shops. Most of these still preserve their original linear arrangement along major arterial streets radiating out from the core of the city.[21] They also retain some of the vestiges of late nineteenth and early twentieth-century trading structures, as seen in the 'inertia' of small, family businesses and a continued dominance of food selling.

The spatial pattern of urban retailing and the importance played by the different components of the retail hierarchy can be illustrated by an examination of the Rhineland city of Bonn (Figure 5.3). Within the administrative limits (post-1969 boundary), there are two 'regional' shopping centres; central Bonn itself and the newly built *Einkaufszentrum* of Bad Godesberg. In 1975 these accounted for 52 per cent of the city's total retail turnover and 78 per cent of its durable sales.[22] The citizens of Bonn are also served by eleven 'community centres', the largest two being those which are located within the inner-city districts of Bonn-Nord and Bonn-Süd. The rest of the city's shopping provision is distributed amongst 25 neighbourhood centres, which in the majority of cases characteristically have a very high leaning towards the food trades.

Since the mid 1960s an increasing number of West Germany's large urban areas have experienced the construction of major 'out-of-town' shopping complexes (Figure 5.4). The earliest two developments of this type were the Main-Taunus Zentrum (1964), near Frankfurt, and the Ruhrpark-Zentrum (1965), lying between the Ruhr cities of Bochum and Dortmund. Significantly, both of these ventures pioneered the way in using locations with direct Autobahn access, and taking advantage of positions within easy car travel from major centres of population. The Ruhrpark, in fact, represents an extreme demonstration of these two locational principles, for it is situated at the intersection of the 'Ruhrschnellweg' and Cologne-Wuppertal-Recklinghausen Autobahn, and moreover, has a catchment area which includes as many as 2.7 million potential customers.[23]

By 1976 West Germany could claim to have 44 'out-of-town' shopping centres, each with a 'regional' status. From an initial concentration within the Rhine-Ruhr and the Rhine-Main areas, they have spread in two principal directions: first, to the fringes of the Hamburg urban agglomeration; secondly, into southern Germany, where their development has been encouraged by favourable demographic trends and above-average increases in personal spending power.

Figure 5.3: Bonn-Bad Godesberg: Spatial Patterning of Retailing

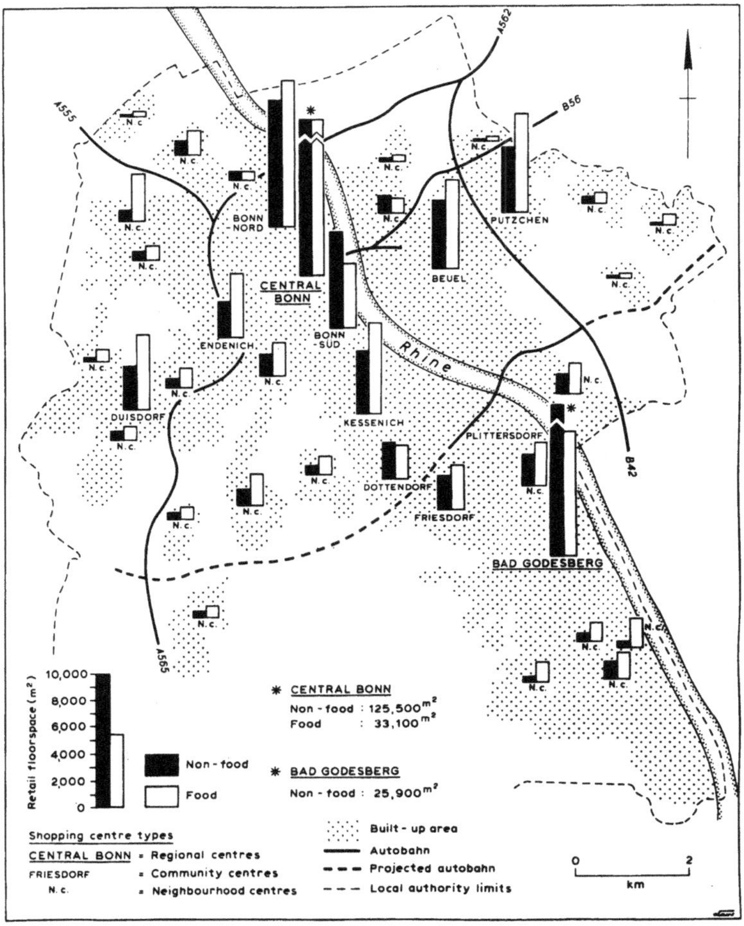

Source: Stadt Bonn, ***Planung von Verbrauchemärkten und Einkaufzentren im Gebiet der Stadt Bonn*** (Stadt Bonn, Bonn, 1976).

Central-area Retailing

Like those in most other developed countries, the central retail areas of West German cities have been under considerable pressures from changes in consumer mobility, the suburbanisation of the retailing function and the growth of 'out-of-town' shopping complexes. However, the central

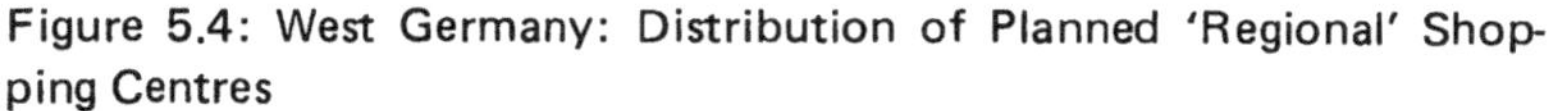

Figure 5.4: West Germany: Distribution of Planned 'Regional' Shopping Centres

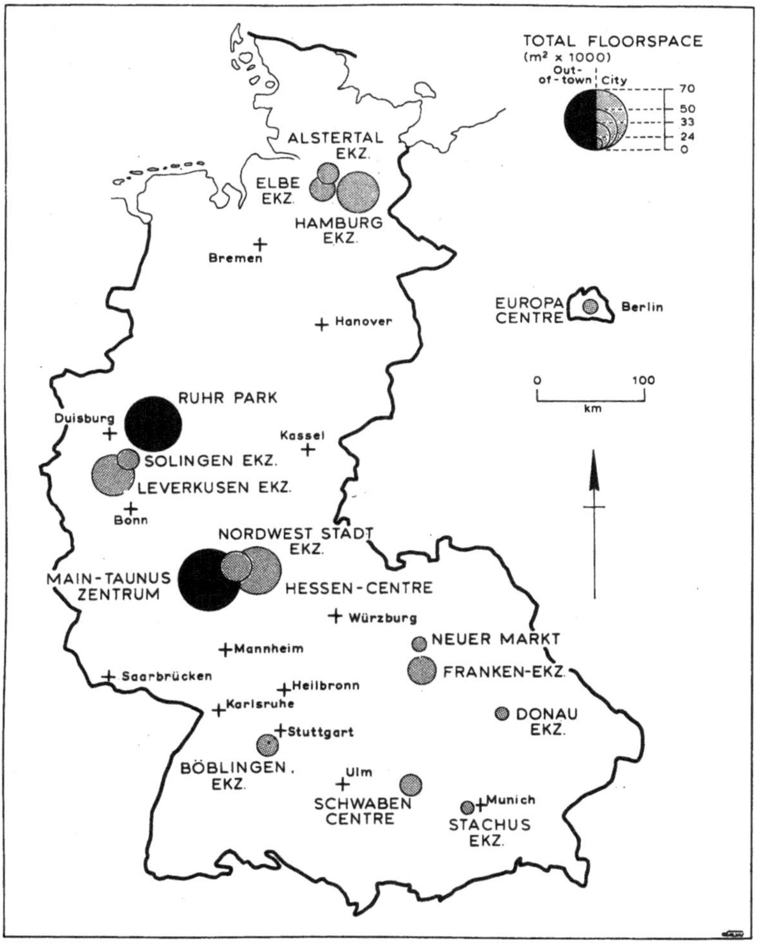

Source: Based upon information contained in Bundesforschungs/anstalt für Landeskunde und Raumordnung, *Untersuchung Kundenverkehr 1976* (BfLR, Bonn, 1977).

positions can still claim to represent by far the largest concentrations of fixed investment in shopping facilities, and accordingly any adverse effects on their continuing prosperity is viewed with considerable concern. Consequently, planning authorities are taking special pains here to improve the general shopping environment and reinvigorate trading activity.

In order to comprehend the nature of retail provision within the centres of West German cities, it is first of all necessary to comment upon certain aspects of their temporal change. In prewar times urban retailing, despite some spread of small shops into the nearmost suburbs, was heavily concentrated within the historic, commercial cores, usually with a strong spatial emphasis along streets leading to the main railway station and tramway terminus. It is important to stress that most centrally situated retail foci were closely surrounded by densely populated residential districts, and because of this they possessed large numbers of traditional convenience-type shops.[24] Mostly trading in a specialised range of products, these businesses more often than not tended to form distinct quarters within the central business district, where they tended to be geographically differentiated from, but functionally linked to, the 'prestige' streetblocks dominated by department stores and other forms of capitalised retailing.[25] The recognition of these different areal components of the retail core was to play an important part in the formulation of postwar plans for the reconstruction of West German cities.

In a large number of instances the initial stimulus to change in central areas arose from the destruction by wartime bombing and the very urgent need for city reconstruction. The situation provided many local authoritities with a great deal of scope to adjust physical layouts to accord with the various needs of modern urban society. However, it was often the case, especially in cities where reconstruction proceeded too quickly, that town plans came to reflect the personality and ideas of just one, particularly influential, official.[26] From the outset, therefore, a diversity of approaches to city-centre planning was established, with some schemes achieving unqualified success and standing as models for later designs, but just as many floundering on account of hasty vision and inadequate expertise.

The highly individualistic nature of city reconstruction in West Germany had a major effect on retail provision and central-shopping environments. As far as the environmental question was concerned, there were two basic types of change. The first came hand in hand with the earliest plans, in which the rebuilding of central areas was dominated by the desire to cater for envisaged increases in traffic flows. It mainly took the form of widening, or sometimes complete alteration, of long-outdated street layouts, invariably with the prime objective of easing traffic congestion.[27] Ultimately, however, these adjustments to the morphological fabric served only to emphasise the problem of incompatibility between traffic and pedestrian movement. Very often the larger of the 'modernised' streets attracted a far greater volume of vehicle flow than could ever have been expected, and this made it harder and harder for planners to provide a suitable environment for central-area shoppers and other pedestrian visitors.

The realisation of the problems arising from increased vehicle access led to a fresh approach in the drawing up of new reconstruction plans. In these later versions special significance was attached to the introduction of pedestrianisation schemes. It would be wrong, however, to view these as a recent phenomenon, for in certain German cities they have a history which dates back to prewar times. For example, the Limbecher Strasse of central Essen was first closed to traffic as long ago as the 1920s, whilst in Cologne two of the city's principal shopping streets – the axial Hohestrasse and the adjoining Schilder Gasse – were partially pedestrianised in 1939.[28] Nevertheless, it was not until the 1960s that these schemes became common, rather than exceptional, features in the spatial structures of West German cities.

In the large majority of cases the initiatives for pedestrianisation schemes were taken by those cities which were suffering the greatest quantity of traffic congestion. Throughout the 1960s these were almost invariably the major urban centres with large car-commuter and car-visitor catchment areas. Since about 1970, however, a rapidly increasing number of smaller towns and cities, particularly those which stand at important foci of main roads, have followed the example. In doing so they have been greatly encouraged by the generous financial assistance which is now available from federal government sources. The money comes mainly in the form of direct subsidies on pedestrianisation expenditure, which were first introduced as part of the 1971 Municipal Transport Assistance Act. As part of this legislation and its subsequent improvements, all new pedestrianisation programmes, including public plazas and subways, are eligible for federal subsidies, which can amount to as much as 60 per cent of the construction costs. In addition to this, local authorities can apply for Land subsidies ranging from 10 per cent to a maximum of 30 per cent.[29]

Usually the pedestrianised areas focus on an axial, main shopping street linking two or more nodes of attraction, especially concentrations of department stores and access points to public transport. A major benefit arising from the prohibition of motor vehicles (except at specified times) is the opportunity which is given to planners to enhance the visual appearance and attractiveness of city centres. To this end much thought and effort has gone into the provision of street 'furnishings' and facilities for outdoor relaxation. Moreover, important historic features of city-centre townscapes, such as market places, town halls and cathedral precincts, are normally incorporated into the plans. This aspect of the planning of pedestrianised areas is typified by the example of central Nuremberg (Figure 5.5). Here, the longitudinal Königstrasse, which runs from the main railway station (outside the city walls) to the Hauptmarkt, forms the principal axis. Characteristically, it also links together all the other pedestrianised streets, including the main shopping alignments of Karolinenstrasse and Breite Gasse, which contain the three major department stores of Kaufhof, Hertie and Karstadt. As has happened in many other large cities, considerable attention has been placed on providing customer access. Nuremberg's pedestrianised zone, with its three 'U' Bahn stations, has a liberal distribution of underground-tramway entrance points. In addition to these, a subway was opened in 1979 to provide easier pedestrian movement from the Hauptbahnhof to the pedestrianised section of the Königstrasse. For people visiting central Nuremberg by motor vehicle, a system of car-parking spaces, including some large underground developments, has been introduced around the edges of the retail core and inside the orbital inner-ring roads.

The success of these schemes is underlined by their growing popularity, both among customers and shop owners. Indeed, in many cities it is the retailers, rather than the planning authorities, who are now the main supporters for further extensions of pedestrianised streets. For example, a survey of Essen found that 85 per cent of all central-area retailers were in favour of expanding the area of pedestrianisation.[30] Furthermore, an analysis of retail change between 1972 and 1978 in central Marburg indicated that the creation of a pedestrianised zone not only presented a substantial impetus for increased trading, as witnessed by an 18 per cent rise in its share of retail turnover within the duration of six years, but also significantly strengthened the ambience of the city.[31]

The important role of pedestrianised areas in the centres of West German cities seems to be assured, although some potential problems have already been recognised. Amongst these, there is some growing concern within planning circles that successful schemes tend to force up shop rentals, and consequently there is a tendency for small retail businesses to be priced out of central-area locations. There is also a tendency for the consumer's image of the central area to diminish and focus almost entirely on the pedestrianised streets. Thus, shops along

Figure 5.5: Central Retail Core of Altstadt Nuremberg

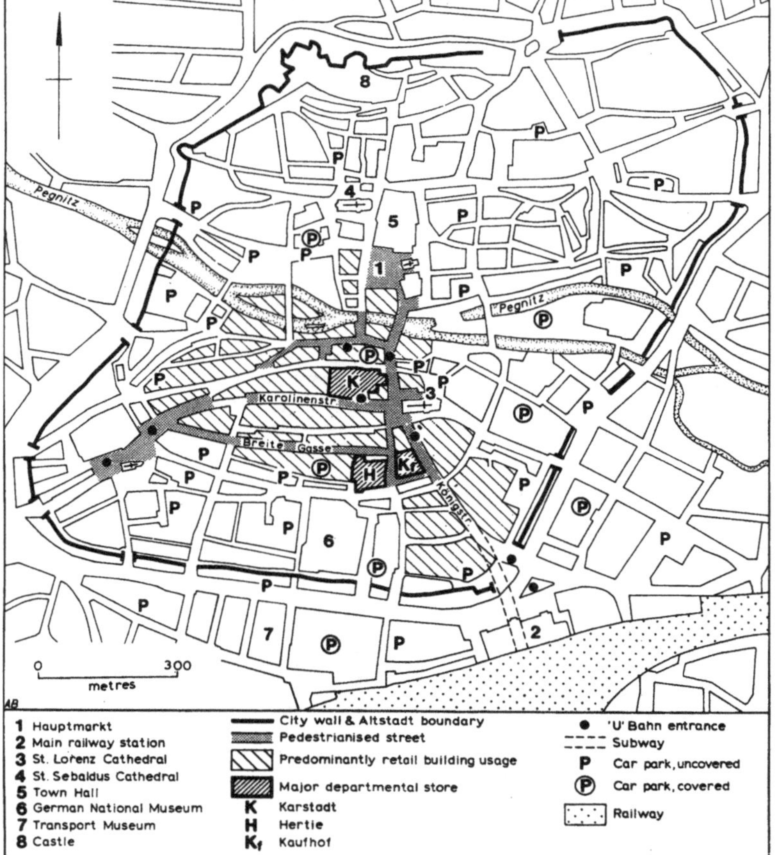

Source: Based on information in Stadt Nürnberg Arbeitsgruppe Nürnberger-Plan, *Bericht zur Entwicklung der Altstadt*, edn E, vol. 12 (Stadt Nürnberg Beitrage zum Nürnberger-Plan, Nuremberg, 1975), Karten 1-5.

streets which are still open to traffic movement at all times of the day are becoming increasingly disadvantaged by the progressive diversion of trading. Clearly, the lesson to be learned for the future is that any new project, or indeed extensions to existing schemes, need to be placed within the context of a general strategy of central-area planning. This approach is essential if further disruption to traditional retailing structures is to be avoided.

Notes

1. Statistical Office of the European Community, *Eurostat Review, 1970-79* (Statistical Office of the European Community, Luxembourg, 1980).
2. H. Soldner, 'West Germany', in J.J. Boddewyn and S.C. Hollander (eds), *Public Policy Toward Retailing* (MIT, Boston, 1972), pp. 405-29.
3. Ibid., pp. 406-10.
4. Ibid., p. 409.
5. Committee of the European Community, *Synoptic Tables of the Measures taken by Member States of the European Community in the Field of Commerce* (EEC, Brussels, 1977).
6. Ibid.
7. G. Hallett, *The Social Economy of West Germany* (Macmillan, London, 1973).
8. M.T. Wild, *West Germany, A Geography of its People* (W. Dawson and Son, Folkestone, 1979, and Longman Group, Harlow, 1981), pp. 50-4.
9. Ibid., pp. 112-17.
10. Bundesforschungsanstalt für Landeskunde und Raumordnung, *Untersuchung Kundenverkehr 1976* (BfLR, Bonn, 1977).
11. G. Shaw, *Retail Development and Structural Change in West Germany* (Retail and Planning Associates, Cambridge, 1978), pp. 15-27.
12. Ibid.
13. Statistisches Bundesamt, *Statistisches Jahrbuch für die Bundesrepublik Deutschland*, 1961 and 1971 edns (Kohlhammer Verlag, Stuttgart and Mainz, 1961 and 1971).
14. Bundesforschungsanstalt für Landeskunde und Raumordnung, *Standortprobleme bei Verbrauchermärkte* (BfLR, Bonn, 1977).
15. Ibid., p. 28.
16. Ibid., p. 29.
17. BfLR, *Untersuchung Kundenverkehr 1976*.
18. N. Perry, 'The Federal Planning Framework in West Germany', *Journal of the Town Planning Institute*, vol. 54 (1968), pp. 91-3.
19. W. Solesbury, 'Local Planning and the German Bebauungsplan', *Journal of the Town Planning Institute*, vol. 54 (1968), pp. 117-22.
20. BfLR, *Standortprobleme bei Verbrauchermärkte*.
21. R. Seyffert, 'Der Standort der Einzelhandelsbetriebe', in R. Seyffert (ed.), *Handbuch des Einzelhandels* (Poeschel, Stuttgart, 1932), pp. 151-63.
22. Stadt Bonn, *Planung von Verbrauchermärkten und Einkaufzentren im Gebiet der Stadt Bonn* (Stadt Bonn, Bonn, 1976).
23. E. Grepl, *Einkaufzentren in der Bundesrepublik Deutschland* (Munich, 1972).
24. H. Friedmann, 'Alt Mannheim im Wandel seiner Physiognomie, Struktur und Funktionen, 1606-1965', *Forschungen zur deutschen Landeskunde*, vol. 168 (1968).
25. Seyffert, 'Der Standort der Einzelhandelsbetriebe'; also, R. Stewig, 'Vergleichende Untersuchung der Einzelhandels-strukturen der Städte Bursa, Kiel und London/Ontario', *Erdkunde*, vol. 28 (1974), pp. 18-30.
26. T. Greene, 'Politics and Planning for Reconstruction in Western Germany', *Urban Studies*, vol. 1 (1964), pp. 71-8.
27. An extreme example is Dortmund where, during the period 1945-61, the total area covered by streets and car-parking spaces in the city centres rose by a huge 52 per cent.
28. R. Monheim, 'Fussgängerbereiche Setzen sich durch-über 200 Stadtzentren haben Fussgängerstrassen', *Der Städtetag*, Feb. 1974.

29. E. von Einem, 'National urban policy; the Case of West Germany', *Journal of American Planning*, vol. 48 (1982), pp. 9-23.

30. R. Monheim, 'Fussgängerbereiche Setzen sich durch-ürber 200 Stadtzentren haben Fussgängerstrassen'.

31. E. Buchhofer, V. Julich and P. Jungst, 'Zur Effizienz Zentralitätsplänerischer Massnahmen', *Erdkunde*, vol. 34 (1980), pp. 22-9.

6 DEVELOPMENTS IN TRANSPORT

John North

The far-reaching economic and social developments in postwar West Germany have been accompanied by major changes in transport at the national, regional and local scale. During the period from 1948 to the beginning of the 1960s, the national communications pattern continued to be dominated by the arteries of nineteenth-century and early twentieth-century industrialisation. The first fifteen postwar years were also a time when transport investment was largely geared to the redevelopment, re-orientation and technological improvement of roads, railways and waterways to assist industrial production and the movement of export traffic. Since 1960, however, there have been dramatic changes in the relative importance of these three transport media, while the rapid development of pipeline and airline systems has added to the competition. There have also been massive investments in Autobahn and urban-road construction, together with schemes for modernising, expanding and integrating urban-passenger transport. Furthermore, growing political and economic interdependence in western Europe has opened up the West German communications network which, occupying a key nodal position, has been subjected to increasing international flows of goods and people.

Since the early 1970s the effects of economic recession, tighter budgetary controls and growing opposition from the environmentalist lobby have brought about a sudden reduction in the rate of approvals for major transport projects. Nevertheless, there has been a continuation of the West German commitment to the creation of an integrated, multi-modal, national communications system which is intended to provide maximum energy-saving and environmental benefits.

Before examining specific trends in the West German communications system, it is necessary to briefly consider the nature of the relationship between transport developments and processes of economic and social change. In addition, it is also worthwhile to identify a number of special factors and influences which are of recurring significance in the West German context, as this will avoid undue repetition in subsequent discussion.

The relationship between developments in transport and general economic and social change is complex and accordingly difficult to assess with any precision. The extension, improvement or adjustment of transport systems may represent a response to changes in the intensity and spatial patterns of movement generated by economic and social forces. At the same time, however, the provision of newer, faster and cheaper transport facilities can also create significant multiplier effects at all geographical scales. Such multiplier effects may be positive or negative, since developments in communications will enhance the accessibility of certain favoured locations while also diminishing that of others. Favoured locations may derive positive benefits, such as new jobs and housing; on the other hand, the diminishing attractiveness of other localities may be reflected in declining levels of economic activity and out-movement of population. The West German experience provides ample evidence of the complexities of this relationship.

Turning our attention to the recurring influences upon West Germany's postwar transport development, we find that the impact of changed political and economic alignments becomes clearly apparent. The division of Germany and the imposition of the 'Iron Curtain' severed many of the important prewar transport and trade links between West Germany and East Germany, Czechoslovakia and central Europe. Accordingly, West Germany has become increasingly dependent upon her west European neighbours for trading purposes, a trend which has been accentuated by the emergence of the European Economic Community. At the time of the formation of the EEC the original five partner countries accounted for 27.6 per cent of West Germany's export trade.[1] By 1979 the collective share of the enlarged EEC was 48.2 per cent, while France, Italy and the Benelux countries were accounting for almost 40 per cent of total (import and export) trade.[2] This trend has encouraged the re-orientation of the West German transport system from its traditional west-to-east emphasis towards one which now caters primarily for north-to-south movements. Closer integration of the West German networks with those of neighbouring west European countries, especially Holland, Belgium and France, has also been a continuing objective. In addition, the changed political and economic alignments have served to enhance the significance of the Rhine axis in the European context, with almost inevitable repercussions in terms of increasing strain on the capacity of existing transport systems.

The configuration of the Federal Republic itself has naturally influenced network orientation. With maximum distances of approximately 900 km from north to south and 450 km from west to east, there was an urgent need for the redirection of traffic towards longitudinal axes.

Important too has been the spatial distribution of major cities in West Germany and their functional status. Reference to any atlas map illustrates both the profusion of large urban centres and their highly significant distribution (see also Figure 1.1). A large majority of the major cities are located within, or in close proximity to, the 'banana-shaped' axis which extends from Hamburg in the north towards Hanover, thence westwards along the fringe of the Central Uplands to the Ruhr. From here it turns southwards to follow the Rhine valley before veering southeastwards at Karlsruhe to pass through Stuttgart, Augsburg and Munich. Several of the large cities along this axis have long-standing importance as regional centres,[3] but their functional status has been increased since 1949 by their becoming foci of dispersal of federal government offices and national institutions. The diffuse nature of the urban system in West Germany has meant that particularly heavy levels of interaction exist between the various cities.[4] These in turn play a major part in the evolving pattern of transport developments.

Two additional factors are worthy of note. The first concerns the continuing role of the federal government in transport policy. This intervention has occurred in a variety of spheres, ranging from the determination of an overall transport strategy for the country at large to financial support for individual projects. Significant too have been the federal government's taxation and tariff-setting procedures, which have been a vital factor in determining the 'split' of traffics amongst the various transport media.

Finally, reference must be made to the impact of rising personal affluence and the growth of the consumer society in West Germany from the late 1950s onwards. Increasing travel-mobility, changing residential preferences and the adoption of an ever-widening range of leisure activities have all affected transport, particularly at the urban and subregional level.

The National Transport System

Road Traffic

In West Germany very few people would be prepared to disagree that the most pervasive development in the transport sphere has been the huge upsurge in motor traffic. This has come through a massive rise in levels of car ownership and a rapid growth in commercial road haulage. Until the late 1950s most West Germans were still enduring low personal incomes and limited purchasing power. Accordingly, levels of car ownership had remained low in comparison with those of most other major industrialised countries. Although the numbers of car registrations in West Germany rose from 598,000 in 1950 to just over 2 millions in 1956, the latter figure represented only 43 cars for every 1,000 inhabitants.[5]

From the late 1950s onwards, however, rising personal affluence generated a meteoric advance in car ownership. Between 1956 and 1966 the number of cars in West Germany more than quadrupled; then, during the next ten-year period (1966-76), the figure almost doubled from 10.3 millions to 18.9 millions. By 1980 total car registrations had progressed to as many as 23 millions, giving on average one car for every family.[6] Within the duration of just twenty years, therefore, West Germany had managed to overtake almost all west European countries, including Britain, France and Sweden, to rank in second place behind Luxembourg in terms of motor cars per 1,000 persons (Table 6.1). Significant too is the fact that by 1979 cars accounted for as many as 86 per cent of all registered vehicles in West Germany, compared with only 25 per cent in 1950. At the end of the 1970s also, four out of every five personal journeys within the Federal Republic were being undertaken by this mode of transport.

Table 6.1: Car Ownership in West Germany and Other West European Countries, 1958-79

Country	Motor cars per 1,000 inhabitants			
	1958	1970	1974	1979
West Germany	58	234	280	369
Belgium	60	210	254	312
Denmark	63	219	250	278
France	100	246	289	345
United Kingdom	83	207	251	268
Eire	49	121	158	203
Italy	25	187	258	309
Luxembourg	88	268	365	456
Netherlands	34	199	254	292
Sweden	127	284	324	346
Switzerland	79	221	269	340

Source: Statistisches Bundesamt, *Statistisches Jahrbuch für die Bundesrepublik Deutschland*, 1959, 1972, 1976 and 1981 edns (W. Kohlhammer Verlag, Stuttgart and Mainz, 1959, 1972, 1976 and 1981), tables on *Internationale Übersichten.*

This remarkable advance has produced a tremendous growth in both inter-regional and local traffic, principally for the purposes of conveyance to work, travel to holiday venues and visits to friends and relations. The most dramatic effects were felt in the large cities and conurbations where, during the 1960s, the belated, but none the less very rapid, emergence of the traffic problem threatened to engulf and destroy the existing urban fabric.

The congestion on West German roads and streets also owes much to the expansion of commercial traffic. Widespread recognition of the greater flexibility of road haulage for quick, door-to-door deliveries of low-bulk goods led to an impressive rise in numbers of lorry and van registrations. These rose from just 445,000 in 1950 to 1.3 millions in 1979.[7] During the same period annual traffic tonnages hauled by lorries increased from 32.9 milliards to a massive 294 milliards.[8] Even more significantly, the share of road transport in the total quantity of long-distance freight traffic more than trebled from a modest 11.3 per cent of tonne/km to 36.9 per cent.[9] This was in spite of the federal government's attempts (from the late 1960s onwards) at diverting goods traffic from road to railway, through the placing of additional taxes on heavy lorries and the imposition of severe restrictions on weekend haulage operations.

By 1975 transport of goods by road had replaced the amount which was being carried by the federal railway system. Legislation during the late 1960s did bring some temporary halt to the advance of lorry traffic, but by 1972 it began to accelerate again. In that year, and also in 1973, the pace of growth of lorry-carried tonne/km of goods exceeded 10 per cent.[10] Since then the trend, although very irregular, continued to be upwards: in 1976 a 15.7 per cent rise was recorded, but more recently the yearly rate has slackened to between 4 and 7 per cent. Today, semi-finished products, machinery, foodstuffs, building materials, chemicals and mineral oils provide the principal stimuli for expansion.

Another important trend has been the growth in international haulage, which gathered strongly in momentum as trade between EEC countries widened during the 1960s and 1970s. In West Germany, however, the increase in international movement also reflected a dependence upon Dutch and Belgian ports, chiefly Rotterdam and Antwerp, on account of their strategic location in relation to the industrial regions of the Rhine axis. Within West Germany international road haulage has expanded from a mere 1.1 million tonnes of cargoes in 1950 to a huge 63.7 million tonnes in 1979.[11] Indeed, it now accounts for more than one-fifth of all long-distance movements on

West German roads. With the single exception of 1951, the inwards flow has always exceeded the volume of outward traffic, although the gap has narrowed, especially in recent years. Meanwhile the 'key' location of the West German road network within the context of the EEC and western Europe in general has been underlined by growing quantities of through-traffic. In this, there has been a trebling of the amount of movement since 1970. By the end of the 1970s more than 8 million tonnes of freight was passing each year from one West German frontier to another.[12] This placed yet one more extra strain on the country's overburdened road network, especially on the congested Autobahn routes of the focal Rhine axis.

The Autobahn Network

West Germany's Autobahn system is the most extensive in western Europe, and during the last two decades has played a central role in the economic and social development of the nation. From an early base of 2,116 km of length in 1950, much of which was a legacy from the military planning of the 1930s, the system was enlarged rather slowly at first. In fact, by 1963 only 820 km had been added – just 68 km per annum since 1950.[13] During the period 1963-70, however, regular yearly additions of between 100 km and 150 km were made. The 1970s saw a further quickening in the amount of Autobahn construction: during this decade a further 3,100 km was added to the system, bringing the total length to an impressive 7,292 km.[14]

The spatial patterns and chronological sequence of Autobahn construction in West Germany are of considerable interest, for amongst other things they are reflective of changing priorities and purposes. The prewar network had been designed to link the principal regions of Hitler's Germany to Berlin. Accordingly, the portion of this system which came to be inherited by the Federal Republic displayed a pronounced west-to-east orientation. It also exhibited a fragmentary pattern: there were no connecting links between the Mainz-Oberhausen-Hanover-Helmstedt and the Munich-Frankfurt-Göttingen routes, while the North Sea ports of Bremen and Hamburg were left very much in isolation.[15]

The first of two maps drawn in Figure 6.1 illustrates the pattern of Autobahn development from 1948 to 1963. During this period completion of the Hamburg-Göttingen, the Karlsruhe-Basel and the Cologne-Dortmund links, together with the vital inter-connections to the west of Frankfurt, provided the basis for a significant shift in traffic flow away from the traditional latitudinal direction, and towards two north-south spinal routes linking most of West Germany's larger and more dynamic industrial and commercial centres. Moreover, attempts to integrate the West German network with those of neighbouring countries were reinforced by progress on the Oberhausen-Wesel-Emmerich and Cologne-Aachen routes. Here, access to Dutch and Belgian ports was a prime consideration, although in both cases progress with linking motorway development beyond the respective frontiers remained slow throughout the 1960s.

One further feature of the 1948-63 pattern of Autobahnen was the incorporation of some of West Germany's more isolated regions and urban centres. This included the provision of a direct link to Nuremberg from Frankfurt, and the building of the Mannheim-Saarbrücken Autobahn. The latter is of special interest on account of its being designed primarily to assist the political and economic integration of the Saarland into the Federal Republic.[16] The Mannheim-Saarbrücken route also provided the basis for a future Frankfurt-Paris motorway. Here again, however, progress beyond the West German frontier has been extremely protracted.

The second map in Figure 6.1 shows the pattern of Autobahn development since 1963. To some extent this involved a continuing pursuit of the earlier objectives of adding to longitudinal flow. However, it also involved the provision of additional capacity on certain existing routes, and the creation of dense networks of urban motorways within the Ruhr and Rhine-Main conurbations. Furthermore, the period after 1963 has seen the emergence of a policy of using Autobahn construction as a means of aiding regional development in backward areas. The duplication of Autobahnen along the heavily-congested middle section of the Rhine axis, between the Rhine-Ruhr and Rhine-Main agglomerations, has been a particularly prominent feature involving the construction of the eight-lane Cologne-Limburg-Frankfurt Autobahn and the 'relief' Dortmund-Giessen-Frankfurt route. Both of these avoid the congested and meandering Rhine valley: instead they cut across the flanking uplands of the Sauerland, Westerwald and Taunus plateaux several kilometres away to the east. In so doing they have helped to revitalise the economies of numerous intervening rural communities, especially those of the Lahn valley and Limburg areas.[17] A third example of a parallel Autobahn, and one which was likewise designed primarily to ease congestion, is to be found in the Upper Rhine section of the Rhine axis. Here, the Frankfurt-Mannheim Autobahn follows the valley floor, and for much of its length runs almost side by side with an older route from Frankfurt to Karlsruhe.

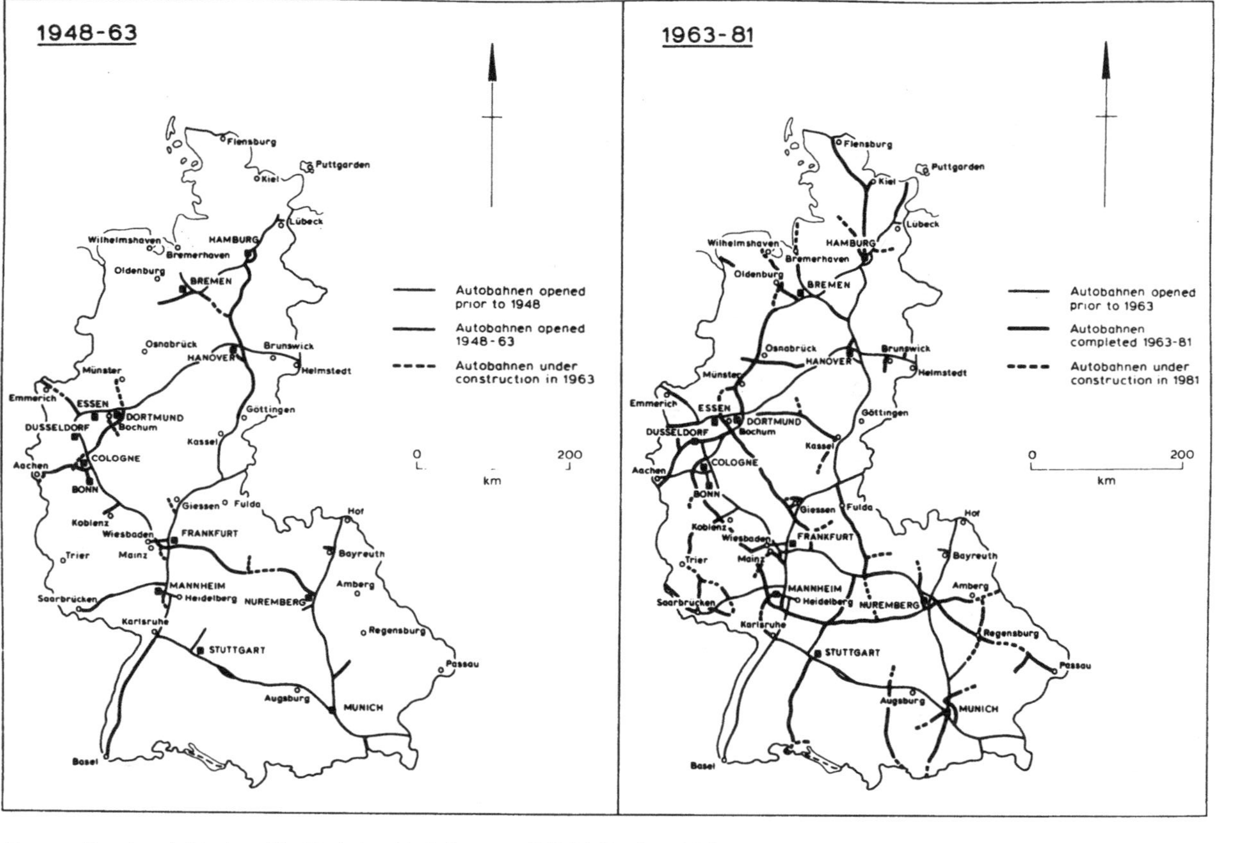

Source: Bundesministerium für Verkehr, *Verkehrswege* (BMfV, Berlin, 1964), p. 116; also, Bundesministerium für Verkehr, *Netz der Bundesautobahnen und Bundesstrassen* (BMfV, Frankfurt, 1981), 1: 750,000 scale maps.

Away from the Rhine axis, the progressive extension of the Cologne-Trier-Saarbrücken Autobahn (still to be completed) is intended to provide an economic stimulus to the backward Eifel region. In southern Germany the improvement of access, together with efforts to promote tourism, were the main reasons for the southwards extension of Autobahn routes from the Karlsruhe-Stuttgart-Munich axis towards the Allgäu and Bavarian Alps. It is intended that several of the south Geman routes will eventually join up directly with the Austrian and Swiss road networks.[18] In addition, completion of the Regensburg-Deggendorf section of the Nuremberg-Passau Autobahn and the continuing eastwards penetration of the Nuremberg-Amberg motorway towards the frontier with Czechoslovakia serve as further indications of the keen desire to improve communication links with West Germany's neighbouring nation states.

The post-1963 period has also seen substantial Autobahn development in the northern regions. The opening of the Dortmund-Münster-Bremen route provided a more effective line of movement between the Rhine-Ruhr and West Germany's North Sea cities. At the same time, the northwards extension of Autobahnen from Bremen to Bremerhaven and from Oldenburg to Wilhelmshaven (not yet completed) has assisted greatly in the port developments of the Weser estuary. Furthermore, communications with Denmark, Sweden and Norway have been substantially improved by the completion of the Hamburg-Flensburg Autobahn, and the construction of the motorway extension from Lübeck towards the Puttgarden ferry terminus on the Baltic.

There are still some important gaps in the West German Autobahn system, especially within the remote regions of the eastern borderlands where, for example, the Coburg area in northern Bavaria and the eastern part of Lüneburg Heath in Lower Saxony still represent extremely inaccessible locations. Their situations are unlikely to be improved, at least in the near future. This is because tighter budgets on new road construction, together with the emergence of a vociferous environmental lobby, strongly opposed to further Autobahn developments, have delayed, and in some cases reversed decisions for, the implementation of current projects.

Rail Transport

In 1950 the federal railways accounted for as much as 62 per cent of long-distance freight traffic and 38 per cent of all passenger journeys within West Germany. By 1979, however, these proportions had shrunk to 31 per cent and just 6 per cent respectively.[19] These figures amply demonstrate the rapid decline in the relative importance of railways during the postwar period. Changes in the structure and composition of goods traffic, competition from road transport, investments in pipelines and, since the late 1950s, the upsurge in car travel have all contributed to the worsening plight of the *Deutsche Bundesbahn* (DB), which has been accentuated further by escalating costs for both labour and essential technological development. By 1980 the annual deficit of the DB had reached DM 4 billion, whilst the accumulated deficit had soared to the colossal figure of DM 32 billion.[20] Government annual subsidies to the railways have increased steadily from around DM 3 billion in the late 1960s to an estimated DM 13.6 billion in 1981.[21]

The response to this situation has been a progressive concentration upon the most remunerative types of freight and passenger business. This has been accompanied by the withdrawal of many rail services on light-traffic routes, together with a steady contraction of the railway workforce from 512,000 employees in 1957 to 337,000 in 1979.[22] However, in spite of its heavy deficits in revenue, the DB has continued to receive strong support for its investment programmes from the federal government. Amongst the various motives for providing this aid, the most outstanding is the growing concern for the environment and energy conservation.

Although the railway's share of total goods traffic has fallen precipitously, the actual quantity of movement has shown an upwards trend, with annual tonnages increasing from 209 million tonnes in 1950 to levels exceeding 350 million tonnes during the early 1970s. Since then the figure has fluctuated between 320 million and 350 million tonnes each year; the only exception being in 1974, when increased amounts of coal movement at the time of the oil crisis were largely responsible for producing a freight-level of 389 million tonnes.[23] Coal, in fact, has consistently accounted for more than one-quarter of rail goods traffic. Accordingly, the decline in West Germany's coal industry since the late 1950s has had a serious effect on the finances of the DB. Carriage of coal fell most dramatically during the period 1963-72 (114 million tonnes to 82.3 million tonnes). Since the mid-1970s, however, the trend has levelled out within the 75-80 million tonnes range,[24] with short-distance movements from mines to thermal power stations representing the most stable element. At one time a potential compensation for the decline in coal haulage existed in the transport of crude oil. Much of this, however, was denied to the railways by the development of pipelines during the 1960s.

Movements of metal ores and scrap, chiefly to the Ruhr, still provide the DB with around 50 million tonnes of goods traffic each year, while iron and steel traffic retains a similar level of importance. However, there has been a catastrophic decline in the carrying of machinery, semi-finished articles and manufactured products. In these the DB's share of tonnage has slumped from 68.5 per cent in 1950 to a mere 25 per cent today.[25] This owed itself to increased competition from road hauliers who, unlike the railways, are able to offer a direct door-to-door service, and are particularly attractive to traders in low-bulk and high-value goods.

During the 1950s and much of the 1960s there was also an alarming decline in railway passenger-travel, with the numbers of persons using the DB falling from 1,473 millions in 1950 to 1,009 millions in 1968.[26] Since the late 1960s, however, the trend has stabilised, mainly on account of the success of the new high-speed commuter systems ('S' Bahnen) which have been developed within West Germany's largest urban agglomerations. Indeed, if the people using the 'S' Bahnen are excluded from the statistics, the decline in rail-passenger operations has progressed to only 600 million travellers in 1979.[27]

Spatial Pattern of the Rail Network. Since 1950 there have been some significant changes in the geography of West Germany's railway network. Additional sections of track and new junctions were required to assist the general redirection of traffic towards north-south axes. More specifically, a new link has been provided between Brunswick and Hamburg, whilst completion of the Gelsenkirchen-Marl-Haltern line served to improve the railway facilities of the Ruhr coalfield. Inevitably, however, the general re-orientation of West Germany's internal traffic, together with the growth of international freight and passenger movements, has placed increasing strains on the capacity of several longitudinal routes, especially those which run along the constricted valley of the Middle Rhine. Recognition of this problem during the 1970s has led to recent announcements for additional lines to be built; one between Hanover and Würzburg, a second between Cologne and Frankfurt, and a third from Mannheim to Stuttgart.

Electrification of the federal railway system has been progressively extended, particularly along the longitudinal routes. By 1970 10,900 km of track, representing 38 per cent of the total length of the DB, had been treated.[28] Nine years later, electrified lines carried as much as 80 per cent of all West Germany's rail traffic. Nevertheless, by 1981 there were still several important long-distance routes, including the

Cologne–Trier, the Bingen–Saarbrücken and a number of well-used south German lines, which were still operated by diesel-powered locomotives.[29]

Since the early 1970s the federal government and the DB have worked together to formulate a continuing programme designed to promote the expansion of both passenger and freight traffic. A key element of this is the decision to concentrate major capital investments on the most remunerative types of traffic. In the freight sector this has brought about a comprehensive reorganisation of conventional traffic operations, together with the recent introduction of specialised services to cater for the growing quantity of container movements. Much emphasis has been placed upon improving the efficiency of the nationwide wagon-load service, which today is an essential ingredient of West German freight operations. Accordingly the number of goods marshalling yards has been heavily reduced, but 36 'key' foci have either been substantially improved or completely remodelled for the introduction of computerised facilities.

The remodelling of wagon-load operations in the Hamburg area provides a striking example of the rationalisation programme. Here, the traffic of five former marshalling yards has been absorbed by the construction of the DM 800-million Maschen complex in open countryside to the southeast of the city. This now handles more than 6,000 wagons per day.[30] The number of transit lines to and from Hamburg has been substantially reduced; a feature of the programme which has created substantial economies, for example, is the saving of almost 24 hours over previous schedules to and from the distant city of Ulm in Baden-Württemberg.

An important feature of the streamlining process during the 1970s has been the growth of inter-modal traffic in the form of container and *Huckepack* ('piggyback') movements. Container traffic increased from 2.1 million tonnes in 1970 to three times this figure in 1979. Huckepack traffic has grown even faster, from 0.8 million tonnes to 4.6 million tonnes during the same period.[31] To cater for these trends, special segregated services (known as the *Grünnetz*) were introduced in 1981 to link 60 inter-modal terminals located throughout the country (Figure 6.2).[32] Regular timetables are operated, with transit times between Bremerhaven and Munich – a distance of 820 km – taking approximately 19 hours. However, continued rapid growth of container and Huckepack traffic in future years could be inhibited by limited terminal capacity at a number of key centres, such as Nuremberg and Stuttgart, where expansion plans have been delayed by environmentalist opposition.

Figure 6.2: West Germany: Container and *Huckepack* Rail Terminals, 1981

Source: Deutsche Bundesbahn, *Geschäftsbericht der BRD*, 1981 edn (Brönners Druckerei, Frankfurt, 1981), p. 50.

In the passenger sector the principal development has been the introduction in 1971 of the Inter-City (*IC Zug*) express network linking 33 large cities and covering a total distance of 3,115 km. At first the services ran at 2-hourly intervals, but frequencies have since been increased to provide hourly inter-city departures from most major stations. The four main routes (Figure 6.3) are interlinked in Dortmund, Cologne, Mannheim and Würzburg in order to ensure that all main stations served by the system can be reached with a maximum of just two changes of train.[33]

Figure 6.3: West Germany: The Inter-City Railway Network, 1981

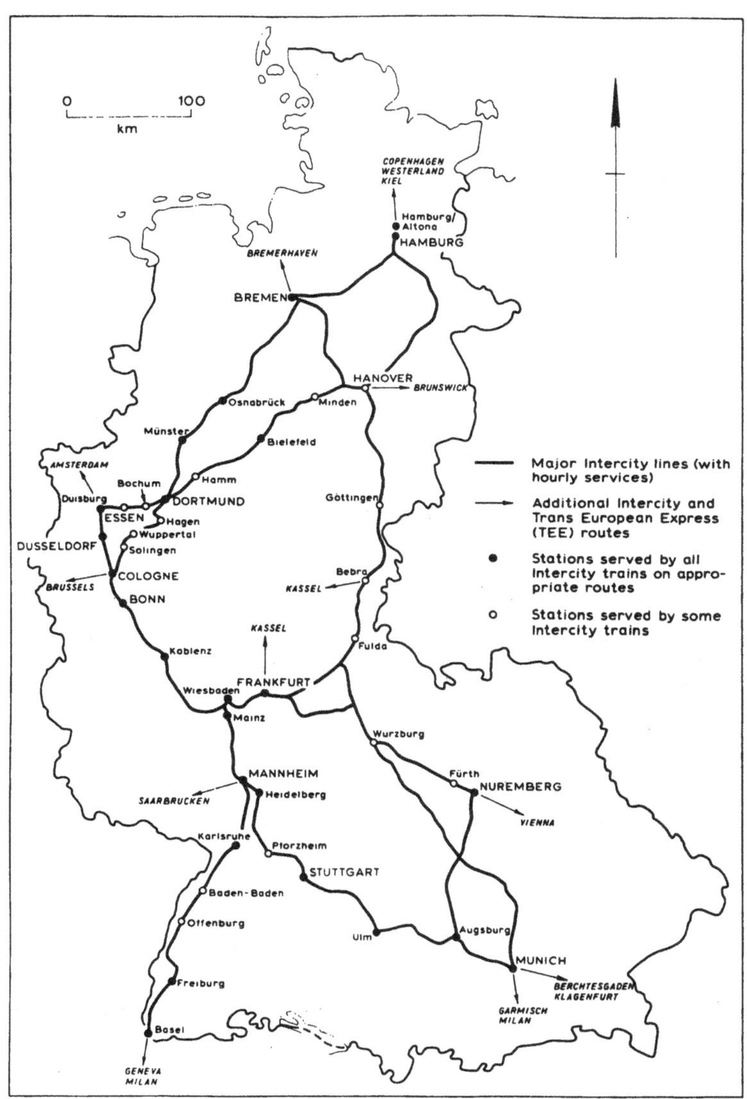

Source: Deutsche Bundesbahn, *Geschäftsbericht der BRD*, 1981 edn (Brönners Druckerei, Frankfurt, 1981).

The 1981 timetable of the DB indicates the favoured position of the Rhine-axis cities within the IC network.[34] Including Trans-European services, Cologne has 90 daily inter-city departures, while Duisburg, Dusseldorf, Bonn, Koblenz and Mannheim each have more than 50. Elsewhere, Munich, Hanover, Hamburg and Dortmund are also well provided, but Stuttgart, Nuremberg and the eastern axis of Hanover-Kassel-Fulda have less frequent services. The pattern as a whole underlines the existence of the 'banana-shaped' alignment of communications which extends from Hamburg, via the Ruhr and the Rhine axis, to Frankfurt and thence Munich.

The introduction of hourly IC services stemmed largely from the competition generated by airlines for long-distance passenger movement. Inter-city trains in West Germany today achieve average speeds of between 120 and 134 km/h on long-distance routes.[35] The average journey-time from Cologne to Hamburg is 4 h 15 m; that between Cologne and Munich is 6 h 15 m, and the lengthy travel from Hamburg to Munich (using the direct line through Hanover and Würzburg) now takes less than 8 hours. Not surprisingly, although there have been losses on other routes, passenger totals for IC services have shown a significant increase as the frequencies and timing of trains have been progressively improved.[36]

Away from the primary inter-city network, the contraction of passenger services has been a much criticised feature. In many rural areas trains have been replaced by buses owned by the DB or the Post Office. During the period 1960-79 the total length of the federal railway network was reduced by 26 per cent from 36,000 km to 28,600 km.[37] Further contraction is inevitable, although implementation of the drastic 1976 proposal,[38] which called for a reduction of 16,000 km by 1980, has been delayed by strong political opposition.

Federal government concern over the deficit of the DB has been tempered by recognition of the contribution which the railways can make in the sphere of energy conservation. Accordingly, in 1981 a further DM 560 million was allocated for the continued development of inter-modal freight services.[39] Continuing development of the most profitable elements of freight and passenger business, together with the closure of many uneconomic rural lines, is essential if the railways are to improve their financial position and competitiveness.

Inland Waterways and Ports

River and canal transport facilities have continued to play a significant role in West Germany, although the share of waterways in tonne/km of goods traffic fell from around 30 per cent in the late 1960s to just one-quarter in 1979.[40] The waterways undoubtedly made a strong contribution to the period of fastest economic advancement in the 1950s. Annual traffic tonnages rose steadily from 71.8 millions in 1950 to 137 millions by the end of this decade, while there was also a significant increase in the waterways' share of total goods-traffic movement (from 26 per cent to 33 per cent). The heaviest gains were made in coal traffic, but substantial increases were also recorded in the movements of oil products, ores, scrap and construction materials.[41]

The quantity of waterway traffic maintained its general upwards trend during the 1960s, with the cargoes carried reaching a level of 240 million tonnes per year by 1970. The conveyance of construction materials and oil products continued to increase, but the problems in the coal industry were reflected in a sharp fall in annual coal tonnages to amounts below those of 1950. During the 1970s inland waterway traffic tended to level off, with annual tonnages fluctuating between 230 and 250 million tonnes.[42]

The unrivalled focus of movement has, of course, been the Rhine, the 'spinal cord' of the European waterway network. Yearly quantities of traffic on the German section of this river continued to grow, even during the late 1970s; by 1979 the figure had reached 204 million tonnes of cargo, equivalent to 83 per cent of all West German inland waterway traffic.[43] More than two-thirds of movement along the Rhine occurs within the stretch between the Dutch border and the premier inland port of Duisburg-Ruhrort (Figure 6.4). Duisburg handled 46 million tonnes of cargo in 1979, of which three-quarters were unloaded goods, with iron ore and mineral products representing the main commodities. Cologne, with 13.8 million tonnes of traffic was the second-ranking Rhine port in 1979, followed by Mannheim, Ludwigshafen and Karlsruhe.[44]

Patterns of traffic on the Rhine have changed considerably since 1950. Downstream movements of coal from the Ruhr and lignite from the Cologne 'brown coalfield' declined sharply during the 1950s and 1960s as Holland became increasingly reliant upon oil and natural gas for its energy requirements.[45] On the other hand, upstream traffic in coal and lignite actually increased, following the canalisation of the Moselle during the 1960s and the opening up of movements to France via Koblenz. Another significant development at this time was the growth of iron-ore shipments upstream from the Rotterdam–Maasvlakte bulk terminal to the Ruhr.

Figure 6.4: West Germany: Freight Traffic on Inland Waterways, 1981

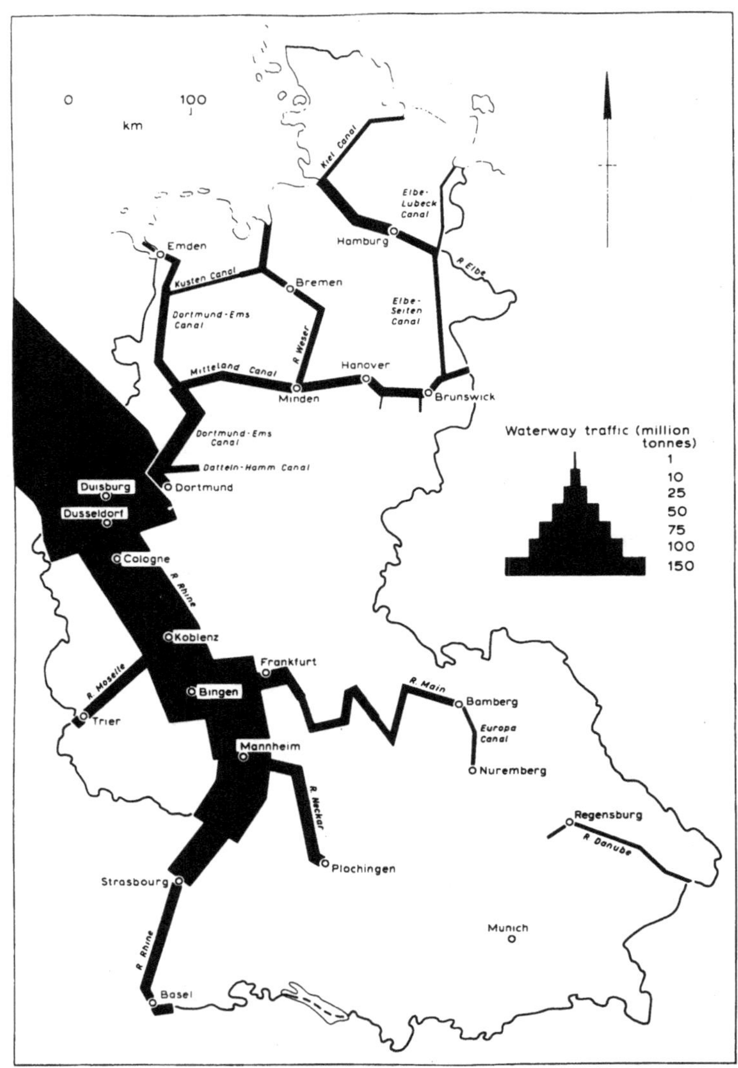

Source: Statistisches Bundesamt, *Statistisches Jahrbuch der Bundesrepublik Deutschland*, 1981 edn (Kohlhammer Verlag, Stuttgart and Mainz, 1981), p. 290.

Superficially, the inland waterway network of West Germany appears to have changed little during the period 1960-79, and the total length has remained just short of 4,500 km.[46] However, some important developments have occurred. The capacity of many sections of waterway has been increased, so that by 1979 as many as 3,038 km (68 per cent) of the total network were navigable by vessels of more than 1,000 tonnes. Moreover, all important links can now handle the standard, 1350-tonne *Europa* barges. Equally significant, only 226 km (5 per cent) of the waterway system is now incapable of handling vessels of more than 250 tonnes, compared with 713 km in 1960.[47] Another important development has concerned changes in motive power, with the advent in the late 1950s of the push-tug system which is capable of propelling four or six barges totalling more than 8,000 tonnes of cargo. The push-tug system has proved very economical, but excess capacity of vessels has been a problem in recent years to the extent that the number of barges in the West German fleet fell by almost one-third during the 1970s.[48]

The postwar period has seen a number of important additions to the national waterway network. The extension of the Middle-Weser navigation between the Mittelland Canal and Bremen, begun in the 1930s, was completed in 1960. More recently in north Germany, the opening of the Elbe-Seiten canal in 1975 has provided improved connections between Hamburg and Lübeck and the rest of the inland waterway system via the Mittelland route. By 1979, however, the Elbe-Seiten carried only 4 million tonnes of traffic.[49] This was largely because this canal failed to attract the expected quantity of traffic in imported iron ore moving from the North Sea ports to the Salzgitter steel plants at Peine and Beddingen near Hanover. This, in fact, was captured by the railways, which provided 5,000-tonne-capacity trains working on a continuous operation circuit.[50] Unfortunately, both for the canal and the railways, economic recession has since brought a sharp slump in levels of iron-ore consumption at the steel plants.

Elsewhere some recent waterway developments have experienced a measure of success. The canalisation of the Moselle, a product of Franco-German co-operation, has enabled more efficient shipments of Ruhr coal to the French steel industry. The Moselle navigation consistently achieved its projected traffic levels of 10 million tonnes during the 1970s. Further south, and on the east bank of the Rhine, the extension of navigation on the river Neckar to Plochingen has brought considerable benefits to the Stuttgart region and central Baden-Württemberg. Traffic along the Neckar navigation varies between

11 and 13 million tonnes per year, four-fifths of which consists of inwards-moving goods.[51]

The most ambitious and controversial project has been the Europa Canal, or Rhine-Maine-Danube scheme, which was conceived with the intention of linking the North Sea ports of western Europe with those of the Black Sea across the heart of the continent. This ambition was to be achieved by the progressive upstream canalisation of the river Main to Bamberg, in combination with waterway regulation and improvement along the Danube below Kelheim. The project also involved the construction of a 171-km canal link between Bamberg and Kelheim. Canalisation of the river Main to Bamberg was completed in 1962, but it took another ten years before the first section of the link-canal (Bamberg to Nuremberg) was opened for traffic. Recently the still-uncompleted Europa Canal has run into mounting difficulties. It was originally hoped that the costs of the project would be recovered from associated hydroelectric power schemes. However, the costs of canal construction escalated alarmingly during the 1970s. Moreover, a number of new developments, including the DB's introduction of specialised iron-ore trains between Hamburg-Hansaport and the Danube city of Regensburg, have cast doubts over whether the Europa Canal can ever achieve its projected traffic levels of 12-15 million tonnes per year. Traffic statistics for 1978 and 1979 seem to confirm this uncertainty, with both Bamberg and Nuremberg already showing declining quantities of movement.[52] A further complication has been the growing fear among West German vessel owners that there will be damaging competition from the state-owned fleets of certain East European countries.[53] By 1981 work on the Europa Canal was at a standstill while the political manoeuvrings over the project continued. At present the completed stretches of the waterway are peripheral to the national network, making it difficult, therefore, to judge the traffic potential of the project; but it does appear likely that the principal benefits will be derived from the secondary functions of electricity generation and water-based recreational facilities.

The crisis over the Europa Canal project, together with the growing success of the DB in competing for long-distance traffic in iron ore and other bulky commodities, has put into question the wisdom of any further extension to the West German waterway system. The Osnabrück-Bremen-Hamburg waterway project appears to have been deferred, while pleas from the Saarland for a direct canal link to the Rhine have not found support. The Rhine will undoubtedly continue to play its vital role, but a number of smaller waterways are likely to experience continued reductions in traffic movement.

West German Seaports. Ever since the first few postwar years seaport traffic has been dominated by the mixed-cargo ports of Hamburg and Bremen-Bremerhaven, and the oil-importing port of Wilhelmshaven. These three ports have consistently accommodated more than 70 per cent of total West German sea trade.[54] The postwar growth of traffic at Hamburg was partly hampered by the loss of much of its traditional hinterland following the division of Germany. But Hamburg also suffered because of its relative isolation from the principal centres of industrial and commercial activity, a problem which has been remedied only gradually by the extension of the Autobahn network and improvements to north-south railway links. Above all, however, Hamburg has experienced severe competition for West German traffic from the Dutch and Belgian ports, especially Rotterdam and Antwerp, which have exploited their more favourable location with regard to the industrial regions of the Rhine axis. Nevertheless, trade at Hamburg has grown from 30 million tonnes per annum to 60 million tonnes over the past two decades.[55] Traffic here is dominated by imports, which outnumber exported goods by a 3:1 ratio in tonnage terms.

A particularly impressive feature of recent years has been the rapid growth of container traffic at Hamburg, with a tenfold increase being recorded between 1969 and 1979.[56] Hamburg at first was slow to react to containerisation, but now handles almost 5 million tonnes of this traffic each year.[57] Container movement at Bremen-Bremerhaven exceeded that at Hamburg until 1976, and is likewise now approaching the yearly figure of 5 million tonnes. New container terminals, with their associated railway facilities, form an integral part of continuing port expansion at both Hamburg and Bremerhaven. At Wilhelmshaven, however, development has been less progressive, primarily because of the heavy reliance on oil imports. In 1950 Wilhelmshaven handled a mere 100,000 tonnes of cargo, but by the early 1970s it was dealing with between 25 and 30 million tonnes per annum, nine-tenths of this being crude oil.[58] Since 1974, however, levels of traffic have stagnated within this range, despite attempts at diversification. The port is linked by pipelines to the Ruhr and also to the major oil refineries of the Rhine axis, while a further pipeline serves plants in the Hamburg area.

Air Transport and Pipelines

Air Transport. Passenger movement by air increased rapidly during the fifteen years which followed the re-introduction of civil aviation in West Germany in 1955. The total number of passengers, including international travellers, using the ten leading West German airports increased from 3 millions in 1956 to 36.3 millions in 1971, the fastest yearly growth-rates being recorded in 1969 and 1970.[59] However, annual increases in passenger traffic then slowed appreciably between 1971 and 1977 before accelerating again to give a total of 49 million passenger movements in 1979. The unrivalled focus of air transport is the Rhine-Main terminal at Frankfurt, which is also a key node in the European network. Frankfurt increased its annual passenger throughput from 2.2 millions in 1960 to 17.5 millions in 1979, and also claimed a larger share of total passengers handled in West Germany (27.7 per cent, rising to 35.4 per cent).[60] Dusseldorf and Munich airports each handled over 6 million passengers at this latter date, while Hamburg and West Berlin both accounted for 4.5 millions. Surprisingly, the Cologne-Bonn airport, which serves the federal capital Bonn, ranks only seventh in the passenger totals of West German airports.

The network of internal air-passenger services in West Germany has been progressively extended in recent years. Services to and from West Berlin have been of vital importance in view of the restrictions imposed upon road and rail travellers. Air services are also competitive over the country's longer north-south hauls, for example Hamburg to Munich, but the introduction of IC railway timetables has had the effect of reducing air-passenger movements over shorter distances.

The growth of air-freight traffic has been just as impressive. Annual tonnages for West German airports increased from a paltry 114,000 in 1960 to 888,000 in 1979, although the quantity has yet to account for even 1 per cent of total goods movement within the country.[61] In the freight sector the dominance of Frankfurt airport is even more pronounced, this airport handling as much as 70 per cent of all West German air cargo in 1979. As one would expect, low-bulk and high-value goods, including electrical articles and small machine components, are the most important sources of business.

The fast growth of traffic at several West German airports, in particular Frankfurt, Dusseldorf and Munich, has required major extensions to systems of runways. In recent years runway extensions have become highly controversial, and have aroused fierce opposition from environmentalist and local protest groups, notably at Frankfurt.

Pipelines. The development of pipelines was extremely rapid during the era of cheap and plentiful oil. This lasted until the early 1970s, by which time 1,597 km of crude-oil pipelines and a further 507 km of product pipelines were in operation in West Germany. Significantly, very few additions have been made to this network since the oil crisis.

The expansion of the pipeline network during the 1960s deprived both the railways and the inland waterways of a share in the then fast-growing traffic in crude oil. In 1960 just over 20 million tonnes of crude oil were transported within West Germany, 64 per cent of it by pipeline and the rest by the DB and the waterway system.[62] By 1973, however, when traffic in crude oil reached a peak of 91 million tonnes, pipelines accounted for as much as 97 per cent of the movement. Nevertheless, as far as the distribution of oil products was concerned, the waterways were able to retain their function, handling 46 per cent of tonnage in this particular field.

The geographical pattern of pipeline developments emphasises the four principal foci of refining capacity – the Lower Rhineland and Ruhr areas, the Mannheim–Karlsruhe area, Ingolstadt in central Bavaria and a grouping of plants within the Hamburg region. The Lower Rhineland–Ruhr focus includes important plants at Dinslaken, Gelsenkirchen and along the Rhine axis to the south of Cologne.[63] Crude-oil pipelines from Rotterdam and Wilhelmshaven serve these refineries, while there are also product pipelines linking Rotterdam and the Ruhr. Refineries in the Karlsruhe-Mannheim area of the Upper-Rhine valley receive crude oil piped from Marseilles and also from Genoa and Trieste via Ingolstadt. The pipelines from Genoa and Trieste also serve central Bavaria, while in northern Germany the Wilhelmshaven oil terminal is linked to a system focused on the refineries around Hamburg.

A further development has been the extension of natural-gas pipelines since the 1960s. West Germany receives supplies of natural gas from her neighbouring countries, but the most significant development has been the agreement with the Soviet Union for gas to be piped via Czechoslovakia to the Nuremberg area in central Bavaria.

Developments in Urban Transport

Until the late 1950s few West Germans travelled significant distances to work, to shop, or to visit entertainment or cultural facilities in the cities. Moreover, the vast majority of personal journeys at this time were undertaken by public transport, motor cycle, cycle or on foot. In addition to the low personal incomes and limited levels of car ownership, two other factors contributed to this situation. First, the postwar reconstruction of residential properties in most West German cities had been characterised by the erection of high-density apartment buildings, most of which were located within the confines of the prewar, inner-city districts. As a result, many people continued to live in close proximity to their place of work and to the shopping and other facilities offered by the rebuilt city centres. The second factor was the limited investment in urban public transport. Interwar networks of tram and bus services were re-established, but few were extended in geographical terms. Many tram and bus routes terminated at the edge of the existing built-up areas and administrative boundaries of cities. The lack of co-ordination of the services of different transport media, and of services operated by neighbouring local authorities within the major conurbations, further handicapped the degree of personal travel-mobility during the early part of the postwar period.[64]

Rising personal wealth and rapidly increasing levels of car ownership from the late 1950s onwards had immediate and drastic effects upon patterns of urban travel. A growing number of families were able to satisfy their desire for newer and more attractively situated houses by moving out from the inner-city districts to small dormitory towns and villages within the hinterlands of large cities. Accordingly, while the populations of most major urban areas began first to level off and then decrease, those of the adjacent urban-rural fringes began to grow dramatically. Thus, journeys to work and other urban visits became progressively longer, and were made increasingly by private car rather than by public transport.[65]

In the cities themselves the growth of motor traffic created mounting problems of congestion, noise and pollution. The historic and symbolic Altstadt cores, with their narrow and irregular patterns of streets, were threatened the most, and already several valued buildings here were being demolished to make way for road improvements. By the early 1960s, therefore, city planners in West Germany faced an acute dilemma. How could they accommodate the motor car, which by now had become a cherished status symbol for many citizens, while still preserving not only the unique character and ambience of Altstadt areas, but also the organic structures of cities as a whole?

By the middle of the decade the authorities in West Germany, unlike their counterparts in Britain, had come to accept the urgent need for a balanced approach to the urban transport problem, an approach which would incorporate not only additional road construction and schemes of traffic management, but also other investments designed to make public transport more efficient and more attractive, especially for work journeys. The commitment of the federal government to such policies was underlined in 1967 by the imposition of a special levy on petrol, the proceeds of which were to be used to help finance road construction and public-transport improvements in urban areas. The revenue accrued by the federal government was to meet 60 per cent of the capital costs of all such projects, the remaining balance being found by the Land and city authorities. Initially, 40 per cent of the total fund was made available for public-transport developments, and 60 per cent for road construction. Subsequently, these proportions were adjusted to 50 per cent in each case, and in addition the levy itself was doubled during the mid-1970s from 3 pfennigs per litre of petrol to 6 pfennigs.[66]

The 1967 legislation gave a considerable impetus to urban transport investment, and in particular to proposals for extending and integrating public-transport services within the major conurbations. Between 1967 and 1977 the federal government provided DM 14.2 billions for improvements in urban transport, of which DM 6.6 billions were ear-marked for the public sector.[67]

Public Transport in Urban Areas

Objectives and Organisation. The objectives of urban public-transport investment in West Germany were clearly defined during the 1960s. The overriding aim in the large urban agglomerations was to create integrated systems of public-transport services in which the various transport media would be complementary rather than competitive. Indeed, competition between parallel routes was to be avoided wherever possible, and public transport was to be promoted as a single cohesive network which would provide an attractive alternative to the use of private cars.

From the outset it was recognised that individual modes of public transport were best suited to particular tasks. In these, a hierarchy of services would be created. Thus, for peak flows of traffic between the suburbs and city centres, fixed-rail, rapid-transit systems were the most appropriate, while buses could be used to provide feeder services and distribution along the less busy of the across-town axes.

Other key elements in the public-transport strategies of recent years have been the establishment of common fares structures, together with the introduction of single-ticket tariffs effective for travel on entire city, and even regional, communications systems. Co-operation between the various transport operators was crucial for the achievement of these objectives, especially within the polycentric conurbations. Accordingly, the formation of *Verkehrsbunde* – joint marketing companies owned by all the transport operators and charged with the task of planning and selling of public transport on their joint behalf – has become an important organisational feature in Hamburg, Munich, Stuttgart, Frankfurt and the Rhine-Rhur.[68] In these areas the Verkehrsbunde establish the fares structures, plan the network and co-ordination of the various transport media, and devise the formulae for dividing the revenue amongst the member operators. Elsewhere, several city authorities have copied the basic principles embodied by the Verkehrsbunde, marketing their transport services under a single banner and often using very attractive pamphlets and posters to advertise their networks. The *Verkehrs Aktion Gesellschaft Nürnberg* (VAGN), for example, embraces local bus, tram and 'U' Bahn operations over the entire Nuremberg conurbation.

In four of West Germany's largest monocentric urban agglomerations (Hamburg, Munich, Stuttgart and Frankfurt) the Verkehrsbunde also involve a partnership with the DB, which operates the specialised 'S' Bahn rapid-transit systems in addition to its conventional train services. The polycentric urban structure of the Rhine-Ruhr region has made this area a special case, both in terms of its Verkehrsbund organisation (with its 22 member operators) and the character and pattern of transport facilities that have been developed.

Implementation and Operation. The 'S' Bahn networks of Frankfurt, Stuttgart, Hamburg, Munich and the Rhine-Ruhr (Figure 6.5) provide the most spectacular and best-publicised examples of the West German approach to public-transport provision. From the outset a distinction must be made between the systems which operate in the four monocentric agglomerations and that of the polycentric pattern of cities within the Rhine-Ruhr. However, there are a number of common features. In essence 'S' Bahns are specialised electric trains which operate a frequent service between the suburbs and the city centre, using existing suburban and main-line railways on a track-sharing basis with conventional passenger and freight traffic. However, where conventional traffic is heavy, segregated 'S' Bahn tracks may be provided, as on the Munich-Augsburg axis, where the poor timekeeping of international trains from Italy and the Balkans presents special difficulties.

A distinctive and very expensive feature of 'S' Bahn engineering, particularly within the monocentric urban areas, is the *Verbindungsbahn* (connecting tunnel) which serves to bundle the several radial routes into

Figure 6.5: West Germany: 'S' Bahn Networks, 1980

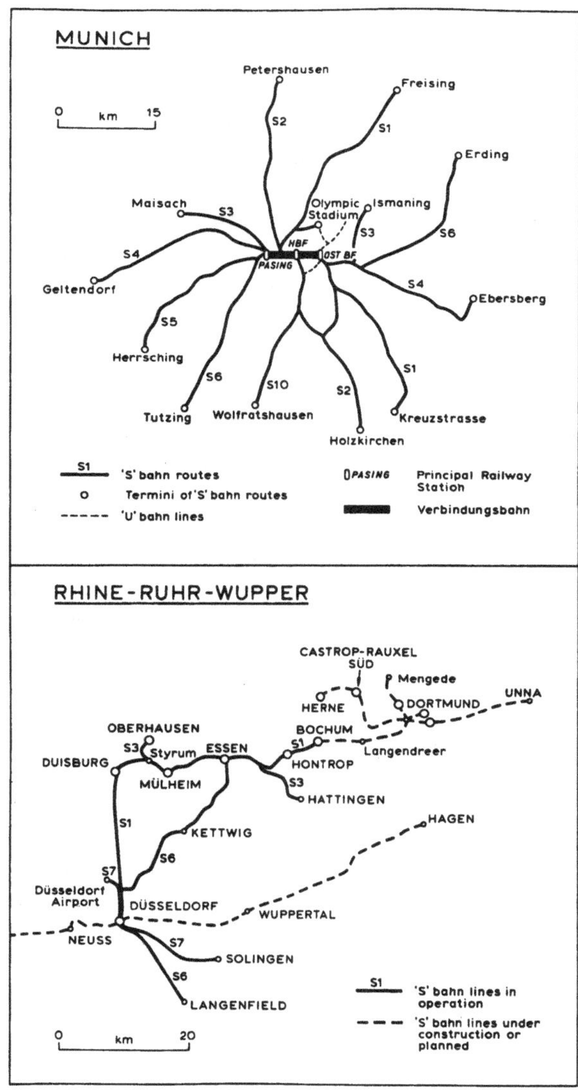

Source: H. Weigelt, 'S-Bahn systems in Germany: Concepts, Operation Strategies and Components', *DB Information* (updated), p. 12; also, Deutsche Bundesbahn, *Kursbuch 1980-81*, timetables, nos. 180-97 and 990-8.

and beneath the city centre. Usually running for 4-6 km, the Verbindungsbahn forms the hub of a whole 'S' Bahn system, for it carries the heaviest traffic, and normally includes four or five stations to provide maximum access to the city centre.

The example of the Munich 'S' Bahn, completed in 1972, illustrates the nature of the system within a monocentric conurbation. Here, the Verbindungsbahn brings twelve radial lines into the city centre. The Munich network is the most extensive system to date, and reaches several dormitory communities situated well beyond the local authority's area of jurisdiction. Service intervals from the outer termini are 40 min, and the frequency increases to 20 min in the inner suburbs and just 2-4 min on the city-centre link. Journey-times from the outer termini to the city centre average 40 min. On the more compact Hamburg network, however, journey times of between 10 and 15 min can be maintained.[69]

Both the Frankfurt and Stuttgart 'S' Bahn systems are still far from completion, while only about one-third of the proposed Rhine-Ruhr network is in operation. Early in 1982, following protracted negotiations between DB, Land Bavaria and the Nuremberg city authorities, agreement was reached for the development of an 'S' Bahn within the Nuremberg conurbation. Here, the system is intended to operate through the existing main railway station, as the size of the Nuremberg agglomeration does not justify massive expenditure on a separate connecting tunnel.[70]

Some indication of the contribution of 'S' Bahn systems towards the easing of the urban transport problem in West Germany can be gained from passenger statistics. For example, prior to the opening of the Munich system, the city's pre-existing railway services carried 160,000 passengers per day. During its first year of operation the 'S' Bahn attracted as many as 250,000 daily travellers, and within five years this figure was doubled.[71] In the Rhine-Ruhr, passenger levels on the Dusselforf-Essen line also doubled during the first five years of 'S' Bahn operation. Not only have the 'S' Bahnen proved themselves in terms of passenger popularity, but they have also brought important social and environmental benefits. Travel-times for numerous suburban and urban-rural-fringe communities have been substantially reduced by these systems, while city dwellers have been provided with much better accessibility to outlying leisure and recreational facilities.[72] Just as important has been the reduction of car journeys and associated pollution levels. Estimates for the Munich area, for example, indicate a decline in car usage of 70,000 vehicles per day, while CO_2 pollution levels have dropped by 11 per cent.[73] It can also be argued that the 'S' Bahn systems have provided an attractive image-maker which adds to the prestige of those cities which possess such networks.

'U' Bahn Systems. 'U' Bahn systems have been constructed in several West German cities. One which has already been mentioned in Chapters 2 and 5 is the evolving Nuremberg network, and this is worth describing now in some detail. The first section of the Nuremberg 'U' Bahn was opened in the early 1970s, linking the satellite town of Langwasser (8 km to the southeast of the city centre) to the central railway station. Since then the 'U' Bahn system has been extended beneath the commercial quarter of the Altstadt, and development is now continuing towards the neighbouring city of Fürth. The growth of passenger movement has been impressive, with figures increasing from 5.4 million passenger journeys in the first year of operation to 34.3 million in 1980. Meanwhile, its share of total VAGN traffic has increased from 4.6 per cent to 21.7 per cent.[74]

However, the financial situation with regard to 'U' Bahnen, and indeed the 'S' Bahnen and some of the Verkehrsbunde operations, has aroused growing concern in recent years. Most systems cover less than 60 per cent of total costs from fares revenue, and several have incurred substantial financial losses. The 1967 legislation did not provide revenue support for urban public transport, but merely assistance for construction costs. This neglect has led to considerable argument in political circles as to who should bear the operational deficits. Meanwhile, the most recent passenger statistics for the Verkehrsbund areas indicate yet another worrying trend – a pronounced deceleration of annual growth-rates in passenger totals. In Hamburg, for example, the 1980-1 increase was only 2.8 per cent, while in Munich it was a very disturbing 0.5 per cent.[75]

Public-transport investment in the near future will be safeguarded by the revenue on oil tax which the federal government has augmented in recent years to offset the effects of depressed demand for petrol and oil. Nevertheless, it is clear that future proposals will be more closely vetted, not only in terms of the social and environmental benefits which they could provide, but also with regard to the willingness of local authorities to assume an additional share of the financial responsibilities.

The West German commitment to investment in transport at all scales remains unaltered, but the era of unlimited expenditure is clearly at an end. Increasingly, new projects are being more closely screened, and there is a tendency today for construction and operating costs to be given greater priority than social and environmental benefits. Progress towards the objective of an integrated, multi-modal transport system will doubtless continue, but the imposition of financial constraints may ultimately restrict its achievement to a limited number of favoured localities.

Notes

1. M.T. Wild, *West Germany, a Geography of its People* (W. Dawson & Son, Folkestone, 1979, and Longman Group, Harlow, 1981), p. 67.
2. Commerzbank, *Die Bundesrepublik Deutschland in Zahlen, 1979-80* (Commerzbank, Frankfurt, 1980), table on *Aussenhandel.*
3. M.T. Wild, *West Germany*, pp. 190-1.
4. H.H. Blotevogel, and M. Hommel, 'Structure and Development of the Urban System', in P. Schöller, W.W. Puls and H.J. Buchholz (eds), *The Federal Republic of Germany: Spatial Development and Problems* (Bochumer Geographische Arbeiten, Bochum, 1980), ch. 1, p. 30.
5. Bundesministerium für Verkehr, *Verkehr in Zahlen*, 1976 edn (Deutsches Institut für Verkehr, Berlin, 1976), p. 114.
6. Statistisches Bundesamt, *Statistisches Jahrbuch für die Bundesrepublik*, 1981 edn (W. Kohlhammer Verlag, Stuttgart and Mainz, 1981), p. 280.
7. Presse- und Informationsamt der Bundesregierung, *Gesellschaftliche Daten 1979* (A. Bernecker Verlag, Melsungen, 1979), p. 231.
8. Bundesministerium für Verkehr, *Verkehr in Zahlen*, 1980 edn, p. 122.
9. Ibid., 1976 edn, p. 175.
10. Ibid., 1976 edn, p. 164.
11. Ibid., 1976 edn, p. 131, and Statistisches Bundesamt, *Statistisches Jahrbuch*, 1981 edn, p. 273.
12. Statistisches Bundesamt, *Statistisches Jahrbuch*, 1981 edn, p. 273.
13. Bundesministerium für Verkehr, *Verkehr in Zahlen*, 1976 edn, p. 102.
14. Ibid., 1980 edn, p. 106.
15. Bundesministerium für Verkehr, *Verkehrswege* (BMfV, Berlin, 1964), p. 116.
16. The Saarland did not become a constitutional part of the Federal Republic until 1957.
17. R.E.H. Mellor, *The Two Germanies: a Modern Geography* (London, 1978), p. 314.
18. Bundesministerium für Verkehr, *Netz der Bundesautobahnen und Bundesstrassen* (BMfV, Frankfurt, 1981), 1:750,000 scale maps.
19. Bundesministerium für Verkehr, *Verkehr in Zahlen*, 1976 edn, pp. 150-62, and 1980 edn, pp. 165-77.
20. G. Freeman Allen, 'Freight on the German Federal Intermodal and Unit trains', *Modern Railways* (April 1982), p. 172.
21. Ibid., p. 172.
22. Deutsche Bundesbahn, *Geschäftsbericht der BRD*, 1979 edn (Brönners Druckerei, Frankfurt, 1979), p. 50.
23. Bundesministerium für Verkehr, *Verkehr in Zahlen*, 1980 edn, p. 171.
24. Ibid., 1980 edn, p. 185.
25. Ibid., 1976 edn, p. 186, and 1980 edn, p. 201.

27. Deutsche Bundesbahn, *Geschäftsbericht*, 1979 edn, p. 18.
28. Compare this proportion with that of just 5 per cent in 1950.
29. Deutsche Bundesbahn, *Kursbuch 1980-81* (Deutsche Bundesbahn, Frankfurt, 1981), *Übersichts Karte*.
30. Freeman Allen, 'Freight on the German Federal Intermodal and Unit trains', p. 121.
31. Ibid., p. 174.
32. Ibid., p. 125.
33. K. Burk, 'West German railways: timed to perfection', *Transport* (July/August 1981), p. 7.
34. Deutsche Bundesbahn, *Kursbuch 1980-81*, IC Fahrplan.
35. Deutsche Bundesbahn, *Geschäftsbericht*, 1979 edn, p. 22.
36. K. Burk, 'West German railways', p. 7.
37. Bundesministerium für Verkehr, *Verkehr in Zahlen*, 1980 edn, p. 63.
38. Mellor, *The Two Germanies*, p. 313.
39. Freeman Allen, 'Freight on the German Federal Intermodal and Unit trains', p. 172.
40. Bundesministerium für Verkehr, *Verkehr in Zahlen*, 1980 edn, pp. 176-7.
41. Ibid., 1976 edn, pp. 166-87.
42. Ibid., 1980 edn, p. 171.
43. Statistisches Bundesamt, *Statistisches Jahrbuch*, 1981 edn, pp. 290-1.
44. Ibid., pp. 290-1.
45. D. Burtenshaw, *Economic Geography of West Germany* (London, 1974), p. 48.
46. Bundesministerium für Verkehr, *Verkehr in Zahlen*, 1980 edn, p. 110.
47. E. Otremba, 'Constraints and changes in traffic', in P. Schöller, W.W. Puls and H.J. Buchholz (eds), *The Federal Republic of Germany: Spatial Development and Problems* (Bochumer Geographische Arbeiten, Bochum, 1980), p. 36.
48. Bundesministerium für Verkehr, *Verkehr in Zahlen*, 1980 edn, pp. 74-5. See also D. Wulf, 'Inland navigation in Europe, its tasks and problems', *Geojournal*, vol. 1, no. 2 (1977), p. 28.
49. Statistisches Bundesamt, *Statistisches Jahrbuch*, 1981 edn, p. 290.
50. Freeman Allen, 'Freight on the German Federal Intermodal and Unit trains', p. 176.
51. Bundesministerium für Verkehr, *Verkehr in Zahlen*, 1980 edn, p. 76; and Statistisches Bundesamt, *Statistisches Jahrbuch*, 1981 edn, p. 290.
52. Statistisches Landesamt Bayern, *Umschlag der wichtigsten Häfen am Main und Main-Donau Kanal* (SLB, Munich, 1980).
53. D. Wulf, 'Inland navigation in Europe', p. 30.
54. Bundesministerium für Verkehr, *Verkehr in Zahlen*, 1980 edn, pp. 82-3.
55. Ibid., 1980 edn, pp. 82-3.
56. Ibid., 1980 edn, p. 87.
57. Ibid., 1980 edn, p. 87.
58. Ibid., 1976 edn, p. 87, and 1980 edn, pp. 84-5.
59. Ibid., 1976 edn, pp. 96-7, and 1980 edn, pp. 98-9.
60. Ibid., 1980 edn, pp. 98-9.
61. Ibid., 1980 edn, pp. 100-1.
62. Ibid., 1980 edn, pp. 186-7.
63. Mellor, *The Two Germanies*, p. 218.
64. Wild, *West Germany*, pp. 97-8.
65. Ibid., p. 99.
66. H. Weigelt, 'New developments in heavy railway systems', *DB Information* (undated), p. 280.
67. H. Weigelt, 'S-Bahn systems in Germany: concepts, operation strategies

and components', *DB Information* (undated), p. 12.

68. Weigelt, 'New developments', p. 281.

69. Deutsche Bundesbahn, *Kursbuch 1980-81*, timetables, nos. 180-97 and 990-8.

70. Weigelt, 'New developments', p. 281.

71. Ibid., p. 295.

72. V. Kreibich, 'The successful transportation system and the regional planning problem: an evaluation of the Munich rapid-transit system in the context of urban and regional planning policy', *Transportation*, vol. 7 (1978), p. 137.

73. Weigelt, 'New developments', p. 295.

74. E. Wetzel, 'U-Bahn, Nürnberg-Fürth', *Modern Tramways*, vol. 45, no. 532 (1982), p. 141.

75. G. Freeman Allen, 'Underpinning public transport in West Germany', *Modern Railways* (May 1982), p. 203.

7 THE RESIDENTIAL DIMENSION TO RURAL CHANGE

Trevor Wild

The traditional image of the inhabited part of the West German countryside is one of a strongly humanised rural landscape which is characterised widely by quiet agricultural villages, timber-framed farmsteads and a centuries-old tapestry of tiny fields, lush meadows and dark tracts of forest. Today, however, this romantic picture, although still popularised in tourist literature, is disappearing rapidly from all save the most isolated and backward farming regions. It is being replaced by a plainer and more functional type of man-made scenery, which bears not only the hallmarks of West Germany's postwar 'agricultural revolution', but also the physical manifestations of the ever-widening diffusion of urban influences. It is with this latter process of rural change, and more specifically the phenomenon of 'rural suburbanisation', that this chapter is primarily concerned.

Strikingly observable as the explosive intrusion of modern residential development, rural suburbanisation, or to use the German term, *Ländlichesuburbanisierung* is exerting a major impact in the countryside around more or less every sizeable city throughout the developed western world. But, in considering its effects today, it is still easy enough – even in this present age of seemingly growing uniformity of general patterns of urban-rural interaction – to recognise salient differences from one culture 'province' to another. Geographic variations of this nature are particularly well in evidence amongst the nation states of western Europe which, with their highly diverse physical conditions, depth of historical traditions, different rates of economic growth and divergent approaches to the management of land use and settlement fabric, demonstrate the dangers inherent in adopting the more extreme versions of global-type theorisation and conceptual ordering which all too frequently appear in our general literature on urban growth. Arguably, there is nowhere else where this criticism can be more strongly exemplified than in West Germany, for in this country residential dispersal from city to surrounding countryside has its own distinctive qualities. The three most salient of these qualities may be mentioned now as themes to be reviewed in the course of this chapter: first, the lateness and suddenness of the full outbreak of the process;

secondly, the impressive character of its spatial expression; lastly, the 'shock' which it has presented to systems of local and regional planning. However, before consideration can be given to these themes, it is necessary to turn our attention in some detail to the main causal factors of rural suburbanisation, dealing first of all with the quantity of postwar housing construction, and then moving on to such pertinent issues as the decline in the apartment tradition, the escalating costs of development land, the upsurge in personal, daily travel-mobility and the dispersal of job opportunities.

Factors of Residential Dispersal

Quantity of Housing Construction

The sheer magnitude of West Germany's postwar housing programme could hardly have been accomplished without some considerable extension of residential land use. The statistics on housing construction speak very much for themselves; 17.6 million dwellings built between 1945 and 1979, an average yearly completion rate of 518,000 homes and (bearing in mind that there have been more than one million demolitions in the interim) a net increase in the nation's total stock of residential accommodation from around 8.5 millions to 24.7 millions.[1] Measured in terms of new homes per standard number of population, there are very few developed countries which can match West Germany's level of achievement. Since 1950 its annual index of 'building intensity' has averaged 9.1 dwelling completions per 1,000 persons. This rate of progress is significantly higher than the corresponding average of 8.1 in the USA, and easily surpasses the figures for most other industrialised countries including France (7.5), the United Kingdom (6.1), Belgium (5.6) and Italy (4.7).[2]

These are convincing measures of the scale of West Germany's 'housing miracle', an accomplishment which, in spite of the addition of more than 12 million extra households since 1945, has brought a remarkable advance from a position of chronic accommodation shortage in the early postwar years to one of sizeable (if by no means nationwide) surplus by the early 1970s. However, as is shown by the graph of annual dwelling completions (Figure 7.1), progress has been far from even in temporal terms. Three phases of particularly heavy activity can be identified: first, the years 1953-7 when annual completions were consistently just above 550,000; secondly, the period 1959-67 when they hovered around 600,000; lastly, the property boom of 1971-4 which, with the graph peaking at 714,200 new dwellings in 1973, saw the breaking of all previous records.

Each of these 'growth phases' lay between occasions of what, by West German standards, must be regarded as poor performances. The first of these belonged to the early postwar years when limited financial resources and shortages of materials hindered the building industry's capacity to meet the huge needs of replacing wartime losses, and also to provide housing for the mounting influx of refugees and expellees. Estimates put the number of destroyed homes at approximately 2.5 millions; but even this large figure was dwarfed by the 5.6 million new dwellings which were required for the first five years of the refugee–expellee influx.[3] The second and third depressions in the graph came respectively in 1958 and during the years 1968-70. Reflecting sudden, but short-lived, falterings in the nation's general economic wellbeing, these irregularities certainly caused concern at the time, yet they were of minor significance compared with the severity of the most recent downturn. This commenced in 1975 when the completion rate fell by a staggering 26 per cent. By 1978 it had plunged to 368,100, the lowest annual recording since 1949. The trend can be partly blamed on the adverse economic climate of the mid- and late 1970s, but it can also be viewed as an inevitable reaction to the so-called *Wohnungshalde* (housing mountain) created by the 1971-4 property boom.

Decline of the Apartment Tradition

Rather surprisingly for a country which in many other important respects is blessed with excellent statistical coverages, West Germany has undertaken only two national surveys on the composition of its *aggregate* housing stock. These were the now much outdated housing census of 1968 and the rather unreliable 5 per cent sample-survey of 1972. Fortunately, however, consistent information does exist on certain vital features of annual dwelling completions.[4] Beginning only a few years after the end of the Second World War, this is suitable enough for charting the two most salient responses to the affluence movement: first, the general trend away from the apartment tradition; secondly, the corresponding shift towards detached, semi-detached and terrace-row houses (henceforth to be described collectively as individual homes or *Einfamiliehäuser*).

In West Germany apartments are normally defined as homes which exist within residential buildings of at least three dwellings (*Drei-oder Mehrfamilienhäuser*). As elsewhere in western Europe the origins of apartment-type housing can be traced back several centuries, but it was

Figure 7.1: West Germany: Trends in New Housing Completions during the Postwar Period

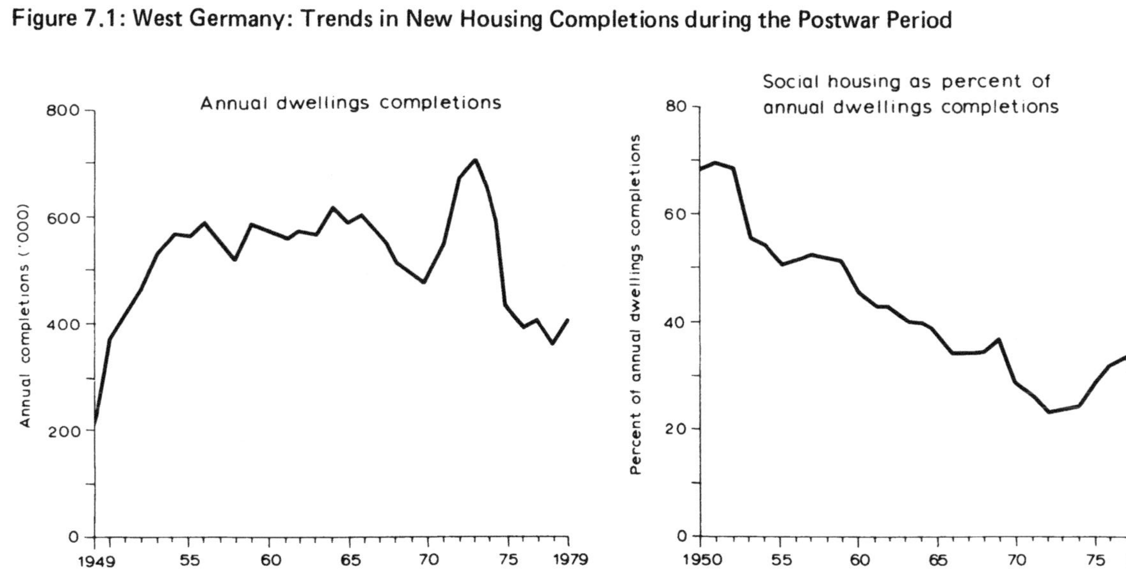

Figure 7.1: Continued

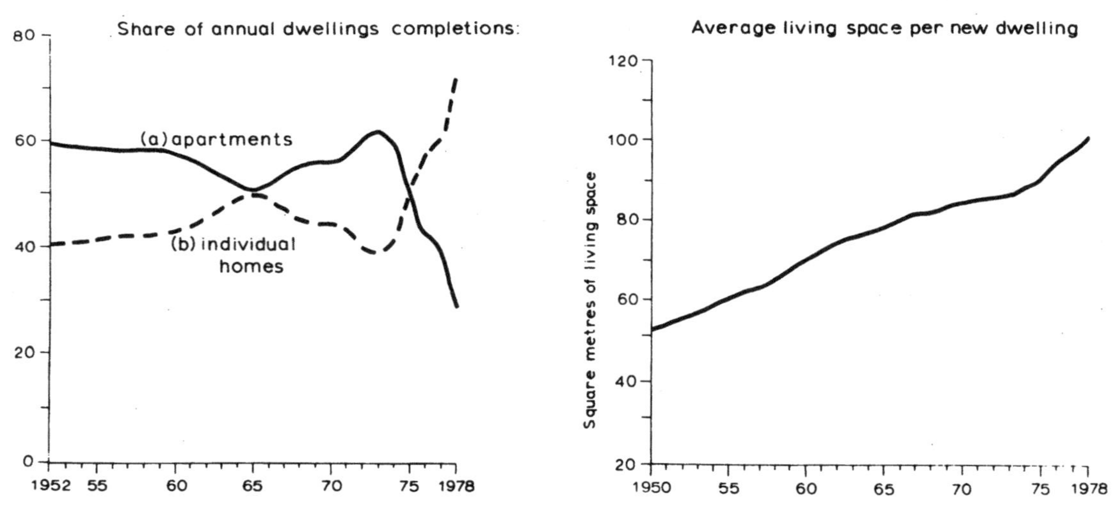

Source: Presse-und Informationsamt der Bundesregierung, *Gesellschaftliche Daten 1979* (A. Bernecker Verlag, Melsungen, 1979), Tables on 'Wohnungsbestand' and 'Qualität der Wohnungen', pp. 236-45; also, annual edns of Statistisches Bundesamt, *Fachserie E: Gebäude- und Wohnungszahlen* (SB, Wiesbaden).

not until the vigorous, yet highly concentrated, urbanisation of the industrial revolution that it reached a predominant position. Thus, during the period of the Second Empire (1871-1918), apartments were reported to have accounted for as much as 61 per cent of Germany's total residential development.[5] Since then, however, their popularity among builders has fluctuated considerably. The first of several quite abrupt changes of direction in fact came during the 1920s and 1930s when, as a response to the widespread implementation of new concepts of working-class housing provision, the apartment share fell by 19 percentage points.[6]

But such early inroads into the apartment tradition came to a sudden end immediately after the Second World War, when most German towns and cities were confronted with the overriding urgency of replacing blitzed homes as quickly and cheaply as possible. For several years the great need for speed and cheapness of residential reconstruction was the paramount reason for the renewed emphasis on apartments. However, one should also bear in mind that within the devastated cities it had been this particular type of housing, with its tight concentrations in the innermost ring of residential suburbs, that had suffered by far the heaviest wartime destruction. Accordingly, when hostilities ended it was here where the greatest demand for accommodation was focused. One further point which is worth mentioning is that the early postwar years were a time of very low car ownership and largely unrestored urban transport systems. Thus, few city planning departments could, at the time, think much more than in terms of recreating the crowded residential environments of the inner cities.

A major stimulus for apartment construction came in 1950 with the introduction of the first Federal Housing Act. This legislation is known principally for its greatly increased financial support for the building of social housing (*Sozialwohnungsbau*), but significant too were the various stipulations concerning the allocation of public subsidies. As a normal rule the highest priority was given to encouraging the construction of new rental accommodation, especially simple two-bedroom apartments with between just 50 and 70 m^2 of floorspace. It is interesting to note that these small and often crudely built dwellings accounted for almost three-quarters of the 1.9 million subsidised homes completed in West Germany during the years 1950-5.[7]

In 1952 the Fe 'eral Statistical Office (Housing and Buildings Department) began to compile information on the qualitative characteristics of all annual dwelling completions.[8] The earliest set of figures showed apartments accounting for 59.7 per cent of new homes, and this was a substantial increase on their 42.0 per cent share during the interwar period. However, during the rest of the 1950s and continuing until 1965 when a 'mini-trough' of 50.3 per cent was recorded, the trend was one of slow but steady decline in the apartment proportion (Figure 7.1). Then, against all expectations, the direction of the graph suddenly altered. By 1970 it had climbed to 55.9 per cent, and three years later a postwar record of 61.1 per cent was established. This phase, which has been described aptly as the *Mietwohnungsbau Nachsommer* ('Indian Summer' of apartment construction), owed much to the strong intervention of large-scale property and finance companies into a field of building activity which had formerly been dominated by private individuals, co-operatives, housing associations and industrial sponsors.[9] Encouraged by a major wave of price inflation in the market for residential properties, these companies not only played a leading part in producing the controversial 'housing mountain' but they also, by concentrating on apartments and flats, turned their backs against the growing popularity of individual homes.

The ill-judged boom in apartment construction reached a peak annual rate of 436,400 units in 1973. However, immediately after this there came a dramatic decline in the figures of apartment completions, with yearly totals falling steeply to 226,300 in 1975, 167,200 in 1976 and just 109,000 at the end of the decade (Figure 7.1). Significantly, the post-1973 contraction in housing demand in West Germany has had much less effect on the numbers of Einfamiliehäuser completions. At first, figures for this sector did show a marked drop (falling from 278,000 in 1973 to 210,500 in 1975), but more recently the trend has been upwards, rising to 245,000 in 1977 and passing 250,000 one year later.[10]

The net results of these trends has been the sudden displacement of apartments as the predominant type of new housing provision in West Germany. This distinction now belongs to the various categories of individual homes, whose collective contribution to annual dwelling completions moved to just above 50 per cent in 1976, and then advanced to a remarkable 71 per cent in 1978. In spite of the much reduced quantity of building activity since the early 1970s, this late but rapid swing to Einfamiliehäuser has had the immediate effect of intensifying pressures on the country's resources of development land, and through this acting as a major encouragement to the process of residential dispersal. The reason why becomes apparent when one considers the figures presented in Table 7.1. Here, information for seven different categories of dwellings has been compiled from the list of planning guidelines first drawn up under the terms of the 1965 *Bundeswohnungsbaugesetz* (Federal Residential Building Act).[11] Of particular interest are the maximum permissible densities for new residential development, although it should be noted that these limits apply only to estates with areas of at least 1 ha. Among the four varieties of individual homes, the densities range from 25 dwellings per ha for bungalows to exactly twice this figure for terrace-row houses. But more significant is the amplitude of difference between the weighted means of 32 dwellings per ha for all Einfamiliehäuser and 85 dwellings per ha for the three types of apartments. To all intents and purposes this means that residential planning policy in West Germany is working on the principle that, for equivalent numbers of dwellings, each new estate of individual homes requires nearly three times as much land as an apartment.

Table 7.1: West Germany: 1965 Guidelines for New Residential Development

Housing type	Floorspace in m²	Land required per dwelling in m²	Net residential density[a]
Bungalow	160	400	25
Detached house	130	320	31
Semi-detached house	120	300	33
Terrace-row house	90	200	50
Individual houses, weighted mean	128	310	32
Apartment in res. building			
3-dwellings	90	125	80
6-dwellings	90	120	83
9-dwellings	90	109	92
Apartments, weighted mean	90	118	85

Note: a. Measured as dwellings per ha of development land.

Source: Bundesministerium für Raumordnung, Bauwesen und Städtebau, *Das Wohnen in der Bundesrepublik Deutschland, Ausgabe 1965* (BRBS, Bonn, 1966).

Cost of Development Land

To understand why the spatial distribution of the various forms of new housing development in West Germany tends to be particularly sensitive to variations in the cost of building sites, one must look first at the inflation factor. Since the early 1960s there has been a tremendous upsurge in the prices of development land, with average valuations (per 100 m^2) rising from DM 1,150 in 1962 to DM 4,660 in 1978.[12] This increase was about five times faster than the country's general inflation rate and nearly three times faster than the rise in costs of residential construction. Moreover, the trend has been accompanied by intensifying geographical differences, with broad regional imbalances now being easily outweighed by the rapidly magnifying contrasts between urban and rural prices. Some impression of the scale of urban-rural differences can be gained from the statistics which are presented in Table 7.2 and 7.3. Table 7.2 gives averages of building-land prices (1978 figures) for all size-categories of settlements, ranging from small rural communities to the largest cities. The latter, of course, attract by far the heaviest quantity of land-use competition, and accordingly produce easily the highest valuation. Indeed, their figure of DM 16,772 per 100 m^2 is almost double the price which is represented in the next largest group of centres (cities with populations between 200,000 and 500,000). Proceeding further down the scale, it is not until one comes to settlements of just 10,000-20,000 inhabitants that the cost of building land at last drops short of the national average. The figure of DM 2,550 in communities with populations less than 2,000 falls furthest below this level, and stands at only 15 per cent of the valuation at the opposite end of the settlement spectrum.

Table 7.2: West Germany: Average Prices of Building Land According to Settlement-size, 1978

	Population-size of settlements								
	under 2,000	2,000-5,000	5,000-10,000	10,000-20,000	20,000-50,000	50,000-100,000	100,000-200,000	200,000-500,000	over 500,000
DM per 100 m^2	2,550	3,360	4,030	4,650	4,660	6,980	8,440	8,890	16,720

Source: Statistisches Bundesamt, *Statistisches Jahrbuch für die Bundesrepublik Deutschland*, 1979 edn (W. Kohlhammer Verlag, Stuttgart and Mainz, 1979), tables on Baulandpreise.

Even more impressive than the range of differences according to settlement size are the gradients of price decline as one proceeds outwards from urbanised areas. These are likewise expressive of spatial differences in the degree of competition for development land, in this case the general distance-decay of pressure from cities to the extremities of their rural hinterlands. The price gradients, therefore, are steepest within the built-up areas of cities where there is a very pronounced concave curve of falling values from the commercial core to the outer suburbs. This feature has been measured by Polensky in a study based on land-sale transactions in Munich during the years 1971-2.[13] His findings showed prices of development land reaching a peak of DM 214,400 per 100 m² within the heart of Munich's central business district. In the inner-city zone, however, they averaged DM 53,600, while in the outer suburbs the figure was DM 18,000. As shown in Table 7.3, the falling trend continues well beyond the city boundary, with land prices dropping progressively right through the urban-rural fringe and not stabilising until locales of truly rural quality are approached some 35 km away. Table 7.3 also shows the effect of inflation during the years 1971-4, when the valuations for the 0-5-km and 40-45-km distance-intervals rose by DM 7,902 and DM 1,475 respectively, and produced a 46 per cent steepening in the overall amplitude of the price gradient.

Table 7.3: Munich Region: Prices of Building Land According to Distances from City Boundary, 1971-4

Distance range (km)	Number of Gemeinden[a]	Average price in DM per 100 m²		Absolute difference
		1971	1974	1971-4
0-5	8	14,604	22,506	+7,902
5-10	7	8,700	10,800	+2,100
10-15	24	7,250	10,684	+3,434
15-20	24	5,388	7,718	+2,330
20-25	30	4,466	6,472	+2,006
25-30	32	3,356	5,096	+1,740
30-35	31	3,114	4,604	+1,490
35-40	34	2,776	4,252	+1,476
40-45	38[b]	2,774	4,249	+1,475

Notes: a. The distances are measured from the median point of each Gemeinde area.
b. Excluding nine Gemeinden which are affected by the proximity to Augsburg.

Source: Statistisches Landesamt Bayern, *Gemeinde Daten*, 1972 and 1975 edns (Statistisches Landesamt Bayern, Munich, 1972 and 1975).

The second reason why variations in land prices exert major influences on the character and spatial distribution of new housing development in West Germany resides in the difficulty of obtaining financial backing for the initial purchase of the residential plots. More often than not prospective house buyers, especially those who intend to use a dwelling for their personal owner-occupance, find that they have to secure the site before any building contracts can be arranged. This may involve a substantial commitment of personal savings, and accordingly special efforts are made by individuals to obtain the cheapest development land. Understandably, therefore, the wide differences in prices can have a very significant bearing on personal locational decisions, and not uncommonly take first priority over other considerations such as distance to place of work, access to basic services and nearness to friends and relations. They also exert a major influence on the geography of housing types, especially the clear contrast between the urban-orientated apartments and the non-urban emphasis of the individual homes (Table 7.4).

Table 7.4: West Germany: Housing Characteristics According to Degree of Urbanity, 1977

Type of environment	Individual homes as % of all dwellings	Apartment homes as % of all dwellings	Dwellings per residential building
Major cities	15.1	84.9	3.6
Small cities	36.3	64.7	2.3
Urban-rural fringes	73.3	26.7	1.9
Rural areas	86.8	13.2	1.5

Source: Statistisches Bundesamt, *Regionalen Daten über Wohnungsbestand und Wohnungsbautätigkeit* (Statistisches Bundesamt, Wiesbaden, 1979).

Daily Travel-mobility

While other influences, particularly dispersal of jobs and services, falling 'activity ratios'[14] and decreasing numbers and length of working days, have done much towards encouraging the trend, it is mainly because of West Germany's remarkable advance in daily travel-mobility that more and more people from an increasing variety of walks of life are now *able* to foresake the crowded cities and join the growing exodus of population to the cleaner, quieter and attractive environments of the surrounding countryside.

The tremendous upsurge in daily travel has been brought about by three positive factors: a greatly improved national and regional road pattern, modernisation and extension of public transport networks and, most significant of all, a massive increase in car ownership. Certain salient facts concerning these developments will suffice to highlight their contribution to the mobility theme. Turning first to West Germany's road system, we find the most important focus of investment has been the construction of over 6,000 km of postwar Autobahnen.

These now cover most parts of the country and leave only a small minority of large urban centres without close access. However, important too has been the expansion of the trunk-road (*Landesstrasse*) and secondary-road (*Kreisstrasse*) networks, whose overall distance has been increased by 35,000 km since 1950.[15]

In the field of public transport West Germany attracts the envy of all other west European countries. Electrification of most main lines and, for Hamburg, Frankfurt, Munich, Stuttgart, West Berlin and the Rhine-Ruhr cities, the introduction of high-speed commuter trains (*'S' Bahnen*) has provided it with one of the world's fastest and most efficient urban railway systems. There have also been substantial investments and innovations in city-focused tramway and omnibus services, whose combined length has nearly doubled from 324,000 km in 1950 to 599,000 km in 1978.[16] This huge increase has come mainly from route extensions (facilitated by the post-1968 enlargements of many urban administrative areas) and integration schemes implemented by regional groupings of local transport departments. Many of West Germany's city tram and bus networks, therefore, are now spread out over quite considerable radial distances: not many years ago very few went any further than the built-up limits.

Despite these developments, private vehicles have risen to a commanding position in West Germany. In 1950 they accounted for only 34 per cent of journeys inside the Federal Republic, but by 1960 their share had climbed sharply upwards to 65 per cent; today the figure is stabilising at around 80 per cent.[17] At first, this 'relative' displacement of public transport by private vehicles owed much to the practice of industrial companies running their own bus and minibus services as a means of widening their labour catchments. But since the mid-1950s the trend has been almost wholly a reflection of the upsurge in car ownership. The growth in car ownership is measured in Figure 7.2, where one can also draw useful comparisons with the USA, the United Kingdom and France. The graphs begin in 1945 when West Germany, with an index of less than one car per 100 persons, stood well behind each of the other three countries. In point of fact its level of car ownership was only one-sixth of the French figure, one-seventh of the United Kingdom's and a paltry 3 per cent of the USA's. A decade of prolonged austerity and, in comparison with what was happening within other developed western countries, low purchasing power meant only a slow advance in the West German graph. During the late 1950s, however, the social fruits of the postwar 'economic miracle' were at last being seen in a sudden acceleration of consumerism and living standards. This was

Figure 7.2: West Germany, USA, United Kingdom and France: Growth in Car Ownership, 1945-79

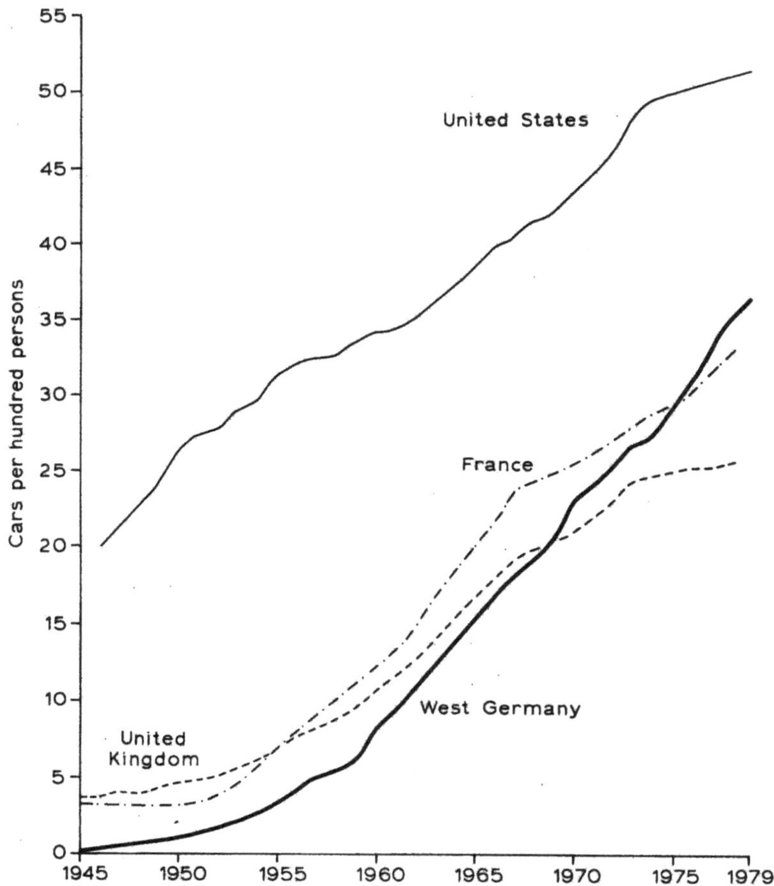

Source: the data for these graphs are from Statistisches Bundesamt, *Statistisches Jahrbuch für die Bundesrepublik Deutschland*, annual edns (W. Kohlhammer Verlag, Stuttgart and Mainz), tables on *Internationale Übersichten*.

accompanied by a quite distinct 'take-off' in car ownership. During the years from 1958 to 1967 car registration increased from 3.0 millions to 10.7 millions. At the end of this short period West Germany, for the very first time, could claim to be a more car-oriented society than the United Kingdom. In spite of the oil crisis and heavy increases in petrol prices there was no slackening in the trend during the 1970s. By 1976 car ownership in West Germany was moving ahead of the French index, and was also rising noticeably faster than in the USA. Today more than two thirds of West German families possess a vehicle, and more than one-quarter are in the happy position of owning at least two.

Dispersal of Employment

One consequence of these spectacular advances in travel-mobility is the tendency for the local geography of job opportunities to have rather less influence on patterns of population distribution than it did during the 1950s and early 1960s. Yet even today, when most workers have a car and few places are without at least one mode of public transport, the growing centrifugal shift of employment from cities into their hinterlands still has an important bearing on the rural suburbanisation process. It has a special significance for low-income families who, generally speaking, are not able to afford long distances to their work-place venues. Because of this, in those parts of the urban–rural fringe where jobs are being created, there exists a much greater degree of social diversity than is to be found in communities more singularly based on the dormitory function.

Until the changing economic circumstances of the 1970s, the dispersal of employment into rural and semi-rural areas was largely generated by the industrial sector. In this, the building of factories within what may be described as 'greenfield' locations was influenced by five conditions: first, West Germany's dynamic pace of economic growth, with its early emphasis on manufacturing output; secondly, with more and more people turning their backs on farming, the freeing of the rural labour force; thirdly, the escalating differences between urban and rural building-land prices; fourthly, the dwindling availability of urban sites either for extensions to existing businesses or for the construction of new factories; fifthly, the generous government assistance which is being offered to enterprises taking up locations within designated rural development areas and development centres, some of which (for example, in the vicinities of Hamburg, Bremen, Hanover, Lübeck and Nuremberg) are situated in quite close proximity to a major city.

The spatial expression of employment dispersal contains some interesting features. As has been demonstrated by Thürauf for the Munich region and Meckelein for the area around Stuttgart,[18] there is a general falling away in the intensity of job creation as one moves further and further away from the city. But irrespective of distance, certain places exert a special attraction. In the large majority of cases these are small to medium-sized towns with well-established service structures, good transport links and quite substantial catchments of local labour. Settlements of this size-range and advantaged by these characteristics are particularly common in West Germany, with large numbers appearing in every major city region. Not only are these places favoured by industrialists but they are also now proving to be well-suited locations for investments in tertiary activities, especially in the fields of retailing and public services. This means that in most cases continued employment growth is ensured despite the widespread contraction in manufacturing jobs over the last decade.

A typical example of the spatial character of employment dispersal can be seen in the territory which surrounds the Nuremberg-Fürth-Erlangen conurbation (Figure 7.3). Outside these three cities more than one-quarter of the population of the Nuremberg region lives in villages, but the settlement pattern also includes 42 outlying towns. These comprise four centres (Ansbach, Schwabach, Forchheim and Neustadt) with populations within the 15,000-40,000 range, ten centres with between 10,000 and 15,000 inhabitants and 28 others with populations under 10,000.[19] Not all of these places, however, have been able to attract a commensurable share of the 120,000 jobs added in the region since 1950. Those which have are nearly all to be found along one or other of the various development axes which radiate outwards from the conurbation core. Comparison between employment figures of 1950 and 1974 reveals that the larger of these axes are being filled by some new centres, the existence of which indicates that (on a very selective basis) villages too are becoming foci for quite sizeable employment growth.

The Outbreak of the Residential Explosion

Following some small and spatially constrained beginnings of the process in prewar times, the late 1940s and early 1950s witnessed a steadily accumulating momentum of rural suburbanisation in most advanced industrial countries. But what was happening in West Germany during these critical years could hardly have been more different. Here, with several millions of people flocking into the cities and very few moving in the opposite direction, the pattern of internal migration was overwhelmingly rural-to-urban and, as such, was taking place on a scale greater even than during the height of the German industrial revolution. During the first few postwar years this massive movement of people inside West Germany was dominated by the return of wartime

Figure 7.3: Nuremberg Region: Employment Dispersal

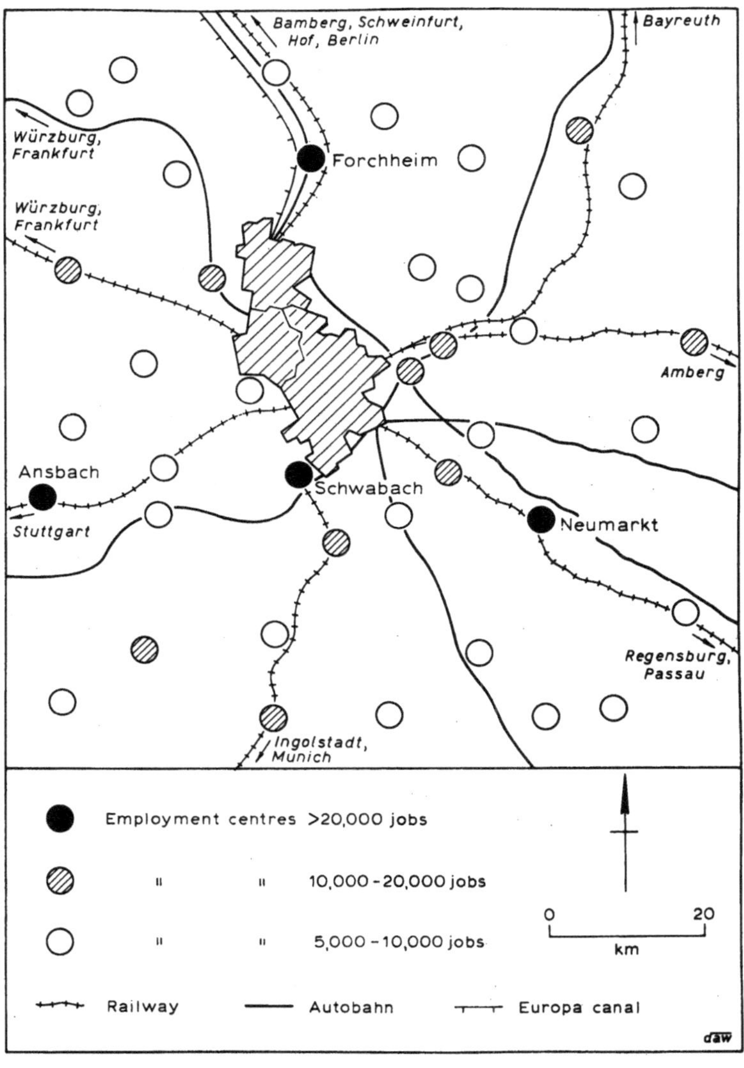

Note: The map shows the distribution and size of employment centres (outside the Nuremberg conurbation) as represented by the 1974 *Gemeinde Daten*.

Source: Statistisches Landesamt Bayern, *Gemeinde Daten*, 1975 edn (SLB, Munich, 1975), tables on *Beschäftigte*.

evacuees leaving their temporary refuges in the countryside. By 1950, however, their flow had become of secondary importance compared with the 'resettlement' of refugees and expellees moving to the cities after a short period of concentration in the rural regions of West Germany's eastern borderlands. Moreover, throughout the decade 1945-55 there were other migrations besides those which had been induced by the after-effects of the Second World War. As has been demonstrated in the writings of Schwarz[20] and Boustedt,[21] there is the underlying rural-to-urban drift to consider. This involved members of the indigenous rural population following a pattern of movement which was mainly one of 'upwards' drift through the settlement hierarchy – from village to market town, from market town to small city, and eventually from small city to a major regional centre. In broad terms this may be regarded as the persistence of a long-established historical process which, after reaching its zenith in Germany during the late nineteenth and early twentieth centuries, appears to have moderated only slowly during the interwar period, and in fact was still involving about 200,000 persons per annum at the time of the 1950 West German census. The turning point came belatedly but very suddenly during the late 1950s when, with more people now leaving the major urban areas than were entering, recordings showed rapidly falling rates of population growth in all save a small minority of West German cities. Thus, the total population of the 138 *Stadtkreise* (urban administrative districts), having risen by a remarkable 15.2 per cent during the six years from 1949 to 1955, was able to increase by only 5.8 per cent during the next eleven years. Then in 1966 there came the start of a steepening decrease in the Stadtkreis population which, despite extensions to city boundaries and large influxes of urban *Gastarbeiter*, has continued without interruption to the present day.[22]

The abrupt ending to the early postwar phase of extremely rapid population growth in West German cities was matched by the speed of demographic change in the urban-rural fringes. Some years ago these areas (henceforth to be described also as *Umlandzonen*) were delineated by the Federal Institute of Regional Research as 'the areas of rapidly changing countryside that extend from the administrative limits of cities to the points where measurable urban influences begin to give way to truly rural qualities'.[23] Their distribution (Figure 1.2) has already been illustrated and commented on in the introductory chapter of this book. However, it is worth emphasising certain salient points. In total the 68 Umlandzonen cover nearly one-third of West German territory, and they vary considerably in size and configuration. In the most developed parts of the country, in particular the Rhine-Ruhr, Rhine-Main, Rhine-Neckar and Middle-Neckar regions, they overlap each other to form extensive and highly complex tracts of urbanising land. But in other localities, notably around the 'isolated' cities of Bavaria, southern Baden-Württemberg and eastern Hesse, they appear as simple, concentric areas whose dimensions are generally in accordance with the size and dynamic qualities of their enclosed urban centre.

The first decade after the end of the Second World War was one of heavy out-migration from all but the innermost parts of the Umlandzonen, although it should be mentioned that the losses incurred were partly offset by above-average birth-rates. However, as was the case within the cities, the mid-1950s represented a critical turning point, for this was the time when the balance of demographic interaction between large urban centres and their hinterlands swung emphatically in favour of the latter. Thus, if one takes Boustedt's and Schwarz's calculations,[24] from 1956 to 1961 the number of people living within the urban-rural fringes increased by as much as 10.4 per cent, and in so doing easily outpaced the 6.0 per cent rise recorded for the country as a whole (Table 7.5). The next few years saw the full force of population dispersal both as a relative and a literal process. During the four years from December 1961 to December 1965, the Umlandzone population grew by a further 12.6 per cent, a rate of increase which was now almost three times faster than the national trend.

Table 7.5: West Germany: Population Change in *Umlandzonen*, 1956-65

	Population (thousands)			
Year	Inner zone or Ergänzungsgebiet	Middle zone or Verstädterte zone	Outer zone or Randzone	All zones
1956	4,451	3,452	1,521	9,424
1961	5,035	3,792	1,576	10,403
1965	5,645	4,361	1,708	11,714
Percentage change				
1956-61	+13.1	+9.8	+3.6	+10.4
1961-5	+12.1	+15.0	+8.4	+12.6

Sources: O. Boustedt, 'Die Stadtregionen in der Bundesrepublik Deutschland', *Forschungs- und Sitzungsbericht der Akademie für Raumforschung und Landesplanung*, vol. 14 (1961); K. Schwarz, 'Analyse der räumlichen Bevölkerungsbewegung', *Veröffentlichungen der Akademie für Raumforschung und Landesplanung*, vol. 58 (1969), Table 2.

Zonal Differences within the Urban-Rural Fringes

Soon after the 68 Umlandzonen had been defined, the Federal Institute of Regional Research proceeded to divide the areas and their principal urban foci into a collective zonal framework: first, the city itself which, under the title of *Stadtkern*, represented the urbanised 'core' of the model region; secondly, the 'inner zone', or *Ergänzungsgebiet*, which consisted of the most heavily suburbanised Gemeinden, and rarely extended beyond 5 km from the city boundary; thirdly, the 'intermediate zone', or *Verstädterte Zone*, where population densities range from 250 to 500 persons per km^2; lastly, the 'outer zone', or *Randzone*, in which the suburbanisation process has only reached an incipient stage and rural features still dominate the landscape.

Figure 7.4: West Germany: Zonal Population Trends in *Umlandzonen*, 1956-61 and 1961-5

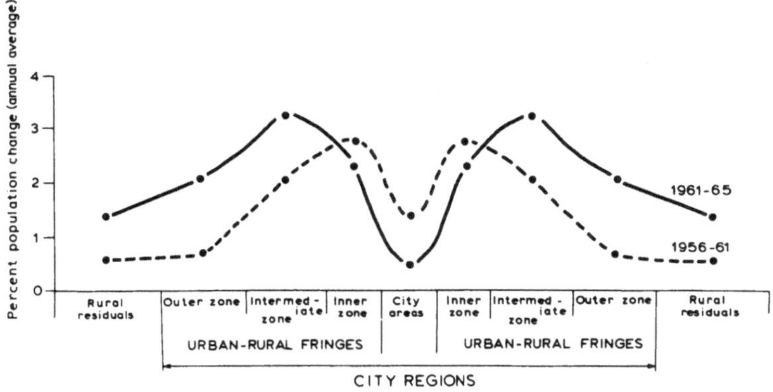

Source: Based upon data in K. Schwarz, 'Neuere Tendenzen der Regionalen Bevölkerungsentwicklung', *Raumforschung und Raumordnung*, vol. 4 (1967), Table 1, p. 146.

Since the mid-1960s many of the Umlandzonen and their spatial divisions have been subjected to a series of boundary alterations. Until then, however, consistency in the information base does allow the type of temporal comparison which is illustrated by the two graphs (one for 1956-61 and the other for 1961-5) in Figure 7.4. The graph for the earlier period shows that the fastest population growth-rate, 2.8 per cent per annum, was in the inner zone of the urban-rural fringe. This was substantially higher than the next highest figure, the 2.1 per·cent annual rise in the intermediate zone, and more than three times the growth-rate in the Randzone. The later graph indicates a marked centrifugal shift in the emphasis of demographic increase. By this time (1961-5) it was the turn of the intermediate zone to experience the fastest population addition, with its 3.3 per cent yearly rise having quickly surpassed the trend in the Ergänzungsgebiet. Significantly too the outer zone saw a considerable advance in its position: here, the growth-rate had more than doubled since 1956-61, and for the first time in the postwar period had managed to overtake the overall West German trend.

As mentioned in the previous paragraph, alterations to the spatial definitions of these areas since 1965 render it impossible to make any meaningful examination of zonal trends for the late 1960s and the 1970s. However, the general impression of an outwards spread of maximum, population growth-rates, starting around the edges of city boundaries and subsequently moving further along the urban-rural continuum, is reinforced and placed in a more up-to-date context by the analysis in Figure 7.5. The graphs in this diagram show annual rates of population change according to distance-intervals from the administrative limits of the Nuremberg-Fürth-Erlangen conurbation. Three periods of time are represented: first, 1950-61 when growth-rates greater than 2.0 per cent were confined to the first two distance-intervals (0-2 km and 2-4 km); secondly, 1961-70, during which the peak figure (3.5 per cent) moved out to the 4-6-km distance-interval, and the whole area lying between 2 to 8 km from the conurbation experienced yearly additions of more than 3.0 per cent; lastly, the years from 1970 to 1974, when further progression of the 'wave-like' effect took place, with the peak in the graph occurring as far out as 8-10 km.

Recent Decline in the Pace of the Dispersal Process

Since the early 1970s there has been a sudden and totally unexpected check to the momentum of rural suburbanisation. This has been in response to two major influences: first, the post-1974 recession in housing construction, which has stemmed from sluggish economic growth, over-provision of new dwellings during the 'housing mountain' years, declining rates of household formation and a perceptible slowing down in the growth of personal spending; secondly, coinciding with the decline in building activity, a discernible change in the evaluation of residential locations.

The recent decline in housing construction has been felt throughout West Germany. For the years 1974-7 this is evidenced by information compiled by the Federal Statistical Office in a special survey on spatial trends in residential building activity.[25] Significantly, the results demonstrated that the fastest fall in annual dwelling completions was in the Umlandzonen. Here, despite some enlargement of their total area, the drop of 38 per cent was 6 percentage points steeper than the national trend (32 per cent): moreover, it surpassed the 33 per cent decline in the cities, and easily exceeded the relatively modest 18 per cent reduction in what were described as 'the sparsely populated rural areas'.

Figure 7.5: Nuremberg Region: Population Growth-rates According to Distance-intervals from Administrative Limits of Nuremberg Conurbation, 1950-61, 1961-70 and 1970-4

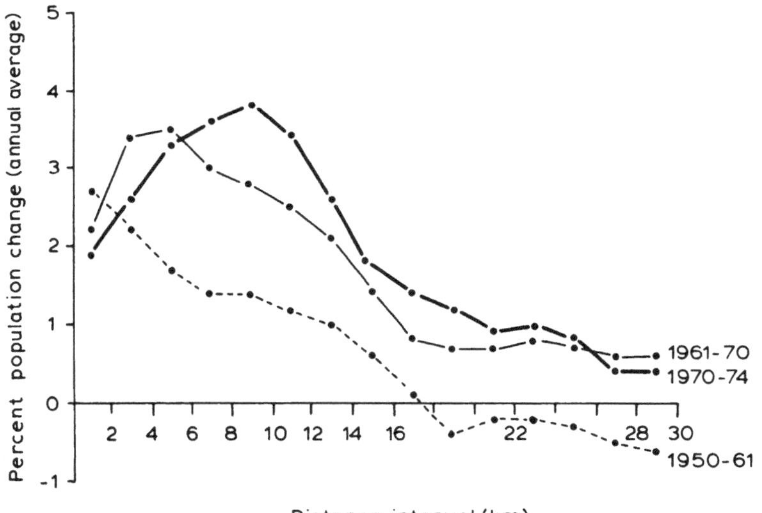

Note: The distances are measured from the nearest point on the conurbation boundary to the median point of each Gemeinde.

Source: The data for these graphs are from Statistisches Landesamt Bayern, *Gemeinde Daten*, 1975 edn (SLB, Munich, 1975), tables on *Bevölkerungsstand*; these provide population figures for each Gemeinde for the years 1950, 1961, 1970 and 1974.

The second influence, the re-appraisal of residential locations, was equally dramatic. Unlike the situation during the 1960s and early 1970s, more and more people began to revalue urban areas as suitable places to live and bring up families. This new perception was partly in response to rising travel costs, especially the inflated price of petrol. Rather more significant, however, were the improvements of urban residential environments; in particular the renovation and modernisation of a sizeable quantity of the prewar housing stock, the implementation of traffic-management schemes and the increasing provision of recreation amenities. While these investments were taking place, a widening range of questions were being raised concerning the 'quality of life' in urban-rural-fringe settlements. In many of these communities, especially those which were at some considerable distance from city-focused employment and service facilities, residential problems were being recognised. Foremost amongt these was the escalation in the costs of building new dwellings; today, even for the simplest and cheapest type of individual house, there are few urban-rural-fringe locations in West Germany where one can find quotations below DM 250,000.[26] Secondly, the trebling of petrol prices between 1974 and 1978 has been very much to the disadvantage of dormitory settlements, where the majority of inhabitants are highly reliant on car or bus travel. A third problem, which had not been fully appreciated during previous years of cheap travel-mobility, was the generally weak amount of service provision in the Umlandzonen. In most dormitory communities fast population growth for several years had tended to outstrip local investments in schools, health clinics, shops and leisure facilities. After the oil crisis, previous expectations that these would eventually be liberally distributed received severe blows from cuts in public expenditure and a poorer economic climate for the fostering of private businesses.

For West Germany as a whole no person yet has attempted to gauge the extent of the decline in rural suburbanisation. However, in instances where temporal comparison has not been invalidated by boundary alterations,[27] examination of population figures in certain appropriately situated *Landkreise* (Lkr.) gives some indication of the trend. A notable example is Lkr. Rhein-Sieg, whose area closely approximates the Umlandzone of Bonn-Bad Godesberg. Like most other Landkreise situated within the urban-rural fringe of a major city, Rhein-Sieg experienced very fast population growth throughout the late 1950s and the 1960s. This continued during the first four years of the 1970s, when the number of its inhabitants increased by 12.5 per cent from 376,800 to 423,800. The next four years (1974-8), however, saw a marked slackening in the growth-rate, with Rhein-Sieg's population increasing by only 5.3 per cent, less than half the previous rate.[28] Other representative examples, using the same two intervals of time, include Lkr. Fürstenfeldbruck in the Umlandzone of Munich (21.0 per cent falling to 10.3 per cent), Lkr. Main–Taunus in the Frankfurt Umlandzone (11.2 per cent and 1.5 per cent) and Lkr. Pinneberg in the Hamburg city-region (10.3 per cent and 1.6 per cent). All these areas convey the point that, while still comfortably exceeding the national population trend (0.7 per cent and minus 1.2 per cent), demographic growth in the urban–rural fringes and attendant housing demand has fallen to unexpectedly low levels. It remains to be seen whether this new situation will be long lasting, or whether future improvements in the West German economy and faster growth in household income will usher in a second phase of rural suburbanisation.

The Spatial Expression of Residential Dispersal

For some time following its 'take-off' in the mid-1950s, the process of residential dispersal from city to surrounding countryside was largely orientated towards conveniently positioned, small dormitory towns mostly with populations ranging from around 5,000 to 30,000. Indeed, during the eleven years between the federal censuses of 1950 and 1961, it was not unusual for such places to experience population increases of 40 per cent, 50 per cent or even higher.[29]

There were several reasons why dormitory towns, as distinct from the later 'rash' of expanded villages, were specially attractive during the late 1950s and early 1960s: first, at a time when car ownership was still limited to a minority of families, these settlements were advantaged by having direct train and bus links to the focal city; secondly, many of them could offer their own ranges of new job opportunities, partly in association with the centrifugal movements of manufacturing industry and partly due to their small concentrations of tertiary activities; thirdly, the rapid inflation of building-land prices had yet to appear, and accordingly costs of construction sites were still very cheap.

At the time in question the character of residential development in these growing dormitory towns reflected the 'inertia' of the apartment tradition and the desire among builders to compromise between urban and suburban styles of housing provision. Thus, much of the housing here was constructed in the form of homogenous estates, each occupying a position on the periphery of the town and each comprising mainly of standard three-dwellings apartment units (*Dreifamilienhäuser*) with shared gardens and entrance ways. However, some diversity was given to the residential and social fabric by two departures from this norm:

first, the sporadic developments of terrace housing (*Reihenhäuser*), and secondly, the building of *Kleinsiedlungen Wohnheime*. The latter are of special interest, since they were designed for accommodating refugee households, carried social-housing subsidies and were laid out as small 'colonies' of utility-style, detached dwellings.

Since the early 1960s the rapid rise in car ownership and increased spatial differentiation of building-land prices has encouraged residential dispersal to orientate itself around village nuclei. This trend, which has been accompanied by a turning away from apartment-type dwellings and an increasing preference for individual varieties of homes, also owes much to the growing predilection for what West Germans describe as *Wohnen im Grünen*. Literally translated as 'living in the green', the phrase is used less vaguely to summarise the upsurge in the desire for living in clean, pollution-free and uncrowded residential environments, which in many parts of the country can only be found in village locations.

The response by house builders to these changes has produced arguably the most outstanding alteration in the West German rural landscape. This, the widespread 'mushrooming' of village dormitory settlements, has parallels in other developed countries; but in West Germany it is imbued with a special identity. This will now be described under two thematic headings: first, the morphogenic structuring of expanded villages; secondly, the spatial selectivity of their development.

Morphogenic Structuring of Expanded Villages

The traditional settlement geography of rural West Germany is one which is dominated widely by compact agricultural villages, mostly with populations of between 300 and 1,500. Deviations from this pattern, namely a dispersed arrangement of hamlets and isolated farmsteads, are largely confined to marshland areas and infertile uplands. Apart from a few notable exceptions, such as in the Taunus hills to the north of Frankfurt, the Siebengebirge to the southeast of Bonn and the reclaimed parts of the Elbe floodplain in the Hamburg region, these scattered settlements do not occur extensively in the vicinity of large urban centres.

By far the most common type of traditional village is the *Haufendorf* which, with its characteristic congestion of buildings and very irregular layout, is prevalent in modernised form within almost every Umlandzone. Throughout the vast length of time from the early Middle Ages to the postwar period, these settlements have functioned primarily as concentrations of farmsteads, smallholders' cottages and craft-industry workshops. But the course of history, with its different phases of rural population increase and intervening periods of demographic retreat, has produced significant variations in village size. Generally speaking, the largest Haufendörfer (prior to rural suburbanisation) were to be found in locales of divided inheritance, areas of high soil fertility and positions close to major historic cities. On the other hand, less developed versions of the Haufendorf were more likely to be encountered in places which not only lacked these encouragements for settlement growth, but had also suffered from such historical 'accidents' as harvest failures, epidemics and warfare.

The sequence of stages through which these antiquated farming villages during the last two decades have been converted into sizeable residential settlements, is typified by the example of Langensendelbach shown in Figure 7.6. Situated within an area of pleasant, undulating countryside, this Umlandzone community is within easy commuting distance southwards to the cities of Erlangen, Fürth and Nuremberg (10 km, 19 km and 22 km respectively). As recently as 1961, more than half the working population of Langensendelbach were farmers: the village had 742 inhabitants and, like the large majority of embryo commuting settlements at this time, had yet to expand in any noteworthy way beyond the confines of its agricultural core. But within this crowding together of farmsteads and cottages, changes, related to what German geographers describe as the preliminary stage of 'internal, residential structuring', were certainly taking place. In conjunction with local agricultural reorganisation, the number of 'active' farmsteads (particularly those with smaller and less productive holdings) was dwindling rapidly, several seeing their function contracting to one of purely residential occupance, and a few others being converted for the accommodation of service enterprises. Some farmbuildings, but only two farmhouses, were abandoned altogether and left in a derelict condition. This retreat from farming, however, was paralleled, and indeed provided the opportunities for, a certain amount of new housing development. Characteristically, this assumed two forms: first, the modernisation and, in some cases, the complete rebuilding of farmers' dwellings; secondly, a significant quantity of infilling inside the curtilages of the village core, often making use of spaces created by the demolition of derelict farmbuildings. In all cases the sponsors were members of the local community. The term 'internal, residential structuring', therefore, is open to two mutual interpretations: in the spatial sense of its connotation it describes a process of village expansion *without* physical extension; in the social and entrepreneural sense it implies little or no intervention from external sources of population and investment. In both cases, Langensendelbach conformed with most West German villages at the same stage of development, experiencing major changes in the fabric of the settlement core, while at the same time seeing this as a product of local investment and functioning almost entirely for local purposes. Indeed, more often than not it was the farmers themselves who sponsored the 'infill' housing. In doing so they were helped by special agricultural-property grants, which were available to assist in the accommodation of relatives who were working, or had worked, on the family farm. Accordingly, the type of residential building usually related to the size and composition of the extended family, with a three-household apartment structure (initially occupied by grandparents on the ground floor and the farmer's offspring and 'sub-families' taking the two other dwellings) being built for large kinship units, whereas a bungalow or detached house sufficed for a smaller family grouping. This opening stage of village expansion, therefore, involved an interesting diversity of new dwellings, a characteristic which, as a demand for accommodating an external clientele began to emerge, was further accentuated by some investors responding directly to the temptation of building high-quality Einfamiliehäuser for speculative purposes.

This incipient 'social externalisation' introduced the second stage of the expansion sequence. This, the 'extension stage', is well shown in Langensendelbach, where it began in the mid-1960s when the Gemeinde council decided to countenance the construction of low-density housing within two small field-parcels (pre-field consolidation), one on the western and the other on the eastern outskirts of the village. Typically, these were laid out as building plots for individual purchasers, the plots being advertised for several weeks in the evening editions of Nuremberg and Erlangen newspapers.[30] In response, the clientele for the 37 dwellings completed in Langensendelbach during the years 1966-9 was mainly drawn from these two cities. Thus, by the end of the decade, the village had assumed something of an external function. The trend accelerated during the 1970s as more field parcels received Gemeinde blessing for housing development. In some cases they were no larger than those of previous years, but in the southeastern quadrant of the growing village a large, post-field-consolidation parcel was assigned for a substantial residential estate. On completion this comprised of 167 dwellings, all save 18 of which were of the Einfamiliehaus variety. Significantly the emphasis here, and also in the other housing developments of the period 1973-9, was firmly on individual homes and,

Figure 7.6: Residential Fabric of Langensendelbach, Middle Franconia

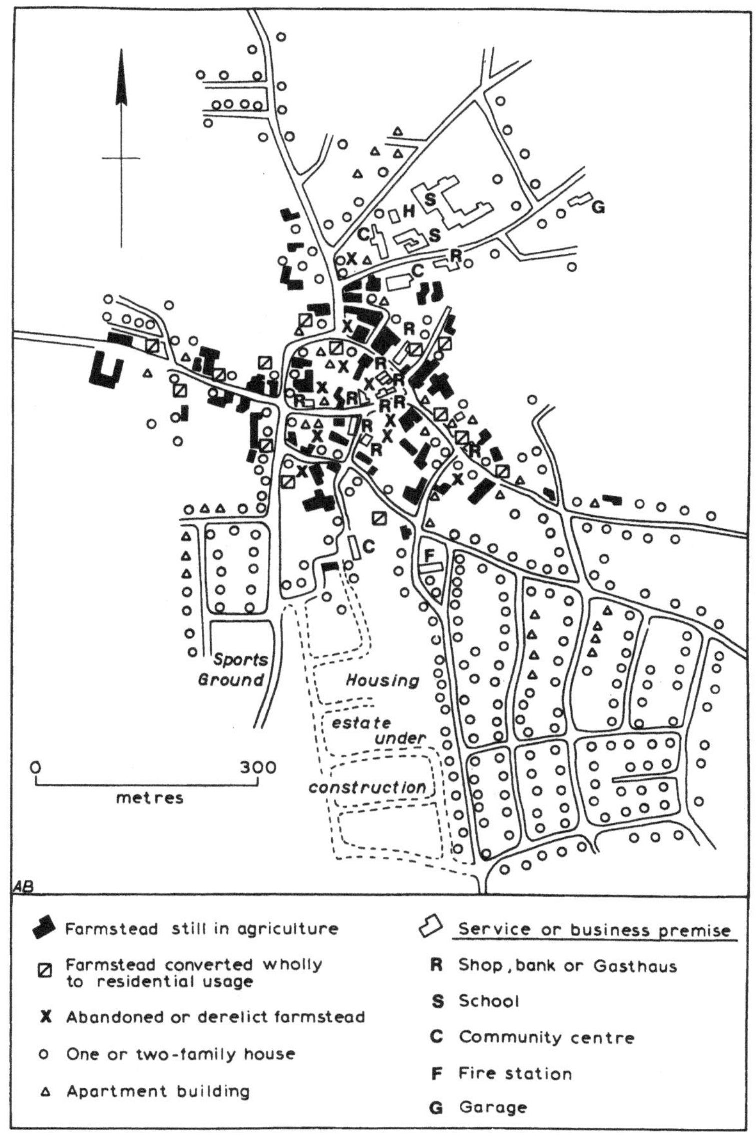

Source: Personal field-survey, conducted in April 1981.

although taking place during a time of growing recession in the building trade, it was very much in accordance with the prevailing direction of housing preference.

The end result of the extension stage, as was the case in countless numbers of similar communities in West Germany, was the creation of a large 'exploded' dormitory village. Typified by the example of Langensendelbach, it saw a trebling of the physical size of the village, more than a doubling of its population (742 inhabitants in 1961 to 1,892 in 1980)[31] and a sweeping change in its social composition. The last-named change can be further described by comparing information in the 1961 and 1975 editions of Bavarian '*Gemeinde Daten*'.[32] At the earlier date Langensendelbach's active population was divided as follows: farmers 56 per cent, blue-collared workers (*Arbeiter*) 33 per cent and white-collared workers (*Angestellter* and *Beamter*) only 11 per cent. By the later date, however, the proportional standing of farmers in the social structure had fallen to just 21 per cent; the proportion of Arbeiter had hardly altered, but the figure for Angestellter and Beamter had risen sharply to 46 per cent.

The third stage in the evolution of dormitory villages is clearly defined as a phase on continued physical extension which, unlike previous development, does show a conscious effort by Gemeinde planners to infuse a greater social mix among the incoming population. This is done through recognising the different social and family-life-cycle responses to variations in housing prices,[33] and insisting on a greater balance between cheaper (usually Reihenhäuser) and more expensive (detached houses and bungalows) types of dwelling construction. It must be stated too that over recent years this policy has been aided by the upsurge in prices of building land in the urban–rural fringe, a trend which tends to discourage low-density residential development. In Langensendelbach the result of this interaction between Gemeinde policy and inflation of building-land prices will shortly be seen on the southern outskirts of the village. Here, yet another housing estate is in the process of construction, but unlike those completed during the years 1973-9, the accent will be on providing for younger, 'lower-middle-class' families by encouraging the building of 'semi-urban' types of dwellings.

It is fitting to conclude this description of village expansion by reasoning why, in the West German experience, so much emphasis is placed on accretive residential growth attached to established settlement nuclei, and, correspondingly, why so little independently positioned development has occurred. In part, the explanation lies in the planning legislation of the 1960s which codified a general policy for Gemeinden to ensure a *contiguous* form of settlement growth. But important too were the problems of basic infrastructure provision, especially the need for modern housing developments to be preceded by the installation of adequate sewerage systems, piped-water supplies, electricity mains and street lighting. It should be noted that until the 1960s a large proportion of traditional West German villages were lacking in most, if not all, of these prerequisites. Then, when funds were eventually made widely available for their provision, it was logical, and of course very much cheaper, to install them only as an outwards process of investment focusing on the village core. Accordingly, at distances some way apart from the extending built-up edges of villages, it was the normal rule that, with the notable exception of relocation of farmsteads, residential development was prohibited, not only because it contradicted planning policy but also on account of physical inexpediency.

Spatial Selectivity of Village Expansion

By no means all urban-rural-fringe villages have become dormitory settlements: many, including some which are situated quite close to large cities, have yet to progress any further than the initial state of functional conversion, while here and there one can find villages which are more-or-less entirely undeveloped. The principal factors that combine to produce what, in the hinterlands of West German cities, is a highly complex pattern of settlements of different degrees of morphogenic evolution can be identified with reference to the area shown in Figure 7.7. This, a cross-section of the northeast quadrant of the Nuremberg-Fürth-Erlangen Umlandzone (and bordering rural area), is particularly suitable for this exercise. It includes 137 villages which are categorised as follows: first, 33 undeveloped villages which are dominantly agricultural in character and have yet to enter even the initial stage of expansion; secondly, 43 villages which have experienced internal alteration, but very little more; thirdly, 61 communities where major residential extension has taken place.

As to be expected, the most noticeable feature in Figure 7.7 is the general distance-decay of levels of village expansion as one proceeds northwards and northeastwards away from the conurbation boundary in the southwest corner of the map. However, closer inspection of the distribution patterns reveals several interesting distortions. Amongst these, the most prominent is the effect of the road and railway network, and in particular the alignment of major communications running from Erlangen northwards down the Regnitz valley. This axis comprises the electrified Nuremberg-Bamberg railway, the *Frankenschnellweg* Autobahn, the Europa Canal and an important linear concentration of industrial plants and construction works. Its existence explains why almost every village along its course has progressed to an advanced stage of residential expansion. Two smaller communications axes, one which follows the Wiessental valley northeast of Forchheim and the other (part of the emergent Nuremberg-Bayreuth axis) which appears in the southeastern corner of the map, have also exerted some positive influence along their alignments.

Figure 7.7: Spatial Selectivity of Village Expansion

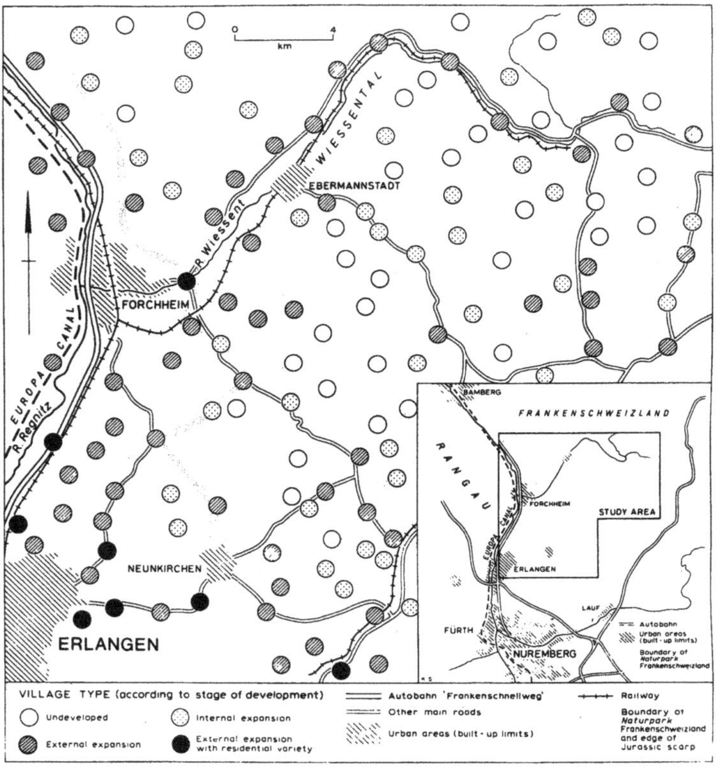

Source: Personal field-survey, conducted in April 1981 and April 1982 with assistance from final year students in Department of Geography and Institute of European Studies, University of Hull.

The area also includes an illustrative example of how a sizeable outlying town can add a further element of disturbance to the general distance-decay pattern. This is demonstrated by the ring of expanded villages around the industrial-cum-historic market town of Forchheim (population 24,500). As well as providing local job opportunities, this centre, with its two hospitals, several schools and large quantity of shops and entertainments, also offers a good range of professional services. Accordingly, the nearby villages have become prized residential locations for incomers seeking to compromise between a rural environment and easy access to central-place facilities. On a more restricted scale, such an evaluation has evidently also been placed on villages closely adjoining two other urban centres in the area; the small, but rapidly growing market town of Neunkirchen (population 4,200) in the south, and the tourist resort of Ebermannstadt (4,800) in the Wiessental valley.

Topographic conditions also play an important part in determining whether or not villages convert from farming to dormitory communities. In Figure 7.7 a line has been drawn depicting the outcrop of the easterly dipping Jurassic limestone rock-strata. This geological feature has produced the extensive, 400-650-m high, dissected plateau of the *Frankenschweizland*. With its bleak winters and exposure throughout the year to winds and rainfall, this region is markedly different from the lowlands to the west, where the Regnitz valley and the district known as the Rangau have a much more hospitable climate and far superior soil fertility. Largely on account of their adverse physical conditions, the higher parts of the Frankenschweizland have not attracted anything like the same quantity of residential dispersal. Here, apart from the main valleys, the settlement pattern consists only of small and little-changed farming villages, some showing a few signs of residential infilling, but just as many continuing to preserve their totally rustic character.

This easily perceived contrast between the 'fossilisation' of traditional villages in the Frankenschweizland and the strength of settlement growth in the lowland parts of the map, was reinforced by the geography of different sizes and facilities of villages prior to the main wave of residential dispersal. Indeed, the preconditions of adequate initial size and concomitant infrastructure provison are of universal significance in all West Germany's urban-rural fringes, for within these locations it is normally the case that the heaviest pressures on settlement growth tend to concentrate on those villages which from the outset are endowed with the advantages of a sizeable and organised community, basic infrastructure installation and essential-service facilities. At the same time, and often irrespective of their positioning, small rural settlements – few of which two decades ago could claim any of these three attractions – have proved to have much less appeal for builders and home-buyers.

The general effect of this differential evaluation of Umlandzone villages can be gauged from the analysis which is presented in Table 7.6. Here, the 137 village communities of the study area are arranged into three categories of population-size. The smallest communities, those with less than 500 inhabitants in 1961, show a very modest rate of population growth; their 3.2 per cent increase during the period 1961-74 being nearly nine times less in percentage terms than the average trend. The other two categories consist respectively of 31 villages with initial populations within the 501-1,000 range and 49 which fit into a 1,001-2,000 grouping. In both cases they underwent substantial rates of demographic growth; the former achieving 26.8 per cent, while the latter reached 33.5 per cent.

Table 7.6: Sample Area[a] within Nuremberg Region: Population Change According to Community-size, 1950-74

Community-size[b] (inhabitants)	Number of communities	Total pop. in 1950	Total pop. in 1974	% change 1950-74
Less than 500	57	16,615	17,151	+3.2
501-1000	31	23,024	29,202	+26.8
1,001-5,000	49	95,112	126,931	+33.5
Total	137	134,751	173,284	+28.5

Note: a. For location, see Figure 7.7.
b. Based on 1950 population figures.
Source: Derived from data in Statistisches Landesamt Bayern, *Gemeinde Daten*, 1975 edn (SLB, Munich, 1975), tables on Bevölkerungsstand.

Distance from major cities, the nature of the communications network, the location of employment opportunities, the positioning of countryside towns, differences in the natural environment and variations in the original size of villages do not fully complete the list of factors which produce a spatially selective pattern of settlement growth. This is quite evident when one takes a final glance at Figure 7.7 and observes the occurrence of several anomalous villages. The most noticeable of these can be seen, first, in the two 'non-extended' villages which appear within 6 km driving distance from Erlangen, and, secondly, in the group of remotely extended villages lying to the east of the main Frankenschweizland plateau. Some of the anomalies have been produced by the 'initial size and infrastructure' factor; others, however, can only be explained in terms of the operation of geographically 'irrational' local Gemeinde policies.[34] Such policies can stem either negatively as deliberate restrictions on the growth of villages which in fact have a potential for development, or positively as forceful encouragements for village expansion in spite of disadvantaged locations. The former are often to be found in settlements governed by conservative-minded councils whose composition is dominated by farmers; the latter, more often than not, are pursued by village leaders who are particularly anxious to stimulate residential growth as a means of increasing the flow of Gemeinde rates and taxes.[35]

Planning Problems in the Urban-Rural Fringe

The relative and literal transferences of large numbers of urbanites from the cities to the surrounding urban-rural fringes have posed severe tests to a system of town and country planning which traditionally and constitutionally has had to place more importance on dealing with parochial affairs than it can attach to wider regional interests. However, the problems which are created by rural suburbanisation can only be properly resolved by imposing a delicate balance between policies designed for the local scale, and policies which are part of integrated regional strategies.

The problems facing West German planners in the urban-rural fringes are multifarious. The most exigent, however, can be considered under two general headings: first, the threat to the environment; secondly, the under-provision of infrastructure and services.

The Threat to the Environment

The effects of uncontrolled rural suburbanisation are all too plainly visible in many parts of West Germany. However, they are particularly apparent in those localities, the *Zwischenstädtegebiete* (districts lying between two or more closely positioned cities) and the previously mentioned Ergänzungsgebiete (innermost districts of the urban-rural fringe), where the process had the earliest and most dynamic start, pre-dating the introduction of basic mechanisms of land-use planning. In these areas the term 'residential explosion' became an appropriate description as early as the mid-1960s, when it was found in places such as the outskirts of Stuttgart,[36] the immediate hinterland of Bonn[37] and the territory between Frankfurt and Darmstadt,[38] that lack of adequate planning intervention had allowed villages to expand so rapidly and with so little co-ordination that they literally grew into each other. The effect of this was the production of a type of contiguous suburban sprawl which took the form of outwards extending 'conurbations' of dormitory communities.[39] Moreover, the problems associated with this process were not confined to the amorphous structure of the enveloped villages: there were also questions arising from the large quantity of land-wastage, the absence of architectural harmony and the unwelcome inter-mixing of residential development with new roads and industrial sites.

Towards the end of the 1960s it was felt that this growing blight on the suburban landscape would, unless checked, spread quickly into extensive areas of West German countryside. Indeed, it was considered to be the most outstanding of all threats to the rural environment. In recognition of this escalating problem the federal government instituted a series of planning measures, of which the most important was the Federal Building Law of 1968. This legislation gave local authorities stronger powers to involve themselves in the complicated, and hitherto largely undefined field of negative planning. Particularly significant in this context was the introduction of much tighter controls for regulating the scale, function and siting of all new building projects. Nevertheless, the application of these controls was still subject to local differences, with some Gemeinden applying them with utmost rigour but others, irrespective of the environmental threat, making the loosest possible interpretation. Consequently, the production of a highly irregular and environmentally damaging pattern of rural suburbanisation continued in many places with only moderate planning checks.

Two federal decisions in 1969 eventually produced a greater degree of co-ordination: first, the designation of *Verdichtungsräume* (agglomeration regions); secondly, the decision to create a new spatial pattern of Gemeinde areas.

The Verdichtungsräume consisted of 24 major cities and the inner parts of their urban-rural fringes: they ranged in size from the polycentric Rhine-Ruhr agglomeration (6,582 km^2) to the city of Münster and its near hinterland (100 km^2). In total the system covered 7.2 per cent of West German territory, but included more than two-fifths of the nation's population.[40] Its principal planning function was to serve as a framework for co-ordinated, local authority policies in precisely those areas where land-use pressures were at their highest. At first there were arguments concerning the nature of general strategy, but by the beginning of the 1970s these were settled in favour of an approach in which all Verdichtungsraum Gemeinden were obliged to participate in a concerted programme of land-use 'harmonisation' and environmental protection. However, as far as these constraints permit, the Verdichtungsräume are still encouraged to function as suburbanising areas. Indeed, it is argued that 'controlled' depletion here of what were already highly tarnished landscapes was a reasonable price to pay for reducing the pressures on rural areas and the less despoiled parts of the urban-rural fringe.

The creation of a new pattern of Gemeinden has far-reaching implications. The *Neugliederung* (redrawing of administrative boundaries) began in November 1969. Prior to this there had been as many as 24,502 Gemeinden in West Germany, each with its own planning officer. By July 1980, following the near completion of the Neugliederung programme, the number of Gemeinden had been reduced to 8,500.[41] This means that their average area of jurisdiction has nearly trebled from 10.2 km^2 to 29.4 km^2. Accordingly, whereas in former years there had been many parts of the country where local decision-making was vested in 'single-village' Gemeinden, today most rural and Umlandzone local authorities preside over at least three settlement nuclei. This allows more selectivity in the application of community planning policies, and avoidance of the previous habit of too much spatial replication of building development. Since the early 1970s most of the newly defined Gemeinden in localities afflicted by rural suburbanisation have adopted the *Siedlungsschwerpunkt* ('settlement-concentration point') approach in the formulation of land-use plans. In this, all types of structural investment, excluding those associated with agriculture, are encouraged to focus within the Gemeinde's most suitably positioned village, thereby leaving other settlements in a preserved state. Rather ironically, the Schwerpunkt approach has met with increasing favour during the present phase of slackening rates of residential dispersal and declining quantity of rural investment. In these two contexts it means that local authorities now have the facility to concentrate a dwindling amount of new rural suburbanisation into selected 'priority' locations which alone have the appropriate combination of positional advantages.

Under-provision of Infrastructure and Services

The suddenness and extreme pace of residential dispersal from the cities soon exposed the inadequacy of the recipient areas' traditional infrastructure and levels of service provision. Until the Neugliederung and the advent of Schwerpunkt planning, this and connected problems were aggravated by the existence of too many population-swollen Gemeinden chasing too little 'extra-urban' infrastructure and service investments. Moreover, much of that which could be provided went to villages that were favoured more in terms of local business entrepreneurship and the political acumen of their leaders, than represented the most logical places in the sphere of planning strategy. As recently as the late 1960s, therefore, it could be said that there were a minority of 'lucky' villages which were in fact *over-provided* with infrastructure and service facilities; on the other hand there existed a large majority, some with large and rapidly increasing populations which, apart from just the basic prerequisites for residential expansion, were very much under-provided.

During the 1970s several influences worked towards improving this situation. First of all, the early years of the decade saw a major wave of infrastructure and service investment in the urban-rural fringes, partly accruing from private initiative and partly coming from large increases in public-sector spending. As a consequence of weaker economic growth, both sources of investment began to recede after 1973, in relative terms at first, but as an absolute trend a few years later. The effect, however, was cushioned somewhat by the slower pace of population dispersal, which of course meant less pressure on the infrastructure and service resources of the urban–rural fringe. In the meantime, the remodelled Gemeinden were free to implement a more rational approach to the positioning of facilities. In conjunction with Schwerpunkt strategy, communities were no longer able to compete against each other; instead, local authorities, within their areas of jurisdiction, deliberately steered public and private investment into those villages which had the largest numbers of inhabitants, and also commanded the best locations for serving all other settlements. This policy has been criticised on the grounds that it fosters, in many Gemeinden, the creation of 'embryo towns' in both the functional and demographic sense.[42] But there is no doubt that, under present economic conditions, it is an effective means of attracting the material essentials for modern 'quality of life'.

In this sphere the Schwerpunkt approach has recently been reinforced by the formation of *Gemeindeverbände*, in which local authorities combine together and pool their resources. Through this, they are able to acquire sufficient funding for higher-ordered, central-place facilities. In providing these, the Gemeindeverbände usually share out the investments between the members of the union: for example, one Gemeinde obtains a secondary school (in which the pupils are drawn from the whole district), while another is given a sports centre, and a third

Gemeinde becomes the location for a public library.

The spatially selective proliferation of services in the urban-rural fringe has posed problems concerning their physical placement. At first, their installation within villages was performed with little attention to ambiance and planning, with shops, petrol stations, professional businesses and public buildings all struggling to find positions as close as possible to the main street. Over recent years local authorities, with their heightened powers of land-use planning, have become fully conscious of the environmental depreciation which is commonly to be associated with this type of development. Several Gemeinden have embarked on carefully designed renovation schemes within the cores of their 'central' villages. As illustrated in Thieme's case-study of the Westphalian village of Brenkhausen (see Figure 9.3), an important feature of these schemes is the clearance of space for the construction of 'internal' service centres. On the other hand, other Gemeinden, normally those which have not implemented *Dorfneuerung*, have favoured the creation of modern, traffic-free foci on the periphery of the village. An illustration of this can be seen by turning once more to the example of Langensendelbach in Figure 7.6. Here the spatial arrangement of services consists mainly of an unplanned cluster in the heart of the village and a more compact grouping on the northern outskirts. The latter, with its shops, community centre, child-health clinic and two schools, is the more recent and dates only as far back as 1976, when the Gemeinde first started developing the site as an alternative to intensifying the congestion within the settlement core. On a wider note, the clusters are symbolic of two markedly different perceptions of the needs of village society; one belonging to an earlier age when just a few shops and a Gasthaus were deemed sufficient for a community which had never experienced urban living; the other being accordant with the present-day evaluation of the requirements of an adventitious and 'psychologically urbanised' population.

Notes

1. Presse- und Informationsamt der Bundesregierung, *Gesellschaftliche Daten 1979* (A. Bernecker Verlag, Melsungen, 1979), tables on Wohnungsbestand and Qualität der Wohnungen, pp. 236-45.

2. Statistiches Bundesamt, *Statistisches Jahrbuch für die Bundesrepublik Deutschland*, annual edns (Kohlhammer Verlag, Stuttgart and Mainz), tables on Internationale Übersichten provide data on population and numbers of dwelling completions for each of these countries. The index of 'building intensity' is

calculated by averaging the completion rate for each country, and then dividing this figure into $\frac{n}{1{,}000}$, with *n* representing the respective national population.

3. D. Claessens, A. Klönne and A. Tschoepe, *Sozialkunde der Bundesrepublik* (E. Diedrichs Verlag, Cologne, 1974), pp. 354-6.

4. This information is quite widely available in various West German statistical reports and handbooks: the most complete coverage is in Presse- und Informationsamt der Bundesregierung, *Gesellschaftliche Daten 1979*, pp. 236-45.

5. Statistisches Bundesamt, *Fachserie E: Gebäude und Wohnungszahlung*, 1968 edn (SB, Wiesbaden, 1968).

6. Ibid.

7. Calculated from Presse- und Informationsamt der Bundesregierung, *Gesellschaftliche Daten 1979*, Table 100, p. 239.

8. Statistisches Bundesamt, *Fachserie E*, annual editions.

9. G. Hallett, *Housing and Land Policies in West Germany and Britain*, (Macmillan Press, London, 1977), pp. 8-16.

10. Presse- und Informationsamt der Bundesregierung, *Gesellschaftliche Daten 1979*, Table 101, p. 241.

11. Bundesministerium für Raumordnung, Bauwesen und Städtebau, *Bundesbaublatt 1966* (BMfRBS, Bonn, 1966).

12. Presse- und Informationsamt der Bundesregierung, *Gesellschaftliche Daten 1979*, Table 105b, p. 249.

13. T. Polensky, 'Die Bodenpreise in Stadt und Region München', *Münchner Studien zur Sozial- und Wirtschaftsgeographie*, vol. 10 (1974).

14. 'Activity Ratios' are taken here to represent the percentages (each year) of total working population over the total numbers of persons (male and female) of insurable working ages. For West Germany as a whole, the ratio has fallen from around 75 per cent in 1961 to just over 60 per cent today. Statistisches Bundesamt, *Statistisches Jahrbuch*, 1982 edn, tables on Erwerbstätigkeit.

15. Presse- und Informationsamt der Bundesregierung, *Gesellshaftliche Daten 1979*, Table 96, p. 231.

16. Ibid., p. 231.

17. Bundesministerium für Verkehr, *Verkehr in Zahlen 1981* (BmV, Bonn, 1981), pp. 122-3.

18. G. Thürauf, 'Industriestandorte in der Region München, *Münchner Studien zur Sozial- und Wirtschaftsgeographie*, vol. 16 (1975); W. Meckelein, 'Der Ballungsraum Stuttgart' in Deutscher Geographentag, *Tagungsbericht und Wissenschaftliche Abhandlungen* (Deutscher Geographentag, Wiesbaden, 1967), pp. 71-85.

19. The populations (1974 figures) for these settlements are given in Statistisches Landesamt Bayern, *Gemeinde Daten*, 1975 edn (SLB, Munich, 1975), tables on Bevölkerungsstand.

20. K. Schwarz, 'Analyse der räumlichen Bevölkerungsbewegung', *Veröffentlichungen der Akademie für Rumforschung und Landesplanung*, vol. 58 (1969) whole issue.

21. O. Boustedt, 'Die Stadtregionen in der Bundesrepublik Deutschland', *Forschungs- und Sitzungsbericht der Akademie für Raumforschung und Landesplanung*, vol. 14 (1961).

22. M.T. Wild, *West Germany, A Geography of its People* (W. Dawson and Son, Folkestone, 1979, and Longman Group, Harlow, 1981), pp. 192-6.

23. Bundesministerium für Raumordnung, Bauwesen und Städtebau, *Raumordnungs/bericht 1965* (BMfRBS, Bonn, 1966).

24. O. Boustedt, 'Die Stadtregionen in der Bundesrepublik Deutschland', pp. 16-18; K. Schwarz, 'Analyse der räumlichen Bevölkerungsbewegung', Table 2.

25. Statistisches Bundesamt, *Regionalen Daten über Wohnungsbestand und*

Wohnungsbautätigkeit (SB, Wiesbaden, 1979).

26. *Der Spiegel*, 12 Jan. 1981, article on 'Neue Wohnungsnot', pp. 36-53.

27. The alteration to the configuration of the large majority of Landkreis districts came after 1968 as part of the Neugliederung programme of redefining West Germany's patterns of administrative areas. Lkr. Rhein–Sieg, Lkr. Fürstenfeldbruck, Lkr. Main–Taunus and Lkr. Pinneberg are examples of early redrawings: their boundaries have been consistent since 1970.

28. Population statistics for all Landkreise and Stadtkreise are available in the annual editions of Statistisches Bundesamt, *Kreise in Zahlen* (SB, Wiesbaden, annually).

29. K. Schwarz, 'Neuere Tendenzen der regionalen Bevölkerungsentwicklung', *Raumforschung und Raumordnung*, vol. 25 (1967), pp. 145-54.

30. *Nürnberger Nachrichten* and *Erlanger Tagblatt*, Friday editions, July and August 1963.

31. Statistisches Landesamt Bayern, *Bayern in Zahlen 1981* (SLB, Munich, 1981), tables on Bevölkerungsentwicklung.

32. Statistisches Landesamt Bayern, *Gemeinde Daten 1961* and *Gemeinde Daten 1975* (SLB, Munich, 1962 and 1975), tables on Erwerbstätigkeit.

33. J. Friedrichs, 'Soziologische Analyse der Bevölkerungs-Suburbanisierung', *Veröffentlichungen der Akademie für Raumforschung und Raumordnung*, vol. 102 (1975), pp. 39-80.

34. K.A. Boesler, 'Spatially effective Government Actions and Regional Development in the Federal Republic of Germany', *Tijdschrift voor economische en sociale geografie*, vol. 65 (1974), pp. 208-19.

35. Ibid., pp. 215-18.

36. W. Meckelein, 'Der Ballungsraum Stuttgart', pp. 71-85.

37. M.T. Wild, *West Germany*, pp. 112-17.

38. T. Neubauer, 'Der Suburbanisierungsprozess an der nördlichen Badischen Bergstrasse', *Heidelberger Geographische Arbeiten*, vol. 61 (1979).

39. H.F. Altrup, 'Die Flächennutzungsplanung im jüngsten Wachstumprozess deutscher Grossstädte', *Kölner Forschungen zur Wirtschafts- und Sozialgeographie*, vol. 6 (1969), whole issue: he describes the urban-growth process around four example cities – Wiesbaden, Karlsruhe, Darmstadt and Osnabrück.

40. R. Grotz, 'Verdichtung als Prozess, Dargestellt am Beispiel des Raumes Stuttgart', *Raumforschung und Raumordnung*, vol. 29 (1971), pp. 201-7.

41. Statistisches Bundesamt, *Statistisches Jahrbuch*, 1981 edn, tables on Gemeindengrossenklasse.

42. R. Grotz, 'Verdichtung als Prozess', pp. 204-7.

8 SOCIAL FALLOW AND ITS IMPACT ON THE RURAL LANDSCAPE

Trevor Wild

During the mid-1950s geographers, rural sociologists and agricultural economists in West Germany began to take note of a sudden upsurge in the abandonment and wastage of formerly productive agricultural land. Interest in this unexpected phenomenon was heightened by the apparent paradox that it could be seen taking place in the landscape at a time of very fast national population growth and mounting pressure on farming resources. Moreover, with the 'economic miracle' at its zenith, living standards were improving rapidly and thereby exerting an extra dimension on the increasing demand for home-grown food.

In 1953 the term *Sozialbrache* (social fallow) was introduced into German academic literature by Kröcker in a paper investigating the processes of social change within a group of villages in the Taunus hills.[1] Its full articulation, however, must be credited to Hartke writing in the 1956 edition of *Erdkunde*.[2] Hartke's key point was that social fallow, in the context of postwar West Germany, is to be seen as the end result of a stage-by-stage sequence of occupational shifts in rural communities – away from the farming tradition and into industrial or tertiary employment. Essentially, therefore, Sozialbrache represents a visual casualty and easily observable indicator of the change from an agrarian-orientated rural society to one which is based primarily on manufacturing and other 'non-farm' activities. This is the reason why Hartke and his followers insisted on the retention of the social element in the description, although some debate still hinges around the adoption of the word 'fallow'. The latter is employed as one way of emphasising that theoretically the land's disuse is restricted in time; certainly, if one leaves aside the question of the cost of clearing the overgrown vegetation, much of it is worth recultivating while, in certain localities, the possibilities exist for various types of alternative uses.

Hartke's pioneering work on interpreting and highlighting the wider significance of social fallow set the stage for a profusion of research inquiries; some arguing the actual reasons for field desertion and attempting comparisons with past phases of land wastage, while others looked more directly at the repercussions on rural landscapes. Thus, towards the end of the 1950s regionally based investigations were presented for parts of the country as different in physical character as Bavaria,[3] the Saarland,[4] Lower Franconia[5] and Hesse.[6] Then, with their customary flair for detail and depth of understanding, the interest of German writers moved into highly specific lines of inquiry. Among these, Wendling's study of the effects of tourism on social fallow within the Ahr valley[7] and Dege's analytical examination of land-use change in the Middle Rhine area[8] deserve to be singled out for special mention.

Social Background to Field Desertion

At the beginning of the 1950s West Germany's agricultural structure was dominated by the *Kleinbauer* (small-peasant) category of farmers whose size of holdings ranged only from 1 to a maximum of 10 ha. This group accounted for as many as 1.3 million, or 76 per cent, of the country's total number of 1,647,000 full-time agricultural enterprises and nearly two-fifths of the total cultivated area.[9] Today, after a long and still continuing period of heavy government investment in programmes of farm reorganisation and general agrarian reform, their numbers have fallen drastically to 407,000.[10] Nevertheless, they still represent just over 50 per cent of farming households, and it is worth pointing out that the increase in average size of all agricultural units (8.2 ha in 1950, rising to 15.2 ha in 1980) is still well short of the initial target of 20 ha recommended in the First Green Plan of 1956.

In its social context the abandonment of land lies very much within the sphere of this large, but fast depleting, band of Kleinbauern. This associationship was demonstrated repeatedly in early studies of social fallow, including a 1957 survey of *Land* Hesse where it was found that only 8 per cent of the state's 5,200 ha of Sozialbrache could be attributed to any other category of farmers.[11] One's immediate impression, therefore, is of another apparent paradox in rural West Germany, in this case discernible in terms of many of the poorest and weakest members of the full-time agricultural population – rather than seeking to extend their meagre holdings – taking the opposite course of action and spearheading the trend towards land wastage.

The restricted material aspirations of the Kleinbauern were accorded due publicity in the Federal Green Report of 1964.[12] This document presented statistics which showed that under normal environmental conditions the 1-10 ha farmer could not expect to earn more than about two-thirds of the national parity-income (*Vergleichseinkommen*).

Furthermore, not only was he faced with such a low potential income, but in comparison with most other occupational pursuits his work was very exacting. Indeed, according to one estimate, as recently as the mid-1960s full-time Kleinbauern were averaging as many as 66 hours per week.[13] This was substantially greater than the *per capita* inputs on larger holdings, and well above the figure of 44 hours per week (including overtime) for the country's industrial workforce. There were several reasons for the arduous nature of small-scale peasant farming at this time, including low capitalisation, little-or-no motorisation and very inefficient marketing methods. The underlying problem, however, was the excessive fragmentation of holdings and the way in which farmland in many regions was divided into tiny field-parcels scattered haphazardly over each community's agricultural area. In 1963 the Federal Ministry of Agriculture produced information demonstrating clearly that the degree of fragmentation varied considerably from one size-category of farms to another. Despite their smallness, it was highest among the Kleinbauer enterprises, whose remarkable average of 14.1 parcels per ha was considerably greater than all other measurements; for example, the figures of 10.7 parcels per ha for 20-30-ha farms and 9.0 for concerns larger than 30 ha.[14]

Social Differentiation in Rural Society

There are various meaningful bases for measuring social differentiation amongst West Germany's farming population. Foremost is the crucial question of farmholding size, for as a general rule family incomes in agriculture still tend to vary in accordance with the quantity of land being worked. Next in importance is the aggregate effect of other elements of agrarian structure, especially the degree of fragmentation, the manner in which field-parcels are distributed and (whenever applicable) the type of produce specialisation. A third group of issues is the size, age-sex composition and general wellbeing of the families themselves. More often than not the poorest people in rural West Germany are to be found among the large numbers of war widows and other single, elderly persons. On the other hand, the most affluent peasant farmers are almost invariably those with healthy maturing families in which husband, wife, offspring and, not uncommonly, grandparents too can all take a share in the work. But however unfavourably these bases may represent themselves, they rarely provide anything more than secondary motives for the abandonment of land. In point of fact, unless other occupational opportunities and sources of income are at hand, even the poorest Kleinbauer will more likely struggle on to the end, continuing to cultivate his field-parcels until retirement, incapacitation or eventual death.

Figure 8.1: Sequence of Occupational Change in a Typical *Kleinbauer* Household

	FULL FARMING STAGE	EARLY TRANSITIONAL STAGE	LATE TRANSITIONAL STAGE	DIVORCEMENT STAGE
farm size (ha)	8	8	8	8
field-parcels in use	30	30	20	0
abandoned parcels	0	0	10	30

	Age	Occupation	Age	Occupation	Age	Occupation	Age	Occupation
husband	50		55		60		65	P
wife	43	D	48	D	53	D	58	D P
son	18	S	23		28			
daughter	16	S	21					
son	13	S	18		23			
daughter	10	S	15	S	20		25	

Family Parity Income				
(a) from farm	70%	60%	40%	0%
(b) from non-farm employment	0%	30%	75%	40%
(c) from pension	0%	0%	0%	35%
Total	70%	90%	115%	75%

farming; employment off-farm; D domestic duties; S school; P pensioner

The real connection between social differentiation and social fallow must be viewed within a background of positive stages in occupational change by small-peasant families, and the way by which the resultant improvements in incomes progressively lessen the need to persevere on the land. Perhaps the simplest method of describing the complex chain of circumstances under which a Kleinbauer household will divorce itself from farming is to take a hypothetical, but no doubt typical, case in point. The example illustrated in Figure 8.1 covers a period of fifteen years and a full sequence of occupational structuring. Four stages of change are identified. The first is described as 'the full farming stage' when, apart from the children's schooling and the wife's domestic tasks, the whole family is geared to farming. However, this concentration of agricultural effort produced a parity-income of only 70 per cent. The next five years see our model entering what may be described as 'the early-transitional stage'. By this time employment opportunities outside farming have already attracted three of the four offspring, though they each continue helping on the land during their spare time. In other words, most of the family are now engaged in part-time farming and accordingly merit the title of 'worker-peasants' or *Arbeiterbauern*. Significantly, whilst there has been no increase in the labour input in farming, the overall family income has actually moved sharply upwards to 90 per cent of national parity.

Usually it is when the third, or 'late-transitional', stage of occupational change is reached that social fallow begins to occur on a significant scale. By this time our example family has come to the critical point when only the ageing parents are still agriculturally active. Apart from the elder daughter, who has married and departed from her parental home, the offspring still remain living on the farm; but they are now fully diverted to their respective industrial and tertiary occupations. It must be stressed that it is precisely at this decisive stage that the family, as a cohesive unit, is able to earn its largest gross income. This surpasses the parity level, but very significantly little more than one-third of it comes from farming. At this point too, with so much money being earned, there is little positive incentive for the two sons and the remaining resident daughter to spend spare time on the land. Nor is there any pressing need for their parents to maintain their slowly decreasing capacity for hard toil over the entire holding. Accordingly, unless it is fortunate enough to find a purchaser or somebody to whom the land can be leased, the family will abandon some of its field-parcels. At first this, the fallowing process, is confined to the smallest and least productive parts of the farmholding; but later its distribution becomes more and more random.

Progression from the late transitional stage to the ultimate step of complete withdrawal from farming commonly takes several years to run its course, and in some cases more than a full decade. Under normal circumstances the end comes immediately after the head of family retires and takes his place in the federal agricultural pension scheme. By the time he reaches the requisite age of 65, most, if not all of his offspring will have married and established their own homes and families. Eventually, the farmstead is left occupied by just the parents and the younger son; no longer is there a farming occupation, and consequently the entire holding is uncultivated.

In areas of adverse environmental conditions, such as are widely encountered within the mountainous regions of southern Germany and in the extensive ranges of uplands which cut latitudinally across the centre of the country, there are few persons prepared to buy up patches of derelict and unwanted farmland. But this is not the only reason why much of West Germany's social fallow remains in the hands of the original owners. To that older generation of farmers which had once had to endure the hunger and insecurity of the Second World War and the austerity years, land (irrespective of its state of neglect) has assumed lasting personal importance. This traditional attachment to the soil is something more than a mere matter of sentiment: it is essentially a question of keeping the land as a 'reserve resource' ready to be recultivated during any future food crisis.[15]

Temporal Setting and Economic Stimuli

Historic Precedents of Occupational Change in Farming Communities

The depletion of the farming occupation upwards through the age-structures of peasant families has been described by Franklin as 'a seemingly irresistible incorporation of the rural population within the capitalist system'.[16] As such, it has had a long and eventful history in West Germany. In some of the major seats of 'pre-technical' industrialisation, such as the Sauerland, the Siegerland, the Black Forest, the Harz mountains and the textile districts of the Westphalian lowlands, the early transitional stage of occupational change in farming communities was quite commonly represented as long ago as the fourteenth and fifteenth centuries. This was the time when large numbers of small-peasant farmers first began to turn their attention to domestic manufacuring as a seasonal means of augmenting their livelihoods. In certain areas this type of binary economy continued in strength until as late as the third quarter of the nineteenth century. Subsequently, however, increased mechanisation and broadening scales of manufacturing organisation, together with a growing tendency for productive effort to be concentrated within urban areas, brought about a mounting crisis in what remained of the traditional version of the worker-peasant economy.[17] From around the 1870s onwards, therefore, there came the final phase of decline in domestic manufacturing, and with this the creation of a situation in which the rural outworkers could only choose between migration or reverting to full-time farming.

Significantly, no writer who has given consideration to the centuries-long era of peasant involvement in handicraft industries has been able to unearth evidence of social fallowing on anything even remotely approaching the scale of its occurrence after the end of the Second World War. Here and there in the more backward rural regions, historians have been able to find occasional reports of poorer land being left to waste. These, however, were almost invariably related to population migration. Only in very exceptional cases were they to be associated with a worker-peasant family from within the ranks of the large numbers who (despite the loss of important sources of supplementary income) preferred not to join in the general drift to the growing towns and cities. In turning their backs against industrialisation, these people were greatly helped by the special financial support and agricultural protectionism of successive late nineteenth and early twentieth-century German governments. But much too can be credited to their tendency in the past to avoid complete family commitment in domestic manufacturing. In the large majority of regions where there had been a traditional symbiosis between this activity and peasant farming; the former had always been viewed as complementary work – usually to be performed by a minority of family members – rather than a replacement occupation.

Under a markedly different system of economic organisation, something of a parallel can be drawn with the situation towards the close of the interwar period. Not only was this a time of quickly expanding demand for factory labour as Germany recovered from the economic and financial crises of the 1920s, but, partly in response to deliberate dispersal policies and partly due to the need for firms to find a cheap supply of labour, it was also one of appreciable spread of industrial jobs into rural areas. Yet although this did have the effect in many localities of producing a new wave of occupational change within the structures of farming families, apparently it was still not strong enough to encourage social fallowing on any really noteworthy scale. Indeed, according to Röhm, working on information contained in the last *Reich* census of 1939, only 54,000 ha of the territory which was eventually to become West Germany could be described as wasted land.[18] By no means all of this small area would have been social fallow in the accepted sense of the term, and the quantity which did qualify for this description quickly disappeared in the Second World War programmes of agricultural extension.

Postwar Economic Stimuli

Whilst to the purist it is wrong to consider social fallow entirely as a phenomenon of the postwar age, it was certainly not until the early 1950s that it began to make its presence felt. As a distinctive and problematic element in the rural scenario, its sudden and very vigorous intrusion must be viewed within a background of unprecedented pace of economic change. In this, certain facts speak largely for themselves.

First of all, West Germany's economic growth-rate – fuelled initially by industry, but later being heavily stimulated by expanding commercial and financial activities – was exceptionally high, averaging 7.4 per cent each year from 1949 to 1959 and surpassing the trends of all other industrialised west European countries.[19] This achievement, set as it was during a period when the national economy was still quite labour intensive and when also the country's imbalanced demographic structure provided a sizeable deficiency of persons of school-leaving age, resulted in a dramatic growth in the numbers, quality and security of job opportunities. The direct benefits of the '*Wirtschaftswunder*' were reflected in the sharp drop in rates of unemployment (10.3 per cent of active population in 1950, 5.1 per cent in 1955 and a very modest 0.8 per cent in 1961) and also the speed by which earnings rose above the cost of living. During the 1950s figures for average 'take home' industrial wages and salaries showed a remarkable 95 per cent increase, but the national index of retail prices was inflated by only 21 per cent.[20] Rather unfortunately, there is a lack of consistent information on the upwards movement of agricultural earnings. However, it is worth noting that from 1950 to 1960 the average value-output of West German farms, measured in terms of annual product per full-time worker, increased by only DM 2,797. This compares very poorly with the DM 7,871 rise which was reported for workers in the industrial and tertiary sectors of the economy.[21]

The economic climate of the 1950s and much of the following decade was particularly conducive for movement away from the farming occupation. This is evidenced by a near halving of numbers of active agriculturalists within the space of only fifteen years (5.2 million workers in 1950, falling to 3.0 millions in 1965).[22] To some extent this depletion was achieved through ageing and retirement, but rather more was brought about through the medium of small-peasant families progressing to advanced positions along the scale of occupational structuring. Accordingly, more and more of West Germany's Kleinbauer category of farmers were reaching the late transitional stage and assumed 'threshold' point at which social fallowing becomes a prevalent feature.

Regional Distribution of Social Fallow

The Regional Pattern in 1965

Although a number of early surveys based on field-mapping and air photographs produced much accurate information at local and regional levels, it was not until the middle of the 1960s that reliable figures became available indicating the nationwide quantity of land under social fallow. In 1965 a new system of land-use classification was adopted for the purposes of compiling national and regional statistics. Previously, each form of uncultivated and undeveloped land had been considered under just two general headings: first, *Unland* to represent land, such as upland moors and undrained marshes, which had no potential agricultural usage; secondly, *Ödland* which referred to all types of fallow without differentiating between the social, urban (i.e. sites awaiting construction of buildings) and normal rotational varieties. Fortunately, the new classification introduced a number of specific categories, including *Brachland*, which was clarified as 'former cultivated land that has been out of production for at least a full year and, whether or not it has retained its original ownership, has not been left to waste in accordance with any productive farming custom'.[23] With development and investment land being distinguished separately as *Rohbauland* and *Baureifesland*, this statement comes as close as anyone could reasonably wish towards a full physical definition of social fallow.

According to official figures, West Germany had 150,600 ha of Brachland in 1965.[24] Its distribution, which is mapped in Figure 8.2, was heavily regionalised, with only 62 of the country's (then) 425 *Landkreis* (Lkr.) districts recording proportions higher than the 1.0 per cent level. Apart from the solitary exception of Lkr. Heidenheim, situated about half way between Stuttgart and Augsburg, these can all be seen concentrated within a broken stretch of shaded territory extending from the Siegerland in the north to central Baden-Württemberg in the south, and from the Saarland adjoining the French frontier to as far east as Franconia and the Bavaria-Hesse border. Inside these limits the proportion of Brachland to the total agricultural area exceeded 5.0 per cent in five regions: the Saarland, including Lkr. Saarbrücken and Lkr. Sankt Wendel where the figure was above 10.0 per cent; the Rhine-Neckar area and the adjoining part of Rhineland-Palatinate; the valley of the lower Main to the east of Frankfurt; the Siegerland, and lastly, the western part of the Westerwald overlooking the gorge section of the Middle-Rhine valley.

By comparing Figure 8.2 with the next map (Figure 8.3) one can confirm that the regional incidence of Brachland in 1965 was closely identified with those parts of the country where the small-peasant farmer was particularly prevalent. As has been pointed out by several writers, including such well-known authorities on the subject as Lütge[25]

Figure 8.2: West Germany: Regional Distribution of *Brachland*, 1965

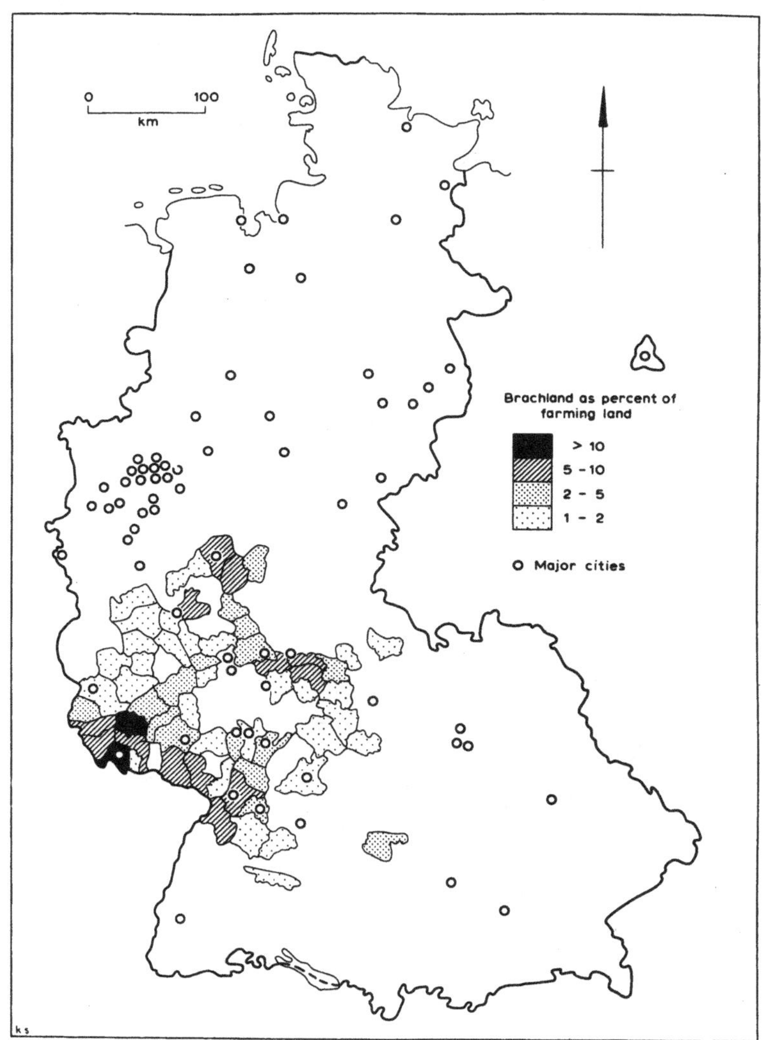

Source: Based upon Bundesforschungsanstalt für Landeskunde und Raumordnung, *Atlas zur Raumentwicklung: 7, Flächennutzung* (BfLR, Bad Godesberg, 1976), Figure 7.07.1.

Figure 8.3: West Germany: Regional Pattern of *Kleinbauer* Prevalence, 1965

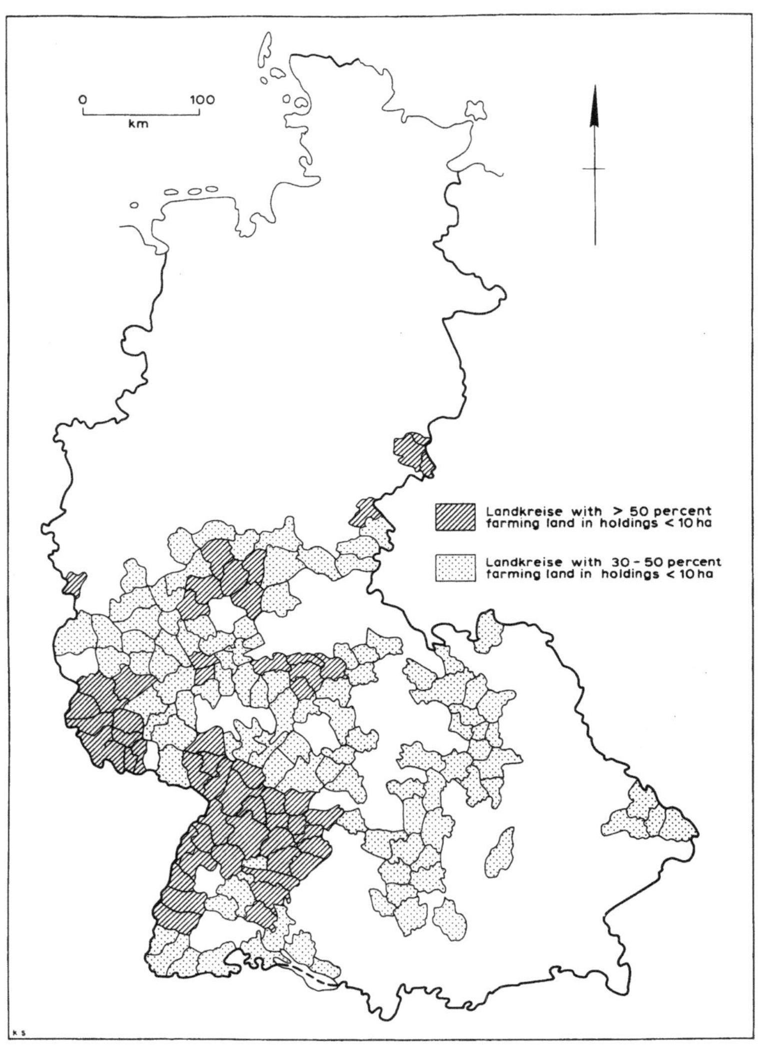

Source: Bayerischer Landwirtschaftsverlag, *Atlas BLV, Die Landwirtschaft der Bundesrepublik* (BLV, Munich, 1967).

and Röhm,[26] these localities in turn tended to show a very close correspondence with those territories in which the custom of partible inheritance had been in operation for the longest and most continuous historical period. A causal linkage, therefore, can be deduced between past processes of historical geography, the creation of regional differences in agricultural structures and, ultimately, the regional localisation of social fallow.

There is, however, one other important observation which must be included in any accurate interpretation of the regionalisation of social fallow in the mid-1960s. For within the broadly defined locale of Kleinbauer predominance fallowed land is particularly well in evidence in and around areas of early and prolonged industrialisation. The most notable cases in point are the Saarland (where as many as 90 per cent of the farms were less than 10 ha), the metal-working Siegerland and the leather-cum-textile working district of the Pfälzer Wald in the southeast corner of Rhineland-Palatinate. But mention too can be made of the northern flanks of the Black Forest, the pottery-working communities of the Westerwald and the 'rash' of small industrial towns and villages which characterised the countryside of the lower Main valley to the east of Frankfurt. In considering areas such as these, one popular argument is that the past existence of a binary economy of small-scale farming and handicraft industry allowed the practice of partible inheritance (with its concomitant fragmentation of farmland and progressive reductions in the sizes of holdings) to proceed to extreme levels without the sort of demographic checks which were periodically suffered in purely agrarian communities. An alternative suggestion, and one that is certainly well worth further investigation, places the relationship between Kleinbauern and early industrialisation the other way round, postulating that in many localities poor farming structures were more of a precondition for than a consequence of pre-technical manufacturing.[27]

In 1965, however, there were certain parts of West Germany where the general spatial associationship between above-average showing of Kleinbauern and significant occurrence of Brachland did not quite hold true. The areas in question were of two different anomalous types: first, some Kleinbauer districts that were too remote from centres of alternative occupations; secondly, a number of others where exceptionally favourable soils and climatic conditions enabled small-peasant farmers to maintain reasonable standards of living by specialising on such lucrative and high-yielding crops as grapes, fruit, vegetables and tobacco. For examples of the former, attention can be drawn to the absence of significant quantities of social fallow, despite expectations, in the eastern Sauerland, eastern Hesse, southern Baden–Württemberg and relevant parts of rural Bavaria. For the latter, the most notable cases which emerge after comparison with Figure 8.2 and Figure 8.3 are the Upper-Rhine Plain south of Rastatt (often described in literature as the 'garden' of Germany) and the wine-producing districts of the Middle-Neckar valley and Rhine-Hesse.

Distributional Trends since 1965

For several years after 1965 the amount of Brachland in West Germany continued to increase at a very rapid rate, passing 200,000 ha in 1967 and reaching 308,000 ha, or 2.5 per cent of the country's total farming area in 1974.[28] One effect of this trend was the creation of a substantially wider regional distribution, even though the drawing of a new framework of larger but fewer Landkreis districts (imposed by the post-1968 reorganisation of administrative boundaries) might have been expected to work towards the contrary. By the mid-1970s as many as 136 of the 250 *new* Landkreise were recording Brachland 'ratios' of more than 1.0 per cent. As shown in Figure 8.4, these had come to represent almost all of the areas of Kleinbauer predominance and in addition a few other parts of the country where the proportion of 1–10-ha holdings was *less* than that of larger-sized farms. It is noticeable too how the distribution of Brachland has spread into some of the remotest regions. Quite clearly, therefore, the late 1960s and early 1970s saw a substantial weakening of the once very tight geographical relationship between the regional occurrence of social fallow and proximity to industrial centres. The principal reason for this change lies in the growing daily travel-mobility of West Germany's rural workforce, a trend which owes itself to increasing car ownership, shorter working days and major improvements to national and state transport networks. Consequently, people living in rural areas were given the means to involve themselves in much longer journeys to and from places of industrial or tertiary employment, with distances of 30, 40 and even 50-km commuting range becoming quite common as the 1960s passed into the 1970s.[29]

These two decades also witnessed a marked increase in *Fernpendelnwanderungen*, the word which German writers use to describe long-distance and across-country movements of unskilled rural workers taking up periodic labour contracts. Typically, these journeys, usually orientated towards new factories or large construction sites, are eventually followed by return visits to the home community, often to spend several weeks helping on the family farm. In some remote regions, as

Figure 8.4: West Germany: Regional Distribution of *Brachland*, 1974

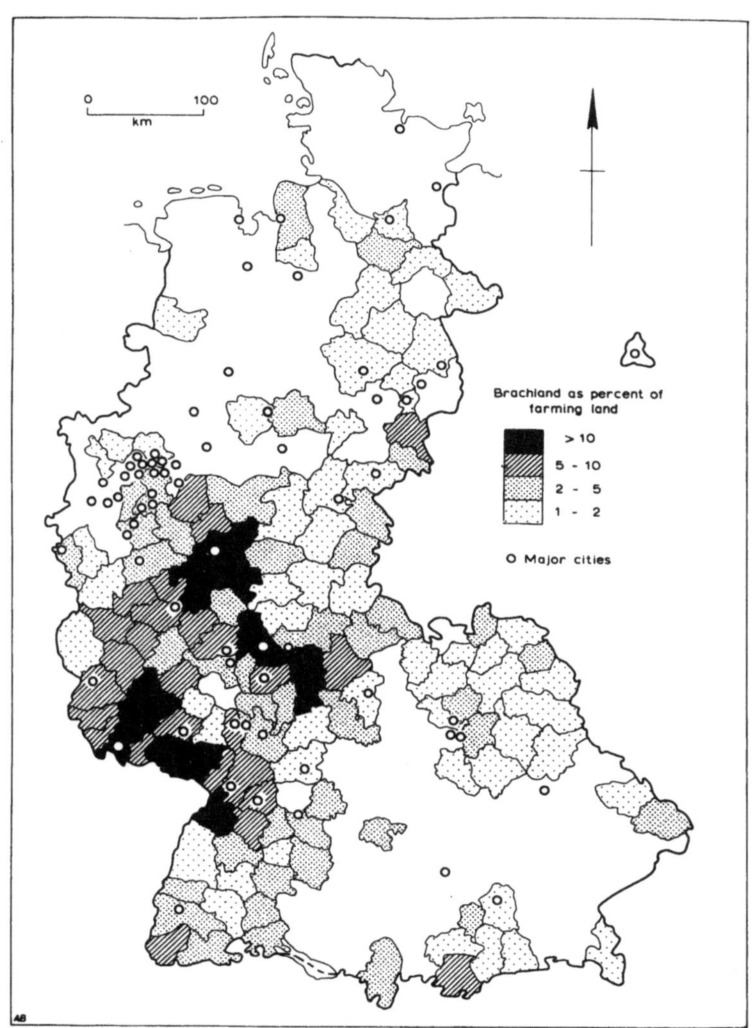

Source: Based upon Bundesforschungsanstalt für Landeskunde und Raumordnung, *Atlas zur Raumentwicklung: 7, Flächennutzung* (BfLR, Bad Godesberg, 1976), Figure 7.07.2.

for example in eastern Bavaria where it is by no means uncommon to find villages in which more than 20 per cent of the active population are *Fernpendlern*,[30] this special type of labour movement must be regarded as an important factor of change in family occupational structures.

Another influence, which likewise relates to the mobility theme, is the rapid upsurge in tourism. In one way or another this is taking place almost everywhere in rural West Germany, but it has a heightened significance in certain scenic regions. Through its own range of additional occupational opportunities, it has undoubtedly played a major part in the spread of social fallow into such well-frequented resort areas as the Bavarian Alps, the High Black Forest, the Spessart-Odenwald hills and the Moselle valley.

As well as showing a wider occurrence of Brachland, the shading pattern in Figure 8.4 continues to highlight the earlier regional concentrations. For, by the mid-1970s, most of the districts here were recording proportions of fallowed land well above the 10 per cent level, while in the Saarland, the Westerwald, the Siegerland and the countryside around Frankfurt there were some Landkreise where the figure was higher than 20 per cent. Moreover, in these areas it was quite common to find villages whose entire farmland had been given over to social fallow.

At this time it was thought by many people that the quantity of wasted land in West Germany would continue its dramatic increase for several more decades. Indeed, one published prognosis predicted that as much as 840,000 ha of Brachland would have to be produced before there could be any long-term stabilisation of the trend.[31] Yet since 1974 it has in fact shown a marked slackening, with the rest of the 1970s seeing only a very modest 5,000 ha being added to the total. There are three main reasons for this quite sudden and unforeseen change in the course of events. First of all, there have been the combined effects of Land and federal programmes of agricultural restructuring, field consolidation (*Flurbereinigung*) and mechanisation. These, together with price guarantees and subsidies, have gone a long way towards elevating the productivity and earning power of the residual farming population, whose average family incomes have risen remarkably from 36 per cent below parity in 1956 to 11.6 per cent above this level twenty years later.[32] The second reason rests in the fact that recent years have seen a heavy reduction in competing work opportunities. This is now occurring in most parts of the country, and owes itself primarily to a widespread downturn in industrial employment.

The worst years were those of the period 1973-6, when a net loss of 940,000 factory and mining jobs were recorded.[33] Little more than one-half of these have been offset by some continued, but strongly regionalised, growth in jobs within the tertiary sector. Not surprisingly, therefore, unemployment has risen sharply in recent years, passing the million mark in December 1975 and climbing above 7.0 per cent of the total working population by the beginning of the 1980s.[34] The third reason why very little social fallow is being added to the landscape is the tendency for an increasing quantity of the affected land to be cleared and reused; some of it as recultivated fields, and some forming sites for recreation schemes, holiday homes and nature reserves.

Social Fallow: a Problem of Rural Land Use?

During the mid-1970s the existence of more than 300,000 ha of social fallow in West Germany raised two immediate objections. First, at a time of rapidly rising food prices and continually growing demand for most types of agricultural products, there was the widely held view that the country should never have allowed the neglect of so much of its potentially productive farmland. During the period 1950-70 West Germany's total agricultural area shrank by nearly 1 million hectares (13.3 million ha to 12.4 million ha), most of this being unavoidably lost to urban growth and various public works undertakings, but more than one-quarter falling to social fallow. The second objection was the seemingly deprecatory and unsightly effect which social fallow had on the rural landscape. As one might expect in a country whose people are noted for their general dislike of waste and untidiness, this became the more prominent focus of criticism.

In the West German countryside the disorderly visual appearance of social fallow is reflective of its own peculiar mode of morphogenesis, in which almost all of the affected land originally consisted of tiny, and very diffusely distributed, field-parcels. When observed at the local level, three stages of physical evolution can be recognised before the cycle of change, from a productive agricultural landscape to a vegetated wilderness, is complete. The sequence commences when the first few members of a farming community decide to abandon the least accessible and least fertile parts of their scattered holdings. After a while derelict land begins to blot the landscape here and there in the form of a loose array of overgrown plots, each separated by field-parcels that are still in cultivation. As time progresses and more waste is created, the second, or 'mature', stage is reached (Figure 8.5). This is characterised by a highly distinctive type of spatial patterning in which social fallow appears as a variegated patchwork of different ages, thicknesses and species of vegetational succession. By this time too so many plots are being abandoned, that inevitably they begin to join together and produce irregularly shaped blocks of blighted scenery. Lastly, the third and final stage of the whole process of landscape conversion is marked by the coalescence of the fallowed blocks: it is the turn now for the fast-dwindling numbers of productive field-parcels to represent exceptional features in the local landscape.

Figure 8.5: Social Fallow in Gemeinde Filsen, Middle Rhine

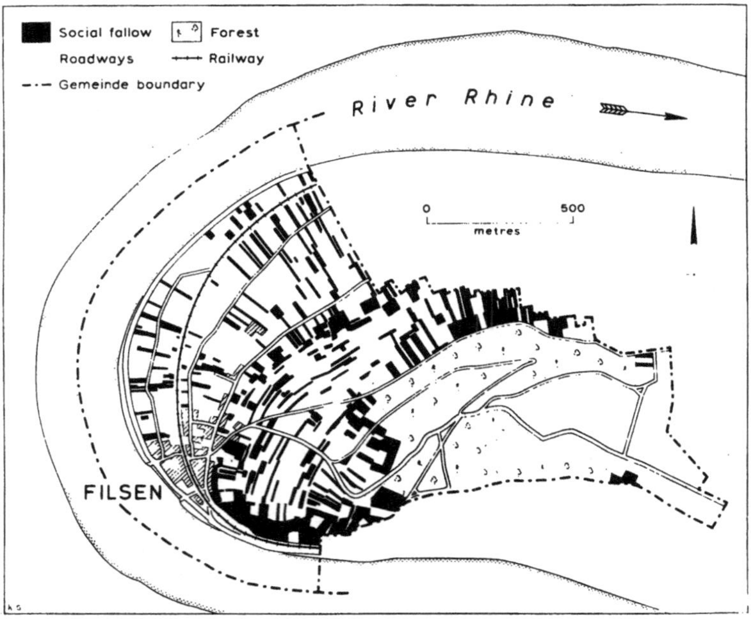

Source: Based upon a map compiled by E. Dege, 'Weinbau, Obstbau und Sozialbrache am oberen Mittelrhein', *Erdkunde*, vol. 27 (1973), Ablatt Beilage 3.

In recent years there has been much debate concerning the possible ways in which social fallow can be removed from the landscape and be put to new uses. The most expensive solution is recultivation. This has been attempted in a number of localities, usually in connection with the implementation of local Flurbereinigung programmes. But it has met with four notable difficulties: first, the not-very-easy task of persuading owners to part with their disused plots; secondly, the heavy cost of purchasing the wasted land; thirdly, the time and effort which has to be spent on clearing away the tangled masses of vegetation; lastly, the often insuperable difficulty of finding farmers willing to take up leases or pay for the new land. Because of these problems, recultivation has proved to be a realistic policy only in areas of intensive cultivation and high agricultural productivity. Specifically these comprise mainly of those parts of the country which have an established tradition in either viticulture or horticulture. Even here, however, there are many places where withdrawal from the farming occupation and attendant land wastage has become so far advanced that there is no longer any locally based desire to embark on any form of agricultural improvement, including the re-working of social fallow. Accordingly, land-use planners have had to consider other courses of action.

One approach, which has been adopted fairly extensively in areas such as the High Eifel, the Siegerland, the Westerwald and the Spessart-Odenwald, is afforestation. But this is only feasible in places where the fallowing cycle has progressed more or less to an absolute state, producing large and unbroken tracts of derelict fields. Another solution, which is becoming very popular amongst local authorities in tourist areas, is to acquire and develop the land for recreational purposes. This has in fact already proved a success as far as it concerns the provision of small-scale leisure facilities, in particular picnic sites, exercise grounds and children's adventure areas. However, as in afforestation, the more space-demanding types of recreational provision can be undertaken only in locales where there is full dereliction. Moreover, for these to be worthwhile it is highly advisable for their sites to be in positions capable of commanding good road access and proximity to special tourist attractions such as lakes, rivers or scenic viewpoints. Thus, the real possibilities of using Brachland for major projects (for example, winter-sports centres, properly equipped camping grounds and estates of holiday homes) are largely confined to just a few well-favoured locations which, more often than not, are to be found only within the upland regions.

Today there is a growing recognition of the ecological value of social fallow, both for its large range of flora species and for its capacity to support an unusually high density of bird and animal life. Its function as a natural habitat may not be popular as far as the nearby farmers are concerned, but in several places it has received official blessing through the designation of some of the oldest tracts of wasteland as nature conservation areas (*Naturschutzgebiete*). Moreover, people in West Germany are now reacting against the monotonous functional landscapes which are being produced in association with field consolidation and general agricultural modernisation. In visual terms, therefore, the deprecatory effect of social fallow, especially the type which is linked with the mature stage of physical patterning, is being called into question. Indeed, the scattering of the overgrown patches, particularly in the spring and in the autumn when their colours and variety are greatly enhanced, is generally considered to be pleasing to the eye. Within the duration of just a few years popular perception of social fallow has swung to the extent that what was once regarded as a problem of crisis proportions, is now becoming widely acceptable as an important environmental resource.[35]

Notes

1. U. Kröcker, 'Die sozialgeographische Entwicklung der fünf Feldbergdörfer im Taunus in den letzen 150 Jahren', *Rhein-Mainische Forschungen*, vol. 37 (1953), p. 46.
2. W. Hartke, 'Die Sozialbrache als Phänomen der geographischen Differenzierung der Landschaft', *Erdkunde*, vol. 34 (1956), pp. 257-69.
3. K. Ruppert, 'Die Sozialbrache als Übergangserscheinung', *Bayerisches Landwirtschaftliches Jahrbuch*, vol. 34 (1957), pp. 622-32.
4. G. Wiegelmann, 'Zur Frage der Sozialbrache im Saarland', *Saarbrücker Hefte*, vol. 5 (1957), pp. 70-86.
5. H. Jäger, 'Sozialbrache in Unterfranken', *Berichte zur deutschen Landeskunde*, vol. 21 (1958), pp. 135-6.
6. W. Frank, 'Der Umfang des Brachlandes in Hessen 1957', *Staat und Wirtschaft in Hessen*, vol. 12 (1957), pp. 270-85.
7. W. Wendling, 'Sozialbrache und Flurwüstungen in der Weinbaulandschaft des Ahrtals', *Forschungen zur deutschen Landeskunde*, vol. 160 (1966).
8. E. Dege, 'Weinbau, Obstbau und Sozialbrache am oberen Mittelrhein', *Erdkunde*, vol. 27 (1973), pp. 34-54.
9. Bundesministerium für Ernährung, Landwirtschaft und Forsten, *Statistisches Jahrbuch über Ernährung, Landwirtschaft und Forsten*, 1977 edn (BMELF, Münster, 1978).
10. Ibid., 1980 edn.
11. Hessisches Statistisches Landesamt, *Hessen im Wandel, 1860-1960* (HSL, Wiesbaden, 1960).
12. Bundesministerium für Ernährung, Landwirtschaft und Forsten, *Bericht über die Lage der Landwirtschaft; Grüner Bericht 1964*, (BMELF, Bonn, 1965).
13. Ibid., tables on Vergleichseinkommen.
14. Initially compiled by the Federal Ministry of Agriculture (BMELF), these figures were first published in B. van Deenen, *Wirtschafts- und Erwerbsstruktur als Bestimmungsgründe der Tragfähigkeit* (Forschungsgesellschaft für Agrarpolitik und Agrarsoziologie, Bonn, 1963).

15. The concept of the 'reserve resource' is discussed at length in J.O. Müller, *Die Einstellung zur Landarbeit in bauerlichen Familienbetrieben* (Forschungsgesellschaft für Agrarpolitik und Agrarsoziologie, Bonn, 1964).
16. S.H. Franklin, *The European Peasantry* (London, 1969), p. 64.
17. The history of the worker-peasant economy in Germany forms one of the underlying themes in F.K. Lütge, *Deutsche Sozial- und Wirtschaftsgeschichte*, 3rd edn (West Berlin, 1966).
18. H. Röhm, *Die westdeutsche Landwirtschaft*, 1st edn (Agrarstruktur, Agrarwirtschaft und Landwirtschaftliche Anpassung, Munich, Basle and Vienna, 1964), p. 48.
19. K. Neelson, *Wirtschaftsgeschichte der BRD* (West Berlin, 1973), pp. 311-16.
20. Ibid., pp. 314-16 and statistical appendices.
21. Bundesministerium für Ernährung, Landwirtschaft und Forsten, *Statistisches Jahrbuch*, 1977 edn.
22. Ibid., 1977 edn.
23. Statistisches Bundesamt, *Fachserie BR 1; Bodennutzung und Ernte 1965* (Statistisches Bundesamt, Wiesbaden and Stuttgart, 1965).
24. Ibid., 1965 edn.
25. Lütge, *Deutsche Sozial- und Wirtschaftsgeschichte*, passim.
26. Röhm, *Die westdeutche Landwirtschaft*, pp. 18-33.
27. As far as the relationship applies to Germany, this view has been discussed at length in H. Linde, 'Die Bedeutung der deutschen Agrarstruktur für die Anfänge der industriellen Entwicklung', *Jahrbuch fur Sozialwissenschaft*, vol. 13 (1962).
28. Statistisches Bundesamt, *Fachserie BR 1*, 1975 edn.
29. See, for example, Statistisches Landesamt Rheinland-Pfalz, *Pendelwanderung und Arbeitszentren in Rheinland-Pfalz* (SLR-P, Bad Ems, 1974).
30. Bayerisches Staatsministerium für Wirtschaft und Verkehr, *Bericht über die wirtschaftliche Entwicklung der strukturschwachen Gebiete Bayerns: Grenzlandbericht* (BSMWV, Munich, 1975).
31. Statistisches Bundesamt, *Fachserie BR 1*, 1975 edn.
32. R. Lawson, 'Poverty and inequality in West Germany', in V. George and R. Lawson (eds), *Poverty and Inequality in Common Market Countries* (Routledge and Kegan Paul, London, 1980), pp. 195-232.
33. Bundesanstalt für Arbeit, *Amtliche Nachrichten* (Bundesanstalt für Arbeit, Nuremberg), annual reports.
34. Ibid., reports for 1975 and 1980.
35. H. Allerman, 'Immer mehr Brachflächen? Extensive Nutzung oder Landschaftspflege?', *Land- und hauswirtschaftliche Auswertungs- und Informationsdienst*, vol. 24 (1973), p. 3.

9 AGRICULTURAL CHANGE AND ITS IMPACT IN RURAL AREAS

Günter Thieme

During the last three decades massive financial resources have been poured into the reorganisation and technological advance of West German agriculture. Yet, despite the widespread transformation of the farming scene and its adaptation to the needs of modern industrial society, there are still some very pertinent questions to be raised concerning its status within the nation at large. Foremost is the unarguable fact that, even after the shedding of 3.7 million farming jobs since 1950 and the loss of 850,000 holdings (mostly belonging to the smallest and least efficient categories of farmers), agriculture continues to be very backward when compared with the performances of other sectors of the economy. Indeed, whilst in absolute terms the position has been improving constantly throughout the postwar period, it is a salient point that the yearly *per capita* contribution of West Germany's farming population to the gross national product remains well below one-half of the average inputs of their compatriots working in industrial and tertiary activities (Table 9.1). The reason for this unsatisfactory state of affairs rests primarily in West Germany's historic legacy of outdated agricultural structures and in its dependence on not very favourable natural conditions for food production.

Natural Conditions and Historic Legacy

While one should always guard against taking a too deterministic view, it can hardly be denied that agriculture, much more so than any other major branch of economic activity, is still strongly subject to the natural factors of climate, altitude, topography, soils and hydrological conditions. Despite all the technology and expertise that is now readily available to most West German farmers, these factors continue to exert profound influences on production costs, types of produce-specialisation, and in some cases even the eventual success or failure of individual farm enterprises. It is not intended here to list and examine all the numerous physical conditions which, in one way or another, may be relevant to the fortunes of farming in the Federal Republic.[1] Instead, attention

Table 9.1: West Germany: Gross Domestic Product (GDP) and Persons Engaged in Farming, 1950-79

	1950	1960	1965	1970	1975	1979
Agricultural contribution to GDP, DM millions	10,130	17,310	19,980	23,070	30,780	32,890
as % of total GDP	10.4	5.7	4.4	3.5	3.1	2.4
DM per farmer	1,981	4,778	6,750	9,738	16,884	21,302
Contribution of other economic sectors to GDP, DM per person	4,737	12,608	17,926	26,103	41,492	55,079
Persons engaged in farming, thousands	5,191	3,545	2,960	2,369	1,823	1,544
as % of total active population	22.1	13.3	10.9	8.9	7.2	6.0

Sources: E. Ballerstedt and W. Glatzer, *Soziologischer Almanach* (Frankfurt and New York, 1979); Statistisches Bundesamt, *Statistisches Jahrbuch für die Bundesrepublik Deutschland*, annual edns (Kohlhammer Verlag, Stuttgart and Mainz).

will be focused on a brief description of the most outstanding natural factors.

Climate and Topography

Because of their considerable temporal and geographic variability, climatic conditions in West Germany exert appreciable controls on crop yields and farm income. To give a topical example: whereas the above-average rainfalls of 1978 resulted in widespread harvest surpluses, the crop failures during and immediately after the excessively dry and hot summer of 1976 brought severe hardships to many agricultural regions, especially those which tend to specialise in the production of cultivated grass and animal fodders. Above anything else, the 1976 drought emphasised the general rule that West German agriculture is much more susceptible to rainfall deficiencies than it is to abnormal wetness.[2]

Significantly, West Germany lies within the transitional area between the cool, temperate, 'maritime climate' of Atlantic Europe and the more extreme, continental regime of central and eastern Europe. In general terms, therefore, there is an increase in the range of seasonal temperatures and a decrease in annual precipitation totals as one proceeds diagonally across the country from the northwest to the southeast. But this broad pattern is greatly disturbed by the existence of a large variety of regional and local topographic conditions. Apart from the two notable exceptions of the North German Lowlands and the Danube Plain, the disposition of major relief features in all other regions is characterised by close alternations of sheltered valley and exposed uplands. These produce a highly differentiated geography of physically advantaged and disadvantaged farming areas, in which environmental differences are not just a matter of contrasts in temperature, insolation and rainfall, but also include acute variations in terrain and soil quality. In the upland regions there are large tracts of steeply sloping land which, although they have been farmed quite intensively during past periods of population pressure, are hardly suitable for the application of present-day agricultural methods. The working of such ground by modern machinery is scarcely feasible: in many instances it is totally impossible. To all intents and purposes, therefore, these hillside and valleyside slopes, which in total cover approximately one-fifth of West German territory, can be exploited only by turning them over to permanent grassland or afforestation. A further problem, which is encountered not only in hilly districts but also in localities with light and friable earth, is the danger of soil erosion. Depending on the type of land use and underlying soil structure, this can occur even on quite gently inclining terrain. Moreover, as recent experiences have shown, in many lowland areas the detrimental effects of soil erosion may often spread themselves well beyond the actual sources of origin, and can commonly cause appreciable damage to good-quality farmland.

Soil Quality

The geography of soil quality in West Germany has the same degree of diversity as has the patterning of climatic and topographic conditions. In theory at least, the application of modern agricultural technology means that soil has no fixed value and within reason can be put to any particular farming usage; but, at the same time, soil quality does have a significant bearing on operational costs. Thus, in reference to West Germany's numerous locales of notoriously infertile soils – for example, the Bavarian Alps, the limestone plateaux of southern Germany, the higher parts of the Central Uplands and the diluvial *Geest* and heathlands of northern Lower Saxony and inland Schleswig-Holstein – agricultural economists prefer to employ the term 'restricted flexibility' (*beschränkte Flexibilität*), and to recognise that in today's economic world there continue to be definable potential limits to the versatility of natural resources.

A simplified method of evaluating soil quality is provided by the so-called *Ertragsmesszahl* (yield-measurement) index, whose values range from zero for completely barren land to a maximum recording of 100 per cent for ground with the very best agricultural potential. About three-quarters of West Germany has yield measurements below the 50 per cent mark. Moreover, as can be seen in Figure 9.1, just over one-quarter of the country has values of less than 33 per cent; this means that there are extensive areas of marginal soils which, under modern economic conditions, can offer little or no chance of profitable cultivation.[3]

Satisfactory soils cover no more than 25 per cent of the area of the Federal Republic. Principally, this remarkably small amount of advantaged territory is made up from the North Sea coastlands and the various *loess* belts of the Lower Rhineland, the Börde regions of Westphalia and Lower Saxony, the Upper-Rhine Plain, the Neckar basin, the South German 'Gäulands' and certain parts of the Danube valley. It is only within these diverse regions that farmers encounter natural crop-growing potentials that can compare favourably with the EEC norm.

Figure 9.1: West Germany: Distribution Pattern of Soil Quality

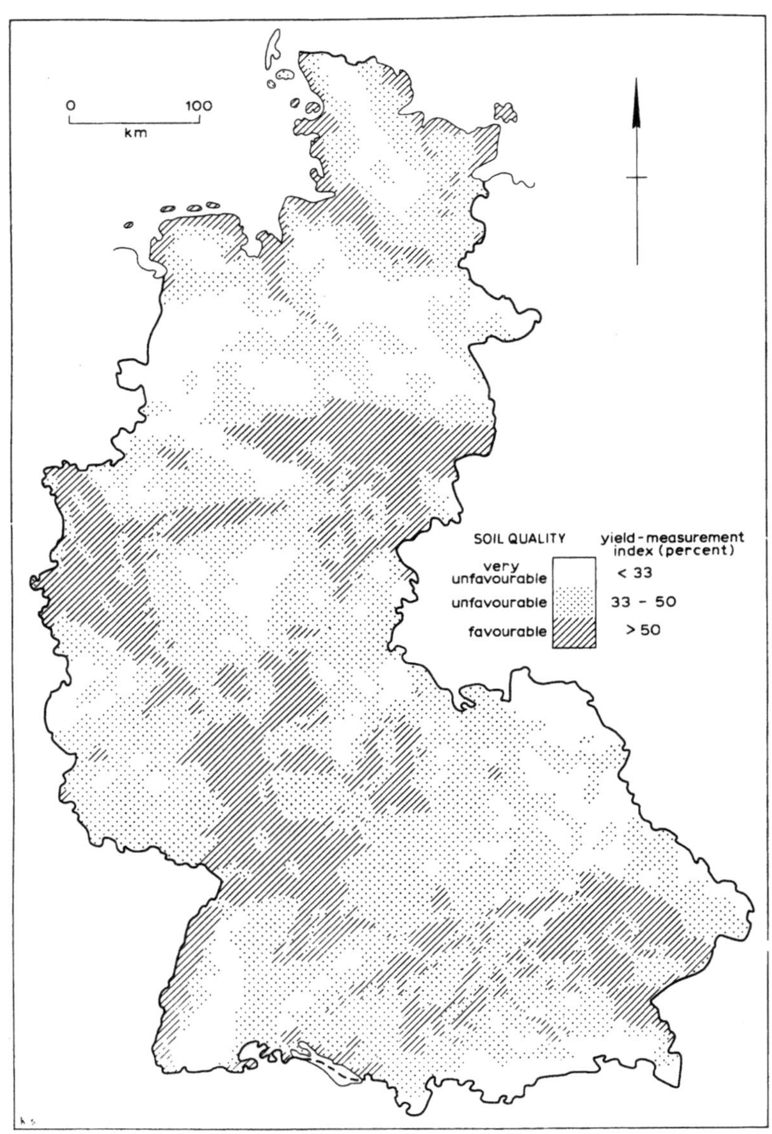

Source: based upon map in *Die Bundesrepublik Deutschland in Karten* (Kohlhammer Verlag, Stuttgart and Mainz, 1965-9), Blatt 2112.

Historic Legacy

While West German farmers in many parts of the country have to operate under adverse physical conditions, they are also forced to bear the heavy burden of coping with long-outdated field systems, farm-size structures and rural settlement patterns. Even after three decades of continuous change, there still remain several backward regions where the farming landscape is essentially one which can only be interpreted in terms of historic bequeathal. Indeed, as far as the effects of land fragmentation are concerned, it is still quite common to find agrarian communities with cultivation plots averaging less than one-tenth of a hectare. Nor is it unusual to come across medium-sized holdings consisting of upwards of 50 field-parcels and more than 200 separate strips of land. Under such extreme structural conditions as these, not only does the farmer have to involve himself in a huge wastage of time and effort, but also the introduction of agricultural machinery and new methods of food production pose insurmountable technical and logistic difficulties.

There are marked regional variations in the degree of land fragmentation and its attendant highly variegated patterns of fields and land uses. These variations are partly a result of the regionally unequal progress of postwar field reorganisation, but are to be seen more generally as a consequence of past geographic differences in inheritance laws and traditional procedures of handing down agricultural property from one generation to the next. In the North German lowlands, large parts of Bavaria and much of the Black Forest Region, the custom of *Anerbenrecht* was practised. In this, one heir only (usually the eldest son) inherited the entire farm, while his brothers and sisters had to be content with settlements of money, furniture and – in localities with a strong tradition of peasant involvement in craft industry – domestic manufacturing equipment. On the other hand, in the Rhinelands, the Saarland and many parts of the Central Uplands, the normal practice was *Realerbteilung*. Almost invariably this, the custom of partible inheritance, led to intense fragmentation and parcelisation of holdings and fields, since under this particular system all the legal heirs were granted more-or-less equal amounts of their parents' land. Moreover, not only was every single piece of farmland divided and shared out among the offspring, but also the farm buildings, tools and stock. Thus, with the succession of each generation, reduction in the average size of fields and farms was bound to occur, and could be checked only by the occasional joining together of field-parcels as a result of marriage or voluntary exchanges of land.

Nowadays, although Realerbteilung still persists in certain parts of the country, it has little practical significance, since there is usually only one heir who is prepared to take up the task of running the farm. However, its historical impact on the regional differentiation of farming structures in West Germany has stood the test of time. It must, therefore, continue to be regarded as one of the most important formative influences on the evolution of contemporary agrarian landscapes.

The same can be said for the traditional patterns and forms of rural settlement. In most rural regions the village, usually large by British standards, continues to dominate over isolated farms and what may be described as 'scatter settlements'. By far the most common and widespread village form is the *Haufendorf*, which is invariably characterised by a distinctive irregular layout and crowded congestion of buildings (Figure 9.3). The historic origins of Haufendorf villages may be traced back to as early as the beginnings of the Middle Ages. Subsequently, the large majority have grown both internally and externally in response to successive phases of rural population increase. Today, their narrow winding streets and cramped positioning of farmsteads pose major problems, hindering the modernisation of farm buildings and greatly impeding the movement and storage of the larger types of agricultural machinery. Moreover, the totally unplanned arrangement of homes and streets adds enormously to the costs of bringing in local electricity and gas supplies as well as the renewal of obsolete sewerage and drainage systems.

General Agricultural Policy: the National and Supra-national Dimensions

Government-inspired agricultural policies in West Germany have never been in full accord with the economic rationale of productive efficiency and free competition. Indeed, in several respects it can be argued that interventionist measures have actually prevented or, at the best, delayed and rendered more difficult sensible structural change and adaptation to modern economic dictates. In any discussion attention must be drawn to the general background of agricultural protectionism. In Germany this has had an almost unbroken tradition ever since the height of the Bismarck era when, for the first time, custom duties were imposed on imported grains as a means of stabilising the decline in domestic food production.[4] Even after the turn of the nineteenth century, when rising prices for cereal crops caused the rapidly growing urban populations to mount a major outcry against the continuance of protectionist policies, the agricultural lobby was still powerful enough to pressurise successive governments into retaining most import duties. The concept of national self-sufficiency and the political expediency of preserving the traditional economic symbiosis between agricultural and industrial Germany constituted two powerful arguments in opposition to all attempts at liberalising the commodities market.

After the First World War the loss of extensive agricultural territories and the onset of a series of severe food crises brought little change in the autarky policy. In fact, during the 1930s the National Socialists made it a major part of their general inclination to elevate the status of the German peasant farmer, who came to be portrayed as the nation's 'life source' and more than the equal of the urban proletariat.

The most critical of all twentieth-century food crises came during the first few years following the end of the Second World War when, in addition to the effects of military invasion and occupation, problems were greatly aggravated by the influx of millions of refugees and expellees moving into West Germany from the east. The need for maximising agricultural production had never been so urgent. In response, the authorities quickly introduced a system of subsidies aimed at the improvement of production resources; in particular the recultivation of war-blighted farmland, the ploughing up of virgin waste and the creation of new farmholdings.[5] During the 1950s the infant Federal Republic was able to enjoy a steady growth of food production, while in the industrial sector of the economy there developed a phase of spectacular and sustained expansion. Yet despite mounting pressure for a change in emphasis to competition and the free market, the general direction of national agricultural policy remained little altered from that of prewar times. Thus, the long-established principles of protectionism and interventionism were retained, both receiving federal government blessing in the 1951-2 series of market-regulation laws. The outstanding feature of this legislation was the fixing of agricultural prices and the discouragement of foreign imports, while the main criticism was focused upon the government's insistence on operating the system without a set timetable. Rather unfortunately from the consumers' point of view, the net outcome was a seemingly permanent rise of domestic food prices above the levels of the world market.

In pursuing this course of action the federal government was, of course, endeavouring to create appropriate incentives for maximum effort among the country's food producers. The Agricultural Act of

1955 was fully in keeping with this intention, and was also designed to cushion the nation's farmers from the allegedly unavoidable 'combination of physical, structural and economic disadvantages which no other productive businesses have to endure'.[6]

The legislation of the 1950s, together with the First Green Plan of 1957, brought several other benefits to the West German farmer besides those which accrued from the artificially inflated level of agricultural prices. In this extra assistance the three most important measures were: first, the special tax concessions for farming families; secondly, the quite substantial handouts of money which were directed to producers of dairy food; thirdly, the generous subsidies on such materials as diesel fuels, machinery spare-parts and manufactured fertilizers.

Whatever the form and scale of assistance, its significance to the farmer depended very much on the type of enterprise, especially the size of its holding and the mode of produce-specialisation. There was no question of government support favouring every category of West German farm. Indeed, apart from the pricing policies (which of course were devised to be of general application), the selective nature of government intervention intensified further during the 1960s. Then in 1970 it became a matter of deliberate policy following the principles laid out in the Individual Enterprise Support Programme (*Einzelbetriebliches Förderungsprogramm*) and its declaration that truly efficient agriculture could only be achieved in West Germany if government aid was focused primarily on those farms which not only had an obvious need for support but, at the same time, also had a clear economic potential. Accordingly, since the introduction of the IESP, highly profitable enterprises, as well as the smallest farms, have found themselves excluded from many federal grant schemes. But the question of economic potential also means that much too depends on the suitability of local soil and climatic conditions. Today, therefore, elegibility for public financial support tends to find its maximum strength within those parts of the country which satisfy the test of 'natural requirements' in addition to having approximately average agricultural structures.

West German Agriculture and EEC Policy

Since 1957 farming in West Germany has been greatly affected by the policies of the EEC. Not only have these progressively reduced the manoeuvrability of federal government strategy, but they have also become targets of heated criticism. At this point, therefore, it is appropriate to present a brief account of the general aims and problems of

EEC interventionism.

Whilst there are certainly many differences in detail, one of the most striking features of EEC involvement in the agricultural sphere is its broad similarity to traditional German farming policies. Particularly familiar is the general emphasis on market organisation, in which there are three underlying features: first, support to the farmer through the adoption of internal threshold-price mechanisms; secondly, the use of heavy import duties to restrict the flow of food from non-EEC countries; thirdly, the employment of external trading subsidies and the fixing of export prices at levels significantly below those of the world market.

Under Article 39 of the Treaty of Rome, the principal aims of the Common Agricultural Policy (CAP) are defined as:

(1) the securing of an adequate standard of living for all persons directly engaged in farming within the EEC;
(2) the stabilisation of agricultural markets;
(3) the provision of farm products to the consumer at reasonable prices.

While in general terms one can hardly disagree that much progress has been made in the direction of the first and second of these three objectives, there has been a rising tide of discontent concerning the seemingly excessive expenditure incurred in fostering these achievements. During the period from 1960 to 1978 the overall cost of implementing CAP initiatives within the original six member-states of the EEC increased from DM 10,000 million per annum to DM 63,000 million at constant money values. As far as the German contribution to this sum is concerned, the increase in the CAP outlay was not quite so staggering in percentage terms; but none the less the rise here from DM 3,000 million to DM 11,000 million was remarkable enough.[7]

To a large extent this massive increase in CAP funding owes itself to certain basic defects in the system of EEC market-regulation and also to the fact that large amounts of expenditure are closely tied to agricultural output. In particular, it must be stressed that in each country and for every type of farming enterprise, the CAP price agreements are operational without restrictions on the quantities of crops grown and animals kept. Accordingly, however much he produces, the farmer is always guaranteed very favourable market conditions, including artificial price-levels which in the large majority of cases are considerably higher than world averages. Accordingly, since he neither has to respond to the real economic forces of supply and demand nor at any time does he have to take much account of specific qualitative orientations in consumer choice, the most obvious and quickest way for the farmer to elevate his income is invariably the short-term expedient of increasing his yields.

The consequences of an EEC policy, which gives far too much scope for uncontrolled self-interest amongst producers and also presents a heavy burden to the taxpayer and consumer, are well in evidence in West Germany. Here, as in all Common Market countries, the main centres of criticism are the huge agricultural surpluses. These not only pose escalating problems of storage, but also stand out unhappily as ostensible symbols of wastage in an age of mounting food scarcity in the Third World. Moreover, it can be argued strongly that the vast amounts of money spent on subsidising production (rather than making agricultural organisation more efficient) are using up finance which could otherwise be directed to improving the farming structures of the EEC's backward rural regions. This crucial task is still left very much to the resources and initiatives of the respective member states. As such, especially when viewed from the West German standpoint, it brings into focus the CAP's caution and apparent lack of a sense of priorities in fields outside the complex realm of market-regulation.

Structural Reform of West German Farming

Heavily disadvantaged both by its generally unfavourable physical conditions and by the various detrimental effects of its historic legacy, farming in West Germany places an overriding demand for sweeping structural improvements. Among these there are three essential issues, each of which will be taken as a focus for separate discussion: first, the reorganisation of the country's anachronistic field and settlement forms, and through this the creation of a new rural landscape which is able to meet the requirements of efficient agriculture; secondly, the enlargement of farms as a means of increasing their potential profitability; lastly, changes in farming methods in terms of increased mechanisation and implementation of technological innovations.

Field Reorganisation and Settlement Modernisation

In the regions of partible inheritance, excessive division of holdings and scattering of field-parcels has made it quite impossible for the large majority of the first generation of postwar farmers to make any proper use of modern technology and agricultural machinery. Understandably, therefore, the first major task in the improvement of operational organisation was *Flurbereinigung* – the joining together of parcels of farmland and the consolidation of holdings. The visual effect of this process can be gauged in detail by comparing the two maps presented in Figure 9.2. The example area is a part of Gemeinde Krombach, which is situated in the Spessart hills approximately equidistant from the cities of Würzburg and Frankfurt. Immediately before its Flurbereinigung Krombach was reported to have had 1,065 ha of farmland: this was distributed in the form of 8,800 strips, giving an average size of only 0.12 ha.[8] To date there has been more than a twelve-times reduction in this number, and with this the elimination of all save a few vestiges of the traditional field pattern. As well as providing an impression of the typical post-Flurbereinigung landscape, the lower map in Figure 9.2 also depicts the extent of one of the largest of the newly reorganised holdings. At one time this farm was divided into as many as 32 fields and 245 cultivation plots, a large proportion of which were scattered randomly in various parts of the Gemeinde. Today, however, as a result of Flurbereinigung, the holding is fully consolidated: its area has been increased from 14 ha to 29 ha, but the number of fields has been reduced to 7 and the number of plots to just 26.

But Flurbereinigung was not simply a matter of rearranging field patterns and removing the problems of fragmentation and parcelisation: it also involved the painstaking construction of new access roads and the installation of field-drainage systems and water-supply facilities. Since 1945 more than 7 million ha of land, 54 per cent of West Germany's present agricultural area, have been treated in this comprehensive manner. But this has needed a massive financial outlay, with Flurbereinigung prices now averaging around DM 2,500 per ha and in certain special cases, such as the highly fragmented, wine-growing, lands of the Middle-Rhine valley and the Plain of Baden, exceeding the colossal figure of DM 100,000 per ha.

During the 1950s and 1960s field reorganisation often took place in conjunction with agricultural resettlement (*Aussiedlung*). Particularly common in those parts of the country where large Haufendörfer predominated, these schemes involved the removal of farmsteads from their cramped positions in the centre of a farming community either to the outskirts of the village or, just as commonly, to sites actually within the newly rearranged holdings. Not unusually, the Aussiedlung process included the creation of hamlet-like collections of modern

Figure 9.2: *Flurbereinigung* in Part of Gemeinde Krombach, Spessart

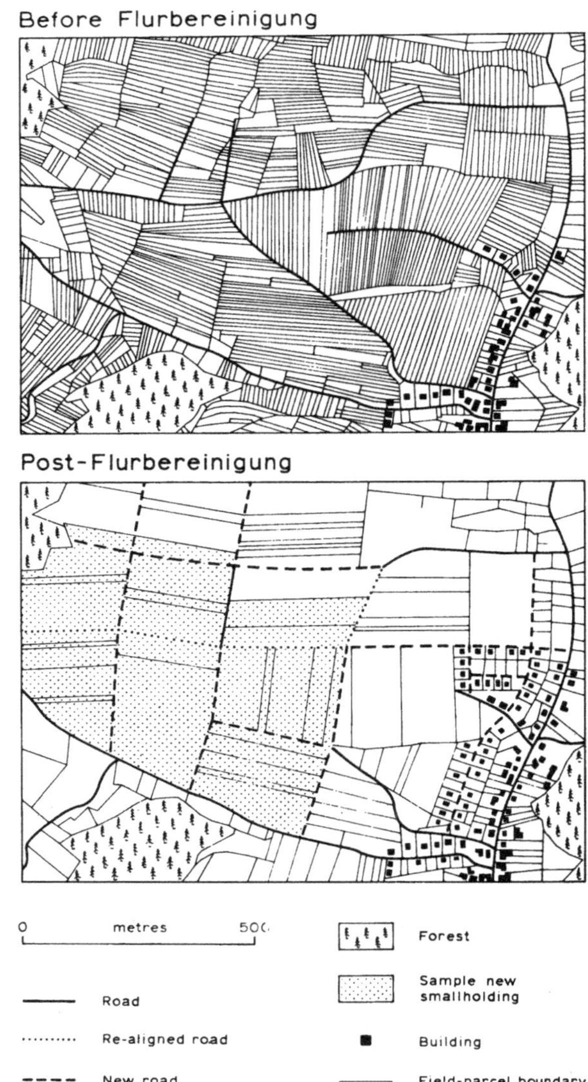

Source: Based upon part of map drawn in Bayerisches Staatsministerium für Ernährung, Landwirtschaft und Forsten, 'Bayern — Agrarleitplan', *Schriftenreihe des Bayerischen Staatsministerium für Ernährung, Landwirtschaft und Forsten*, vol. 15 (1974), pp. 31-2.

farmsteads, with each cluster varying in size from three to five units designed to facilitate infrastructure provision, communication and social contacts. Since its inception during the early 1950s, the Agricultural Resettlement Programme has catered for 23,000 shifts in farm locations. However, within less than two decades of operation its progress came to a virtual standstill, and interest turned emphatically to the renovation of the existing stock of buildings *in situ*. One reason for this is that the financial outlay for Aussiedlung (60 per cent of which has to come from the public purse) has risen to prohibitive levels.[9] The other reason is that, since the late 1960s, greater scope for the modernisation and expansion of village farmsteads was created by an upsurge in the abandonment and dereliction of old agricultural properties.

Today, village renovations (*Dorferneuerungen*) are being pursued on a wider front, not just in the specific context of agrarian restructuring, but also to serve the more general needs of economic and social change in rural communities. Over broad areas of rural West Germany a fast increasing proportion of these settlements are becoming something more than mere farming villages. Many in fact can now be more appropriately described as 'embryo' industrial suburbs, small commuter dormitories or tourist resorts. The intrustion of extraneous functions means that rural planning is no longer able to confine itself singularly to the task of providing for agricultural interests. Just as important in the modern age are such essential investments as the improvement of road and street networks, the installation of adequate public utilities and the fostering of suitable conditions for village trade and local business life. Each of these requirements has become a basic issue in the most recent Dorfneuerung schemes; but they also give rise to difficult problems, especially the delicately balanced conflicts of interest between planners, preservationists and the various social categories of local residents. Over the last few years, therefore, Gemeinde authorities have taken special pains to regulate such sensitive issues as the freeing of development land and decisions concerning the type and amount of new residential buildings. They are also keen to take a positive initiative, as can be seen throughout West Germany in the implementation of a rapidly increasing number of village undertakings designed to meet the three immediate priorities of improving the architectural 'ambiance' of the historic building-fabric, adding to the 'natural' greenery and providing for much-needed leisure and recreational facilities.

A characteristic example of a comprehensive Dorfneuerung scheme

Figure 9.3: Village Renovation in Brenkhausen, Westphalia

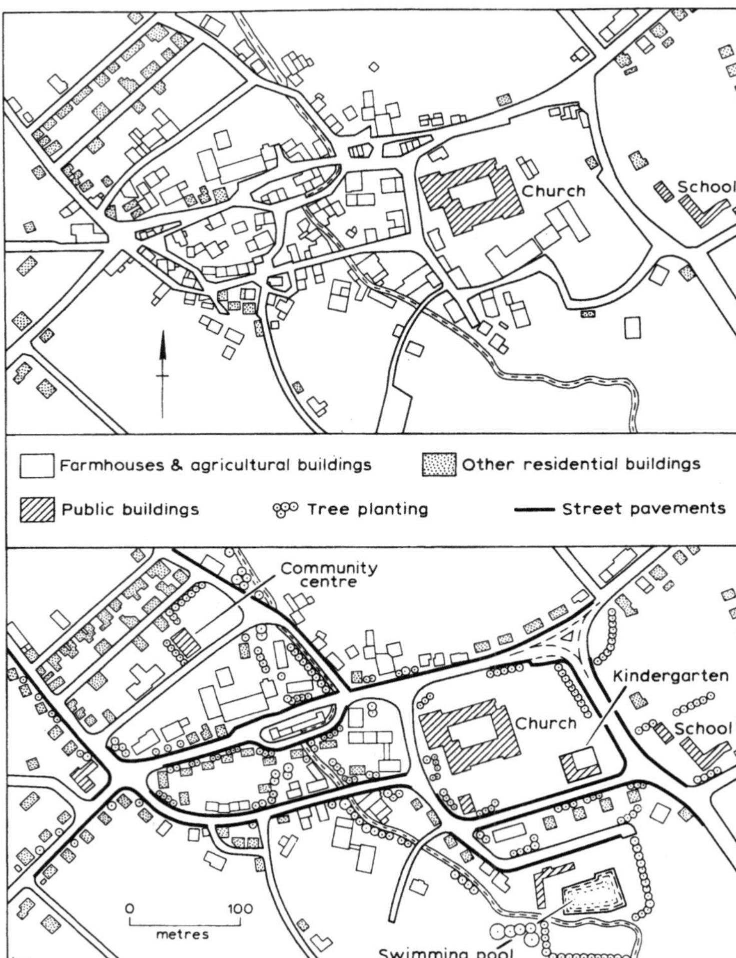

Source: Based upon a survey by E.P. Schmitter in E.P. Schmitter, *Die ländliche Gemeinden; Planung und Gestaltung* (Bayerischer Landwirtschaftsverlag, Munich, 1975), pp. 123-4.

is drawn in Figure 9.3. This shows two plans of the Westphalian village of Brenkhausen; one a few years before renovation, and the other after this had taken place. The former plan, with its highly irregular mesh of narrow streets, tight congestion of buildings and diversity of farmstead sizes, illustrates all the features one would expect to find in a typical Haufendorf settlement of around 800 inhabitants.[10] Partly through the process of voluntary abandonment of agricultural properties and partly also by means of compensatory agreements, it was possible for Gemeinde Brenkhausen to sponsor the pulling down of 38 or the original 82 village farmsteads. Most of the buildings in question had been in a very dilapidated condition, and were considered to have been well beyond repair. Their demolition, however, provided the necessary space for the urgent task of broadening and realigning the internal streets. At the same time, plots of land were made available for the expansion of a number of surviving farmsteads, the creation of public open spaces and the construction of a community centre, swimming pool and new kindergarten school. Three other features which should be noted in describing the Brenkhausen renovation scheme are the extensive tree planting, the construction of pavements alongside the central streets and, finally, the designation of the historic core of the village as a special conservation area.

Enlargement of Farms

In the structural reform of West German agriculture just as much importance is attached to enlarging the quantity of land held by farms as is given to the consolidation of holdings and modernisation of the settlement fabric. But notwithstanding the considerable progress which has been made during the postwar period, the average size of agricultural enterprise in West Germany is still lower than that in the large majority of West European countries, while in the EEC it is surpassed by all nations apart from Italy and Greece. If West Germany's present figure of 15.2 ha is compared with the EEC Commission's recommended targets of 60-80 ha for arable farmers or, as an equivalent, 40-60 milk cows or 150-200 dairy cattle, then it becomes abundantly clear how seriously the Federal Republic is disadvantaged in terms of its extremely weak farm-size structure.

Theoretically, there are two ways of overcoming this critical problem: one is to extend the total amount of agricultural land; the other is to reduce the number of enterprises, with the objective of expanding all viable units at the cost of eliminating a large proportion of holdings within the smallest and least efficient categories. Apart from the first few years after the end of the Second World War when there was in fact some modest increase in the extent of West Germany's cultivated area, the former alternative has not been pursued. To a large degree this is a reflection of the adverse physical conditions of the country's virgin lands: but note too should be made of the fact that the few localised additions that have been made to the agrarian frontiers have tended to be heavily outweighed by losses to urban growth, rural suburbanisation, road construction and social fallow. Indeed, during the period from 1949 to 1980 the total quantity of productive farmland in the Federal Republic shrank from 13.3 million ha to 12.2 millions. The difference between these two figures represents an overall decrease of 7.6 per cent and an average net reduction of 32,160 ha per annum.

With very few exceptions, therefore, the enlargement of farms in West Germany has depended entirely on transferences of land from small to large enterprises, often in the form of complete holdings and commonly in conjunction with Flurbereinigung. However, when one considers the specific categories of farms, these transferences can be seen to have had significantly different points of temporal emphasis. As shown in Table 9.2, from 1949 to 1960 the heavier losses of land came from holdings within the smallest, the 1-5-ha range: their total area fell by a huge 649,000 ha. Yet it is quite clear that by far the largest share of this loss went not to the highly profitable 30-plus-ha enterprises, but to those within the more marginal 10-20-ha grouping.

The situation changed during the 1960s when it was the turn of the 5-10-ha category, with a net loss of 792,000 ha, to become the principal source of land supply for the larger farms. But unlike previous years all of this appears to have gone to the increase in numbers and expansion of holdings of more than 20 ha. The picture altered again after 1970. On the negative side of the dividing line the emphasis of change moved further upwards to the 10-20-ha category (minus 1.2 million ha); on the positive side, it was the turn of the 30-50-ha and 50-plus-ha farms to benefit the most, with gains of 847,000 ha and 896,000 ha respectively.

As a consequence of these trends the average size of farmholding in West Germany has experienced a slow but steadily accelerating increase since the early postwar years, rising modestly from 8.1 ha in 1949 to 9.3 ha in 1960, before producing additions of 2.4 ha during the 1960s and 3.5 ha during the following decade. But the gap between these achievements and the Federal Ministry of Agriculture's periodic raising of desired target-size is continuing to grow in absolute, if not relative, terms. Furthermore, as is apparent in Figure 9.4, the situation is greatly complicated by the persistence of prominent regional differences. Based on statistics compiled for each of West Germany's 38 *Regierungsbezirke* (Administrative Regions), the map shows extensive

Table 9.2: West Germany: Distribution of Farmland According to Categories of Farm-size, 1950-80

Farm-size category (ha)	1949		1960		1970		1980	
	area		area		area		area	
	1,000 ha	%	1,000 ha	%	1,000 ha	%	1,000 ha	%
1-5	2,271	17.1	1,622	12.6	1,058	8.3	660	5.4
5-10	2,860	21.5	2,483	19.2	1,691	13.4	1,086	8.9
10-20	3,543	26.7	3,991	30.8	3,848	30.5	2,636	21.7
20-30	1,740	13.1	1,904	14.7	2,507	19.8	2,508	20.6
30-50	1,505	11.3	1,601	12.4	1,998	15.7	2,835	23.3
50-plus	1,361	10.3	1,335	10.3	1,553	12.3	2,449	20.1
Total	13,280	100.0	12,936	100.0	12,655	100.0	12,174	100.0

Sources: BMELF, *Statistisches Jahrbuch über Ernährung, Landwirtschaft und Forsten*, 1977 edn (BMELF, Münster, 1978); BMELF, *Agrarbericht 1981 der Bundesregierung* (BMELF, Bonn, 1981).

Figure 9.4: West Germany: Regional Variations in Farm-size Structures, 1977

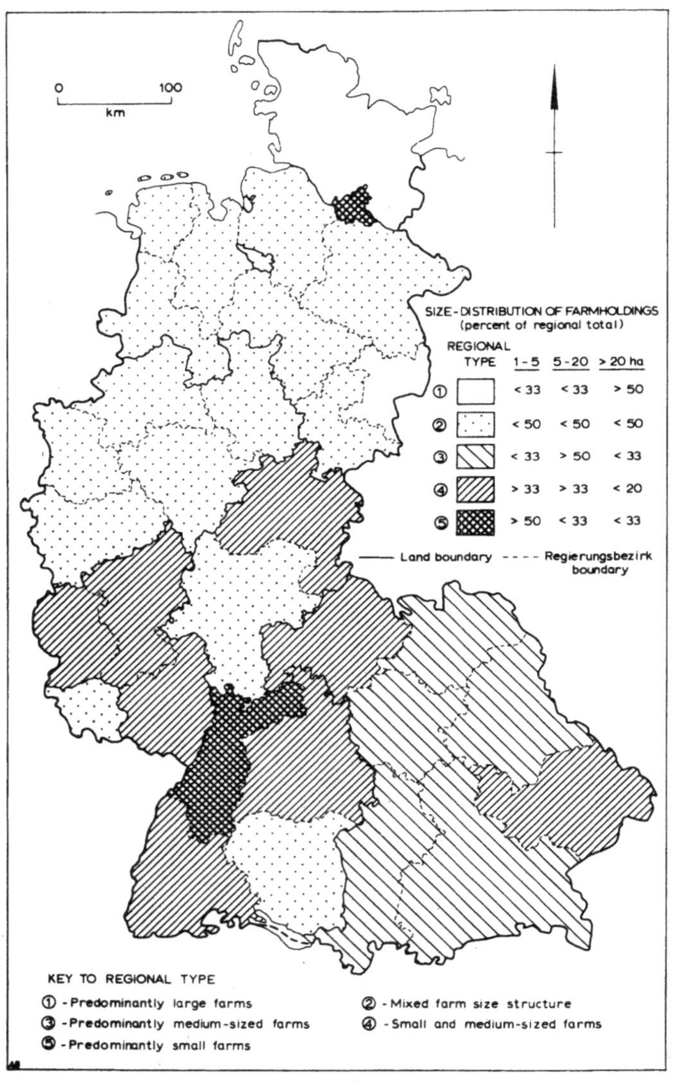

Source: Bundesministerium für Ernährung, Landwirtschaft und Forsten, ***Statistisches Jahrbuch über Ernährung, Landwirtschaft und Forsten***, 1980 edn (Münster, 1981).

parts of the country where even as late as 1977 more than 50 per cent of farmholdings were under 5 ha, but less than one-fifth were larger than 20 ha. The regions in question mostly lie in Baden-Württemberg and Rhineland-Palatinate, two federal states where partible inheritance had been particularly prevalent and long lasting. Here, and one may also include eastern Hesse and Lower Bavaria, the problem of inadequate size-structure of agricultural enterprises continues to prevail in spite of all the efforts which are being made to remedy the situation. In point of fact there is no large area in West Germany where, by the standards of most neighbouring countries, average farm-sizes have reached the requirements of unimpeded profitability. Indeed, in 1977 only two areas – the one which covers Schleswig-Holstein and the other which represents the Brunswick region of Lower Saxony – were able to record substantially lower percentages of farms under 5 ha than the proportions of holdings over 20 ha.

The huge task of improving West Germany's farm-size structure is far from nearing completion. As mentioned earlier, progress is very much dependent upon exchanges of land from small to large farms. To date, most transactions have been effected by means of leasehold arrangements, although in certain regions the selling-off of fields and holdings has also made a significant contribution. Whether through leasing or selling, transferences will continue to be encouraged by the land-surrender pensions which since the late 1950s have been available to all agriculturalists after their sixtieth birthdays. However, less reliance than formerly can be placed on other stimuli for 'unenforced' land exchanges. In particular, one must stress the effect of recent economic recessions on the availability of alternative work opportunities for the families of small-scale farmers; a situation which means that this social group is now much less willing to part with land. The much less favourable economic climate of the late 1970s and early 1980s has in fact provided a setting for the promotion of new approaches to solving the farm-size problem. Amongst these, it appears that co-operation between enterprises (especially those which are within the intermediate size-range of 10-30 ha) has the most to offer. It is envisaged, therefore, that future years will see the proliferation of shared, multi-family farms operating along the same lines as the models which are increasingly being practised in countries such as France and the Netherlands.

Mechanisation and Technological Change

The whole phenomenon of agricultural structure and its multifarious elements is essentially a product of land, labour and capital determinants, whose relative significance has in each case been subject to major temporal changes. The continued backwardness of West German farming, which is clearly apparent whenever one makes comparisons with the *per capita* wealth generated by the industrial and tertiary sectors of the economy, is to be interpreted, therefore, in terms of the inability of the nation's farmers to meet the specific demands imposed by any combination of these three controlling factors. Ideally, all farmers should respond positively to these dictates, and in so doing work towards achieving the objective of 'minimal-cost combination'. But for this to be possible, the amount of money needed to bring a farm up to an optimal level of efficiency has to be carefully evaluated in the light of making the best use of local resources and eliminating unnecessary expense.[11]

Structural change in West German farming, therefore, can be viewed in hypothetical terms as a response to the perception and personal interpretation of cost-combinations and cost-aggregates. Before the Second World War, when labour held a special position as the most important factor of production, an initial phase of concentration of enterprise organisation was followed by one of intensification of occupational effort. However, the phase in the chronology of twentieth-century agricultural development which is usually described as 'the mechanisation stage'[12] had to await the postwar period. It began during the early 1950s, proceeding hesitantly for a while, but once the effects of the Second World War had been overcome, taking place on a massive scale and greatly outpacing all other forms of agricultural improvement. By the mid-1960s, after a little more than one decade of progress, the large majority of farms had already equipped themselves with tractors to replace the cumbersome work which for centuries had been performed by horses or oxen. Taking the opportunities provided by generous investment grants, many farms were also able to display a whole 'arsenal' of agricultural machinery, including such postwar novelties as combine harvesters, electric milking machines and highly sophisticated items of equipment each designed to replace manual labour in a specific branch of food production. Not surprisingly, this type of investment resulted in a drastic decline in the numbers of payroll agricultural workers, especially the traditional farm labourer, who has now virtually disappeared from the rural scene. Today the much diminished group of full-time employees consists almost entirely of highly skilled mechanics and land technicians, many of whom have high educational qualifications. Moreover, the numbers of workers from within the farmers' own families have also shrunk dramatically as mechanisation has made it more and more practical for sons and daughters to transfer themselves into other sectors of the economy.

In West Germany full mechanisation of farming has been in existence since the beginning of the 1970s. Indeed, according to several standard measurements (for example, the present-day ratio of one tractor for every 10 ha of cultivated land) the Federal Republic is ahead of all other EEC countries, and in this respect is arguably over-mechanised. Recently, therefore, the 'mechanisation phase' of agricultural change has been replaced by a new phase of farm enlightenment.

The capitalisation of agricultural techniques has placed heavy pressure on the expertise of West Germany's enterprise owners, and it is a general rule nowadays that competence in running a farm is closely related to the farmer's amount and mode of specialist training. In cases where appropriate professional education has been received, one can usually expect a more rational approach to decision-making than is all too often experienced in situations where reliance is placed only on intuition and tradition. Certainly the technical knowledge and outlook of West German farmers has improved greatly during recent years, but so far this advance has been concentrated within the younger age-groups. Thus, according to a survey conducted in 1980, as many as 70 per cent of farmers aged under 35 years had completed specialist vocational training courses; but this proportion must be compared with the corresponding figure of just 20 per cent for farmers of retirement age.[13]

Environmental Impact

It is fitting to conclude this discussion of the structural reform of West German agriculture by raising the question of its environmental impact. Taking a general view of the countryside as it appears today, one must surely gain the impression that rationalisation of farming, and most notably the comprehensive reshaping of field patterns and the modernisation of rural settlements, has occasioned a marked lessening of those endearing spatial differences which not very long ago were hallmarks of the agrarian landscape. It is true that traditional structures continue to be of some considerable significance, but for more than two decades now there has been an unmistakable trend towards a regional assimilation of field systems, village forms and farmhouse types. From the purely technical and economic standpoints, this heightening trend away from geographic individuality and towards general uniformity in the rural vista has without doubt been urgently necessary. Nevertheless, in recent years there has been a strengthening awareness among the public that economic objectives in the sphere of food production have been pursued at substantial cost to the environment. In this awareness consternation is coming from several quarters, ranging from doubt concerning the future of natural soil fertility to general dismay over the seemingly wanton destruction of the traditional image of the West German countryside. There is, therefore, a growing tide of feeling that too much latitude is being given to the needs of agricultural efficiency. However, a purely nostalgic policy which always places highest priority on the preservation of historic structures does not do justice to the interests of the people who are directly concerned. In fact, such an attitude is typical of the values and ideals of urban middle classes, but not of the people living in rural areas. What is necessary is a careful balance between the desired preservation of the historic heritage and the intention to create living conditions comparable in standards to those of urban and suburban areas.[14]

Social Change in Rural Areas

It has never been possible to speak of a uniform rural society in West Germany. More often than not, the marked diversity of farmholding size has been the most obvious factor working against social homogenity; but differentiation within agricultural communities has also been brought about by varying tenure arrangements and individual responses (or no responses) to innovative change. In areas of locally mixed economies, important too is the role of supplementary work opportunities, the existence of which may add selectively to the incomes of farming families. In the past such opportunities to augment livelihoods were commonly in the form of cottage manufacturing or small-scale mining activities, some of which have still managed to struggle on in parts of the Central Uplands and in isolated localities in southern Germany. Apart from these depleting survivals of pre-technical industry, the nature of supporting occupations has, of course, changed during modern times. Today, in areas beyond the reach of sizeable employment centres, the main emphasis is on participation in local manufacturing industries and the thriving tourist trade. This too is highly selective in its geographic incidence. Interestingly, a large proportion of the regions in question, including such well-known upland retreats as the Black Forest, the Harz, the Fichtelgebirge and the High Eifel, rank prominently in any list of early industrialised localities. Here, therefore, one finds a long, if progressively altering, continuity of peasant involvement in binary economies whose course of development has been one of successive adaptations to changing external conditions.

Since the end of the Second World War there has been a steady disintegration of traditional frameworks of social differentiation in the large majority of farming communities. This has come partly through the internal medium of local economic change and agricultural reorganisation, but rather more so externally in association with the penetration of urban values and behaviour patterns into rural areas. Thus, in human terms, the once very sharp differences between countryside and urban ways of life are becoming heavily blurred. In the rural regions the proportions of extended, multi-generation, families are now in an advanced state of decline, while the average sizes and age-compositions of households are not anything like so insular as they were only two decades ago, when interaction with towns was usually restricted to infrequent shopping trips and rare visits to the cinema, theatre or library.[15] This breaking down of social self-sufficiency, which means that it is no longer an odd exception for friendships and family linkages not to be confined to one's place of upbringing, has been brought about mainly by growing daily travel-mobility and the way this has greatly widened the ranges of personal contracts. However, the mass-media too have played a significant role in the relentless erosion of rural insularity, especially in the spheres of information supply, the diffusion of essentially urban-orientated ideas and the displaying of all forms of sophisticated consumerism. Each of these three psychological inducements to change has found keen acceptance among all except the oldest and most conservative-minded rural inhabitants. Moreover, West Germany has a rural society which, ever since the austerity years of the 1940s and early 1950s, has become increasingly affluent and able to afford the expense of adopting modern lifestyles. As far as the residual farming population is concerned, this has emanated from the substantial betterment of agricultural incomes in both relative and absolute terms. However, it must be stressed that approximately 80 per cent of the working population of West Germany's vast number of rural communities (all Gemeinden with populations below 5,000) have jobs in industry or in tertiary activities. Most of these people work outside their villages and have to travel to the nearest town or city for employment. This is very different from the situation during the 1950s and the years of the postwar economic 'miracle', when spatially concentrated employment growth, together with limited car ownership and restricted ranges of public transport, meant that there had to be substantial migration losses from almost all rural regions. Today, by way of contrast, it is only within the most isolated parts of West Germany that occupational shifts among farming communities still commonly necessitate movements in residential location. Elsewhere, the virtual ending of the classical rural-urban migration drift has ensured a greater degree of demographic stability. This in turn has created conditions that are conducive to more positive local political attitudes and a new confidence for social investments. Indeed, in those areas which lie within reasonably easy travelling distance to and from large urban centres, such changes often serve as a prelude for sizeable centrifugal population movements into villages from town or city. Typically, this reversal of the general direction of migration flow takes the form of influxes of 'urbanites' seeking to fulfill their ambitions of living in newly built houses within attractive 'green' environments. When this process of 'rural suburbanisation' occurs on a large scale, as it has already done so in the hinterlands of most major cities, farming communities are swamped both in the physical sense, by the addition of extensive adventitious elements to the settlement fabric, and also in terms of the destruction of traditional social structures. To a large degree, problems arising from the former process can be reduced by the implementation of thoughtful Gemeinde planning policies, in which the main priority has to be that of catering for modern residential expansion without overwhelming and eradicating the traditional character of the village interior. There is, however, no institutional solution to the various difficulties and frictions which are inherent in the often inevitable confrontation between old-established families and the inflow of newcomers. These can only be resolved by means of creating and developing facilities for greater social interaction and community identity. But this still leaves much responsibility upon the individuals who, in cases where rural suburbanisation has been on such a scale that it has obliterated any real chance of fostering place-identity, may well find no reasons to moderate their prejudices.

Development Prospects of Rural Areas

Since the mid-1970s one of the most pertinent questions to be asked concerning the course of regional development in West Germany has been the future prospects of rural areas under conditions of reduced rates of national economic growth, growing unemployment and increasing political demand for major cuts in public-sector expenditure. From the standpoints of both diagnosis and treatment there is anything but unanimity when it comes to answering possible approaches to this challenge. Some writers present a very gloomy view of the future, despite the fact that most economic indicators (for example, job supply, income-levels and capital investment) put rural West Germany in a far better light today than had once been the case during the late 1940s and early 1950s. In their opinion the last two decades of the twentieth century will see a substantial fall in the quality of life of rural areas, particularly so as less and less disposable national wealth becomes available for maintaining present-day levels of rural infrastructure.[16] Already many country schools, health services and local administrative offices have come under threats of imminent closure; but even more serious is the strong likelihood that, unless there is a return to high economic prosperity, in future years the geographical pattern of job creation in West Germany will contract to just a small number of specially favoured city-regions. Should this occur, it will eventually lead to a forceful renewal of the traditional rural-to-urban migration flow, which will become all the more damaging to rural areas on account of the expected very high involvement of young persons.

The federal ministry[17] which has the responsibility of designing and directing policies of regional planning, however, takes a more optimistic view. According to its own prognosis for the year 1990, population and employment trends in rural areas will differ only marginally from those within the major agglomeration areas.[18] This is not to say that ministerial advisers are not discounting something of a setback to an established regional strategy which primarily seeks to reduce spatial disparities and create an equality of living conditions; but it is indeed a distant cry from the pessimism generated by government critics.

Another commonly expressed point of view is that, in the likelihood of economic growth tending to revert once again to concentrated locations within the urban agglomerations, the rural regions will eventually lose all of their insularity and will function essentially as 'replenishment' areas for city populations.[19] The postwar period has already seen considerable progress in this direction, especially in the fields of leisure and recreation, water supply and the provision of a vast 'land reserve' for urban-derived residential expansion. But, despite all these highly significant connections between city and countryside, rural West Germany, with its increasing food production, its large reservoir of skilled and unskilled labour and its long-established ability to generate local business entrepreneurship, continues to retain important endogenous capabilities.[20] The chances, however, of rural areas being able to make their own internal adjustments to more demanding economic conditions varies greatly from one part of the country to another. At one extreme, there are many well-placed localities close to the major cities whose future appears secure; at the opposite end of the spectrum of potential development lie several very remote regions. Here, as is epitomised in regions as distant from each other as eastern Bavaria, eastern Hesse, the Emsland and the western extremities of Rhineland-Palatinate, massive government assistance is still urgently required in all sectors of the rural economy.

Notes

1. E. Otremba, 'Gunst und Ungunst der Landesnatur für die Landwirtschaft im Gebiet der Bundesrepublik', *Geographische Rundschau*, vol. 23 (1971), pp. 106-8.
2. E. Otremba, 'Der Agrarwirtschaftsraum der Bundesrepublik Deutschland', *Erdkundliches Wissen: Beihefte zur Geographischen Zeitschrift*, vol. 24 (1970).
3. Bundesministerium für Ernährung, Landwirtschaft und Forsten, *Agrarbericht 1981 der Bundesregierung* (BMELF, Bonn, 1981).
4. H. Herlemann, 'Vom Urspring des deutschen Agrarprotektionismus', *Forschungs- und Sitzungsberichte der Akadamie für Raumforschung und Landesplanung*, vol. 30 (1965), pp. 17-40.
5. T. Bergmann, 'Agrarstrukturwandel und Agrarpolitik', in J. Stark and M. Doll (eds), *Strukturwandel und Strukturpolitik im ländlichen Raum* (Stuttgart, 1978), pp. 157-89.
6. C. v. Dietze, *Grundzüge der Agrarpolitik* (Hamburg and Berlin, 1967), p. 189.
7. E.C. Zurek, 'Zwei Jahrzehnte öffentliche Ausgaben für gemeinsame und nationale Agrarpolitik. Die vorprogrammierte Misere', *Forschung und Beratung*, no. 35 (1980), pp. 7-50.
8. Bayerisches Staatsministerium für Ernährung, Landwirtschaft und Forsten, 'Bayern-Agrarleitplan', *Schriftenreihe des Bayerischen Staatsministerium für Ernährung, Landwirtschaft und Forsten*, vol. 15 (1974), pp. 31-2.
9. In 1976 the cost of each resettlement averaged DM 640,000; this large figure is put into perspective when it is noted that this sum was more than twice the price of an average-sized, newly completed dwelling.
10. E.P. Schmitter, *Die ländliche Gemeinde; Planung und Gestaltung* (Bayerischer Landwirtschaftsverlag, Munich, 1975), pp. 123-4.
11. H-D. Laux and G. Thieme, 'Die Agrarstruktur der Bundesrepublik Deutschland. Ansätze zu einer regionalen Typologie', *Erdkunde*, vol. 32 (1978), pp. 182-98.
12. H. Herlemann and H. Stamer, 'Produktionsgestaltung und Betriebsgrösse in der Landwirtschaft unter dem Einfluss der wirtschaftlich-technischen Entwicklung', *Kieler Studien, Forschungsberichte des Instituts für Weltwirtschaft*, vol. 44 (1958), p. 27.
13. Bundesministerium für Ernährung, Landwirtschaft und Forsten, *Statistisches Jahrbuch über Ernährung, Landwirtschaft und Forsten*, 1980 edn (Münster, 1981).
14. This objective is declared repeatedly in the annual volumes of Bundesministerium für Ernährung, Landwirtschaft und Forsten, *Agarbericht der Bundesregierung*.

15. G. Thieme and G. Paul, 'Die Landwirtschaft in der Bundesrepublik Deutschland', *Geographische Zeitfragen*, vol. 6 (1980), p. 46.

16. For example, see K.H. Hübler, 'Zur Problematik der Herstellung gleichwertiger Lebensverhältnisse', *Abhandlungen der Akademie für Raumforschung und Landesplanung*, vol. 80 (1980).

17. This office comes under the *Bundesministerium für Raumordnung, Bauwesen und Städtebau.*

18. Bundesministerium für Raumordnung, Bauwesen und Städtebau, *Raumordnungsprogramm für die grossräumige Entwicklung des Bundesgebietes* (Bonn, 1975).

19. U. Planck, 'Die Zukunft des ländlichen Raums', in Stark and Doll, *Strukturwandel und Strukturpolitik*, pp. 12-40.

20. J. Deiters, 'Industrialisierung ländlicher Räume gescheitert?', *Geographie Heute*, vol. 1 (1980), pp. 57-8.

10 CONCLUSION

Trevor Wild

The foregoing chapters have not only described the principal changes which have (and are) occurring in urban and rural West Germany, but have also focused critical attention on the ensuing problems and their planning solutions. The changes themselves are impressive in their scale and scope, even though most have clear parallels in other industrialised west European countries. In several fields, but most notably so in economic development, social progress, consumerism, travel-mobility, housing and environmental 'modernisation', there is ample justification for speaking in terms of 'miracle' achievements both in the urban and rural spheres. When these and other changes are explored in detail, one is equally impressed with the pace and sudden changes in direction in the advance of West German society. Each postwar decade has been markedly different from its predecessor; most of the 1950s were characterised by extremely rapid economic growth, but at the same time being accompanied by only very tardy social and consumer progress; the 1960s saw the culmination of the fruits of the economic miracle, but in the eyes of several other west European countries were tainted with a philistinistic image; the 1970s were concerned with the energy crisis and the first serious uncertainties over the continuance of high economic growth; lastly, as West Germany moves more and more towards becoming a 'post-industrial' state, the 1980s, with (as far as can be ascertained at the time of writing) the confirmation of economic uncertainty and also increasing challenges at the political fabric of western Europe's 'object lesson in national achievement'.

These sudden and very marked directional changes in the course of West Germany's postwar development have in turn produced severe tests to the nation's evolving system of town and country planning. During the 1950s the problems of the country's urban and rural societies were severe but simply defined, with the principal urgencies being the need for city reconstruction, provision of new houses, the integration of refugees, the reorganisation of agriculture and the creation of new systems of transport to comply with new trends in regional geography. Since then the problems have become more complex and more humanistic in character. The tremendous upsurge in consumerism, with its widespread travel-mobility and pressure on the urban fabric, has been an underlying facet of change in the 1960s and the 1970s. This, above anything else, has brought to the fore the rapidly growing environmentalist revolt, many West Germans now holding the view that the price of sustained economic growth and continued rises in personal affluence is too high when measured against the relentless depreciation of historic townscapes, residential areas and rural landscapes. Moreover, the 1960s and 1970s saw important questions emerging on the social front, for a new generation began to challenge the very premise of the West German version of the Social Market Economy and its claim to have created a 'levelled-out, middle-class' society.

There were tangible reasons for this rising tide of criticism. In spite of massive government support for regional development, broad geographical disparities, especially in standards of living and the material needs for high 'quality of life', have continued throughout the postwar period. Such disparities are to be seen at various scales: between the accessible and the remote regions, between urbanised and rural areas, and, most strikingly of all, between the inner-city districts and the outer suburbs and developing urban-rural fringes. Furthermore, the high degree of social mixing, which was once an important hallmark of the German city, is breaking down conclusively. This is most alarmingly evidenced by the increasing concentration of foreign immigrants, students and 'socially-weak' West German families into obsolete residential quarters, while the beneficiaries of the nation's economic achievement insulate and distance themselves further and further away within mushrooming dormitory settlements.

The problems emerging from these trends can be resolved only by appropriate and carefully designed planning policies at all levels of government. In West Germany's past experiences there has been a praiseworthy degree of adaptability in the vital field of policy formulation, an adaptability which has been all the more remarkable on account of the speed with which problems emerged and changed in nature. The list of postwar achievements is long and impressive. To name the most important, it includes the postwar reconstruction, the integration of millions of homeless refugees, the reform of one of west Europe's most backward agricultural systems, the implementation of new national and regional transport networks, the accommodation of the residential 'explosion' and the combating of the environmental threats of the upsurge in car ownership. These successes would most certainly pose extreme pressures on the resources of most other major developed countries.

It is wrong to ascribe an ethnic explanation for West Germany's postwar achievements in these and other fields. Another theory, that of 'necessity is the mother of invention' has more application, especially during the early years of the Federal Republic. Even truer was the capability of successive West German governments to identify difficulties and to implement and manage efficient strategies of solution. Above all, however, have been the huge backings of financial resources. At first much of these were obtained from external sources, such as American investment and the European Recovery Programme. After the mid-1950s, however, the bulk of the finance was derived from the wealth generated from the *Wirtschaftswunder* and the continuation of West Germany's fast economic growth.

It follows, therefore, that once the financial resources are lessened the ability of West Germany to overcome its internal problems begins to diminish. This is why the timing of this book is all the more important, for today, within a background of intensifying recession and falling expenditure budgets, several clouds are rising on the West German horizon, while those which had already appeared during the preceding decade are becoming progressively darker. These, the underlying elements of the current *Angst* of West German society, have been analysed by the contributors to this book. It remains to be seen in the light of today's widening differences in the ideology of the country's two leading political parties – one preaching the social virtues of the Social Market Economy and the other placing almost complete priority on the economic base – whether or not the management of western Europe's youngest and most enigmatic nation state will continue to attract the admiration, envy and emulation of competing countries.

NOTES ON CONTRIBUTORS

Joe Hajdu is a graduate of the University of Melbourne, Australia, where he also gained his MA and where he is currently a Senior Lecturer in the Department of Environmental Studies.

Philip Jones is a graduate of Birmingham University where he also gained his PhD. He is currently a Senior Lecturer in the Department of Geography at the University of Hull.

John North is a graduate of University College, London. He is currently a Lecturer in the Department of Geography at the University of Hull.

Gareth Shaw is a graduate of the University of Hull where he also gained his PhD. He is currently a Lecturer in the Department of Geography at the University of Exeter.

Günter Thieme obtained his PhD at the Universität Bonn where he is currently an *Akademischer Rat* in the Geographisches Institut.

Trevor Wild (Editor) is a graduate of the University of Birmingham where he also gained his PhD. He is currently a Senior Lecturer in the Department of Geography at the University of Hull.

INDEX

For Product Safety Concerns and Information please contact our EU
representative GPSR@taylorandfrancis.com
Taylor & Francis Verlag GmbH, Kaufingerstraße 24, 80331 München, Germany

www.ingramcontent.com/pod-product-compliance
Lightning Source LLC
LaVergne TN
LVHW010550110826
845149LV00003B/617

* 9 7 8 1 1 3 8 0 5 2 0 8 6 *